Jim Haynes and his sister Jillian Dellit are first generation Australians whose mother migrated from England with her family as a child during the Great Depression. Their father arrived on a British warship at the end of World War II, met their mother and stayed. 'We were brought up to think of ourselves as Australian,' says Jim, 'although the vast majority of our extended family are English and both of us have lived and worked in Britain at various times in our lives.'

Jim went from Botany Public School to Sydney Boys High School and then Sydney Teachers' College. He has two degrees in literature from the University of New England, including a master's degree, and a second master's degree from the University of Wales in the United Kingdom. After twenty years of teaching in New South Wales country areas and in London, Jim became a full-time professional entertainer and recording artist in 1988. He has also worked as a nurse, sapphire salesman, cleaner, songwriter and festival organiser—as well as in radio for 35 years.

Jim wrote his first book in 1995, and this book is his twenty-eighth. In 2016, he was awarded the Order of Australia Medal for 'service to the performing arts as an entertainer, author, broadcaster and historian'. He lives in Moore Park, Sydney, with his wife Robyn.

Jillian Dellit attended Botany Public School and Sydney Girls High School. She graduated with honours from Sydney University before becoming a teacher, principal of an Adelaide girls' school, educational consultant, director of the body co-ordinating digital curriculum content development across all states of Australia and New Zealand, a mother of two and grandmother of four. She has a master's degree from the University of South Australia.

ALSO BY JIM HAYNES

The Big Book of Australia's War Stories
Best Australian Drinking Stories
Great Australian Scams, Cons and Rorts
Australia's Most Unbelievable True Stories
The Big Book of Australian Racing Stories
The Best Gallipoli Yarns and Forgotten Stories
Australia's Best Unknown Stories
The Best Australian Yarns
The Best Australian Bush Stories
The Best Australian Sea Stories
The Best Australian Trucking Stories
The Great Australian Book of Limericks (2nd ed.)
Best Australian Racing Stories
The Big Book of Verse for Aussie Kids

ADVENTURERS, PIONEERS AND MISFITS

AUSTRALIA'S MOST AMAZING TRUE LIFE STORIES

JIM HAYNES

ALLEN&UNWIN
SYDNEY • MELBOURNE • AUCKLAND • LONDON

First published in 2020

Allen & Unwin
83 Alexander Street
Crows Nest NSW 2065
Australia
Phone: (61 2) 8425 0100
Email: info@allenandunwin.com
Web: www.allenandunwin.com

NATIONAL LIBRARY OF AUSTRALIA

A catalogue record for this book is available from the National Library of Australia

ISBN 978 1 76087 762 0

Set in 12/15 pt Minion Pro by Midland Typesetters, Australia
Printed and bound in Australia by Griffin Press, part of Ovato

10 9 8 7 6 5 4 3 2 1

MIX
Paper from responsible sources
FSC® C009448
FSC www.fsc.org

The paper in this book is FSC® certified. FSC® promotes environmentally responsible, socially beneficial and economically viable management of the world's forests.

For Sam

Vita non est vivere sed valere vita est.

Marcus Valerius Martialis

CONTENTS

INTRODUCTION

Having spent a good deal of my life writing and talking on radio about some of the quirkier events, people and circumstances that make up the history of our nation, I have often come across characters whose lives left me amazed, shaking my head in wonderment that one human lifespan, often a very brief one, could contain so many adventures, coincidences, tragedies and achievements.

This is a book about some of those people.

Once I began making the list, it quickly grew until there were over 30 obvious candidates whose lives are, I believe, sufficiently interesting and unusual to deserve their complete history to be told. Not only do they deserve their stories to be told, I was also absolutely convinced that these people's lives were sufficiently fascinating, unusual, bizarre, multifaceted or out of the ordinary enough to make for compulsive reading.

The more I read about and researched the past, the more it became apparent to me that there is always *more* to a story, especially to a life story. Often there was something unknown, something missed, that suddenly explained an aspect of a person's life that had previously seemed out of place in their story. Sometimes it was a fact that gave a totally different perspective to their life and their achievements, something which made it even more incredible and extraordinary that they had managed to do the things they did. These discoveries, of course, only made their lives even more remarkable, more fascinating—more interesting.

That led me to read more widely and carefully, in order to find these long forgotten or hidden facts. What I discovered, of course, was that most of these things were there to be found, often in the research of others who had gone before me, or simply waiting there to be read in the pages of long-forgotten newspapers, now wonderfully available to us all through the miracles of technology and the hard work of the National Library team that compiled *Trove.*

My seemingly never-ending hours spent trawling through *Trove*, plus my frequent and persistent questions and requests for help to my sister Jillian—combined with her amazing detective skills and patience in exploring family histories, census records, shipping lists, and records of births, deaths and marriages—have turned up some amazing discoveries, including facts about the people in this book which we are fairly certain have never been brought to light before.

Many of the most fascinating things, however, were not really hidden at all, just mostly unknown to the majority of Australians.

Who knew, for example, that when she was a teenager, Edith Cowan's father had been hanged for murder? Or that the first man hanged in Australia made an artefact valued at $1 million? Or that an Australian swimmer was the highest paid act on the American vaudeville circuit, and the star of the first movie ever made with a budget of US$1 million?

As you may have expected, doing justice to telling the full extent of these lives, and attempting to be truthful and comprehensive in doing so, has meant that, unfortunately, there are only a dozen 'true life stories' in this collection. The others on the list, which are just as fascinating and incredible, must wait for volume two.

As it seemed particularly important to me to place each of these amazing people into some sort of social and historical context, I have included a kind of 'backstory' in each case, which covers what I hope is an interesting look at one of the elements that made their lives so outstanding, or prompted them to make the first step that led along a path less travelled, to a life so extraordinary and fascinating that it is certainly worth reading about.

PART I

ALL THE WORLD'S A STAGE

Let's start with accounts of the lives of three Australians who were, in their lifetimes, truly world famous.

Although each became famous in a different field of endeavour, there is one thing that all their stories have in common—the memory of their achievements faded over time. Two of them, who shared a commonality in that they were world-renowned in the general area of arts and entertainment, were subsequently 'lost' and then 'rediscovered', to a degree.

It is true that Percy Grainger's place in the world of music was never really forgotten. There is a museum dedicated to his achievements and life, and his music has retained some degree of popularity with orchestras and military bands and in schools and colleges. Throughout the latter part of the 20th century, there was a small group of musicians who found his originality, and the results of his quirky ability to mix folk and classical music genres, pleasant to listen to and interesting to play. His life and achievements have been brought back to public awareness with a renewal of interest in his music in recent years.

Annette Kellerman's achievements, for various reasons which I tried to explain in her story, were almost completely forgotten in the 1960s and 70s, in spite of the fact that she was actually living in Australia at the time. Towards the very end of her life there was some renewed interest in her achievements, and there have been several exhibitions of her memorabilia and archive material, which have helped to keep her memory alive. And she has a community swimming pool named in her honour.

In the case of George Morrison, a man whose role in world politics and Australian affairs was vitally important and influential during his lifetime, it seems that the world has moved on and his memory has now almost faded from the Australian consciousness. The reason for this could be that, whereas Percy Grainger and Annette Kellerman were famous in Europe and the United States, George Morrison's sphere of influence was Asia. Before his achievements became just a mostly forgotten part of history, he was universally known not as George Morrison, but as 'Chinese Morrison'.

Whether they are remembered or not, these three individuals lived truly remarkable lives and achieved things that were, in their time, extraordinary.

1

THE AUSSIE WHO CHANGED THE WORLD

FIGHTING THE RIGHTEOUS FISTS

Australia's first military involvement in Asia occurred 120 years ago.

The conflict was the Chinese Boxer Rebellion of 1899–1900. Chinese Christians and missionaries were slaughtered by members of a group called 'The Righteous Fists', whose members practised martial arts and were therefore called 'Boxers' by the Europeans.

Angered by exploitation and the arrogant attitude of international powers in China, the Boxers attacked and murdered foreigners, missionaries and Chinese Christians, in an attempt to rid their country of their influence. The conflict culminated with all ex-patriot and diplomatic foreigners, along with many Chinese Christians, being blockaded in the walled enclave in Peking (Beijing) for 55 days.

The Dowager Empress Cixi, a royal wife whose son had become emperor, broke with tradition when her son died and held on to power by installing her nephew as emperor. When the new emperor showed reformist tendencies, Cixi had his chief advisers beheaded and kept him a virtual prisoner after most of his supporters fled into exile. She decided to use the Righteous Fists movement as an opportunity to rid China of foreign control, by encouraging the rebellion and ordering the Chinese Imperial Army to support the Boxers. Although many generals hesitated to act on the command and resisted involving their troops, some elements of the army supported the siege.

This led to an armed invasion by American, Austro-Hungarian, British, French, German, Italian, Japanese, Indian, Russian and colonial Australian troops to attempt to lift the siege.

As Britain was already fighting a war against the Boers in South Africa, it was difficult to commit troops to help the embattled embassies, and requests were made for help from the various Australian colonies.

Three colonies answered the call. A group of naval volunteer reservists left Sydney in early August 1900 to join the multinational force. The group comprised 200 Victorians, 260 New South Welshmen and 95 South Australians, who took their own transport, the South Australian navy's gunboat HMCS *Protector.* A controversial decision by the British saw command of the *Protector* given to a British officer, William Rooke Creswell, who was Commandant of the Queensland Maritime Force and, for legal reasons, the *Protector* changed her designation from HMCS (Her Majesty's Colonial Ship) to HMS. (The *Protector* later served as an Australian naval vessel in World War I and was requisitioned as an American vessel in World War II.)

The HMS *Protector* carried out survey work during her tour of duty and was used to carry mail and despatches to Hong Kong during the Boxer crisis. She was released by the admiralty in November 1900 and returned home via Sydney, where she took part in the celebrations to mark the birth of the nation on 1 January 1901.

The New South Welshmen and Victorians arrived at the mouth of the Pei-Ho River on 9 September 1900 and marched to Tientsin, where the Victorian brigade was left to protect local Christians and foreigners. The New South Wales contingent joined other international forces and stormed into Peking to the sound of a pipe band on 20 October. They remained in Peking for five months acting as a peacekeeping police force and, rather amusingly, as the local fire brigade!

The colonial reservists finally returned home to resume their civilian lives in April 1901, only to fall victims to a smallpox scare, which led to them being delayed at the quarantine station in Sydney for two weeks.

It was an Australian who was never in the army or the navy, however, who was the real hero of the siege. His name was George Morrison.

GEORGE MORRISON

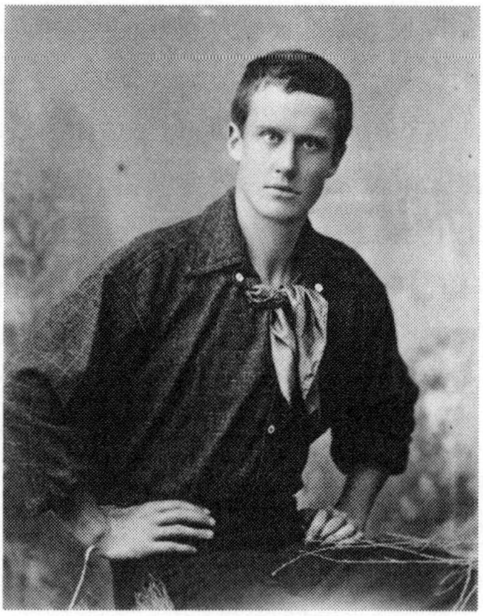

If you asked a thousand Aussies in the street if they had ever heard of George Morrison, I bet the number that answer 'yes' would be zero. Ask if the name 'Chinese Morrison' meant anything and you might get one or two answering in the affirmative, although they would probably not remember what he did, exactly.

Yet, in terms of world history and events, George Morrison was, and possibly still is, far and away the most influential Australian who ever strode the planet. And, boy oh boy, did he stride the planet!

Born in February 1862 at Geelong, Victoria, George Ernest Morrison was the eldest of eight children and was educated at Geelong College. His father, also named George, owned and was principal of the college. Young George remembered that 'we lived healthy, happy lives, giving more time to outdoor play than to study' and, in his childhood, he developed three habits that remained with him throughout his life: keeping a diary, collecting objects and walking long distances.

In 1879, at the age of seventeen, having finished his schooling at Geelong College, he walked from Geelong to Adelaide, around the coast of southern Australia, a distance of about a thousand kilometres.

Having arrived in town he decided to go to the cricket to see the great South Australian wicketkeeper–batsman Affie Jarvis play. George was still wearing his walking clothes and haversack, and later recorded in his diary that he was made fun of by other spectators for his dress and that Jarvis was run out first ball.

Morrison would later walk back from the mouth of the Murray River to Geelong, having travelled the length of the Murray from Wodonga to the sea by canoe, and also walk from the Gulf of Carpentaria to Melbourne. As an adult he walked from Shanghai in China to Rangoon in Burma, a distance of almost 5000 kilometres: it took three months and he spent the grand sum of £20 on the journey, though on that walk Morrison 'cheated' by using boats and horses at times. But that was all in front of the young man who walked to Adelaide to see a cricket match just before his eighteenth birthday.

As well as having a passion for walking, George was already an avid collector and diary keeper when he left school. As a boy he obsessively collected stamps and shells. As a man he amassed the largest collection in the world of Chinese books, maps and manuscripts—which he sold to a Japanese businessman in 1917 for £35,000. It became the foundation collection of the famous Oriental Library in Tokyo.

Everywhere you look in Morrison's autobiography you find surprises, how one man could have managed so many diverse and outstanding achievements in one lifetime is beyond the comprehension of most of us mere mortals. His father and younger brother, Norman, were noted educationalists, both being headmasters of the family-owned Geelong College, which was eventually sold to the Presbyterian Church and is still going today.

George, however, was not interested in the sedentary life of an educator. His first choice of career was medicine and he completed his first year of study at Melbourne University before adventure and an urge to be a journalist took over.

Having sold the story of his walk to Adelaide to a newspaper, he started thinking up other treks and adventures that might make good copy for newspapers eager to thrill their readers with tales of Australia's more exotic and far-flung regions and wildernesses.

He was able to convince David Syme, editor of *The Melbourne Age*, to become involved in one particular scheme he had in mind. Syme was sufficiently impressed by Morrison's journalistic skills to offer to pay him £1 per column for his reports. And so it was that George signed on as a crewman on a blackbirding ship, the *Lavinia*, sailing out of North Queensland, and wrote reports that helped turn the tide of public opinion against the thinly disguised slave trade that provided a workforce for the cane fields. He was able to balance his thrilling seagoing adventures to the exotic islands of the Coral Sea with enough moral indignation to both thrill and influence the readers of his reports. His eight-part series, 'A Cruise in a Queensland Slaver. By a Medical Student', was also published in *The Leader*, *The Age*'s weekly companion publication.

In a retrospective article, written at the end of the adventure, Morrison described graphic details of the *Lavinia*'s operations and exposed the 'Kanaka slave trade' in Queensland. The resulting debate, fermented by *Age* editorials and letters to the editor, led to the election, in 1883, of Samuel Griffith as Queensland premier on an anti-immigration platform. Griffith, who would later become the Chief Justice of Australia, banned recruitment from the New Guinea islands and spearheaded a number of high-profile criminal cases against blackbirding crews. Government intervention to eradicate the practice led to a total ban in 1890 and a scheme to repatriate workers. In spite of these measures, some form of blackbirding continued until Federation in 1901.

The part played by George Morrison in exposing and helping to end the Kanaka slave trade is enough to earn him a permanent place of honour in our nation's history. It is, however, only one in a long list of his remarkable achievements.

The ability to switch between diverse careers and interests was an amazing feature of Morrison's personality. It's no surprise to learn that his adventure down the Murray and his other sporting and collecting interests resulted in him failing his medical exams two years running, having optimistically put himself up as an honours candidate. His account of the results of his examination, written later in life, shows that one of the many qualities possessed by George Morrison was a sense of humour:

> It seems that in the examination in *Materia Medica*, I had among other trifling lapses prescribed a dose of *Oleum Crotonis* of 'one half

> to two drachms—carefully increased'. I confess that I had never heard of the wretched stuff; the question was taken from far on in the text book and, unfortunately, my reading had not extended quite so far. When a deputation from my family waited upon the examiner to ascertain the cause of my misadventure, the only satisfaction we got was the obliging assurance 'that you might as well let a mad dog loose in Collins Street' as allow me to become a doctor.
>
> And then the examiner produced my prescription. But I thought I saw a faint chance of escape. I pointed a nervous finger to the two words 'carefully increased', and pleaded that that indication of caution ought to save me. 'Save you, it might', he shouted with unnecessary vehemence; 'but, God bless my soul, man, it would not save your patient.' The examiner was a man intemperate of speech; so, I left the University. It was a severe blow to the University, but the University survived it.

This minor setback led to George's career change from medical student to crewman on a sailing ship, journalist and moral crusader. His return to medicine would be similarly serendipitous.

As he was in tropical waters, he decided to visit Port Moresby and Thursday Island and then Normanton, on the Gulf of Carpentaria.

Only eighteen years before the Burke and Wills expedition had set out with twenty men, camels, horses and tons of supplies and equipment to cross the continent south to north and had proved a tragic failure; the desert had defeated the best efforts of British know-how, technology and planning.

In typical style, however, late in 1882 Morrison decided to walk back to Melbourne following the route taken by the intrepid explorers, in the middle of summer, alone and on foot. He managed it easily and later described the journey, 3200 kilometres through mostly barren wilderness, as 'a pleasant excursion' which he did not feel was deserving of praise, as it was really 'no feat of endurance'.

The Times of London certainly thought it was a feat worthy of mention and called it 'one of the most remarkable of pedestrian achievements'. The newspaper already had its eye on Morrison who would become, in a later phase of his incredible life, its best and bravest foreign correspondent.

Until that point Morrison's articles had been syndicated through *The Leader,* a regional Victorian newspaper. On his return to Melbourne, however, he wrote a letter to *The Age* criticising blackbirding as 'the Queensland slave trade', which led to questions being asked of the Queensland government, and initiated the first serious enquiry into the trade in Kanaka labour in that state.

Although the Queensland government found no need to act to change things, the governor, Sir Anthony Musgrave, was able to diplomatically concur with Morrison's opinions in letters to influential friends in Britain and the days of the Kanaka trade were numbered from that time.

Another result of that letter, and the preceding articles written aboard the *Lavinia,* was that Morrison was employed and financed by the much-respected *Age* and *Sydney Morning Herald* to explore and cross New Guinea, recently annexed by the Queensland government as a protectorate.

He set out, in July 1883, for the unknown interior from Port Moresby with a party of 25, including renowned bushman John Lyons, some other European adventurers, two Malays and quite a few natives. They trekked into the unexplored jungles and mountains for 40 days until his adventurous spirit and bravery, accompanied by a good dose of youthful recklessness and arrogant bravado, almost cost him his life. He was all of 21 years old at the time.

The local tribes became increasingly hostile as the expedition penetrated the jungle. Finally, there was an all-out raid on their camp and many of the supplies were carried away. In the midst of the attack, Morrison shot and killed a local tribesman. Next day there was a great sound of wailing echoing through the jungle and the men accompanying Morrison, both European and native, were adamant that retreat was essential, at least to neutral tribal territory.

Although Morrison was sick with remorse and 'felt like a murderer' he disagreed with the overwhelming general opinion and went ahead—the others followed reluctantly.

When crossed spears and a shield were found blocking the jungle path, his companions again urged discretion and retreat. Once again, however, Morrison insisted on continuing, past the grim warning, and once again his companions followed, at a distance, only to come across their intrepid leader lying in a pool of his own blood with two spears protruding from his body—one from his head, near his right eye, and the other from his stomach.

Led by Lyons, who broke off the spear shafts and tended the wounds (and to whom Morrison always said he owed his life), the party retreated hastily the way they had come. With Morrison either strapped to a horse or carried in a blanket, they reached Port Moresby, remarkably, in eleven days. There the young adventurer received some emergency medical attention but he did not reach the hospital at Cooktown for more than a month. One day, on the ship returning to Cooktown, Morrison, in constant pain and seriously ill, sat up and blew his nose—and a two-centimetre piece of wood flew out of his nostril.

In spite of what he saw as a failed expedition, Morrison's party had penetrated further into New Guinea than any European.

After a week in hospital at Cooktown, Morrison sailed to Melbourne where, 170 days after the attack, a surgeon removed the remainder of one spear, which had made its way to the back of his throat. This was done by taking it up through his throat and out of his nose—without anaesthetic.

The other spear was still embedded in his abdomen and his father decided to send young George to the famous surgeon, John Chiene, professor of surgery at Edinburgh University, to have it removed.

So George travelled to Scotland and, once the removal of a tapering spearhead 'the size of your second finger' was successfully achieved, he decided that this was an excellent opportunity to resume his medical studies. He duly graduated as a Bachelor of Medicine and Master of Chemistry from Edinburgh University in August 1887.

After his graduation Morrison, having spent several years in the one place, decided it was again time to travel, so he headed to Canada, the United States and the West Indies and worked as a medical officer in several places before returning to Europe, where he became the medical officer at the Rio Tinto mine in Spain.

Tiring of that position after eighteen months, he travelled to Morocco and became physician to the Sharif of Wazan in Tangier.

Although this was only a temporary situation, Morrison stayed in Tangier for the best part of the year, which gave him free time to explore the desert and mountain areas of Africa, where few Europeans had ever travelled. Before long, however, he was once more restless and keen to explore the frontiers of science and medicine, rather than geography.

Morrison had developed an interest in neurology, perhaps associated with his horrific head injuries suffered in New Guinea, and decided to seek out and study under Dr Jean-Martin Charcot, the pioneer of neurological medicine and anatomical pathology in Paris.

Having done that, the 28-year-old George returned to Australia in 1890, and took up a position as resident surgeon at the hospital at Ballarat. He was there for two years before the wanderlust struck again and he was off, after a disagreement with the hospital committee.

This time he travelled through the Philippines, Hong Kong and into Siam (Thailand). He then moved on to China and later Japan. He studied the work of the missionaries and in China, where Christian missionaries were by far the most common Europeans, was often assumed to be one.

While in Japan he decided it was time for another walk. He was now a mature 31-year-old and, for reasons best known to himself, decided he'd like to walk from Shanghai in China to Rangoon in Burma. He set out in February 1894, unarmed and mostly staying with Christian missionaries along the way, or in villages. He spoke very little Chinese and said openly that he started out with the typical racist opinions that most Australians had towards the Chinese. Morrison, however, always seemed to have the ability to challenge his own perceptions and prejudices, take a global view of the world, and objectify his thinking. In his ever-present diary, he wrote:

> I went to China possessed with the strong racial antipathy to the Chinese common to my countrymen, but that feeling has long since given way to one of lively sympathy and gratitude, and I shall always look back with pleasure to this journey, during which I experienced, while traversing provinces as wide as European kingdoms, uniform kindness and hospitality, and the most charming courtesy. In my case, at least, the Chinese did not forget their precept, 'deal gently with strangers from afar'.

He hired guides from time to time and his diary noted that the entire journey cost something in the vicinity of £20. As with his previous walks and adventures, Morrison never claimed to be doing anything particularly extraordinary or brave, although he was undertaking the kind of journey that very few Europeans, since Marco Polo, had dared to contemplate:

> In the first week of February, 1894, I returned to Shanghai from Japan. It was my intention to go up the Yangtse River as far as Chungking, and then, dressed as a Chinese, to cross quietly over Western China, the Chinese Shan States, and Kachin Hills to the frontier of Burma. The ensuing narrative will tell how easily and pleasantly this journey, which a few years ago would have been regarded as a formidable undertaking, can now be done.
>
> The journey was, of course, in no sense one of exploration; it consisted simply of a voyage of 1500 miles up the Yangtse River, followed by a quiet, though extended, excursion of another 1500 miles along the great overland highway into Burma, taken by one who spoke no Chinese, who had no interpreter or companion, who was unarmed, but who trusted implicitly in the good faith of the Chinese. Anyone in the world can cross over to Burma in the way I did, provided he be willing to exercise for a certain number of weeks or months some endurance—for he will have to travel many miles on foot over a mountainous country—and much forbearance.

His journal of his long walk through China was published as a book in 1895. Titled *An Australian in China, Being the narrative of a quiet journey across China to Burma*, it is a detailed, articulate and very readable 93,000-word account of his travels, which gives a unique and fascinating insight into the customs and everyday features of late 19th century life in the cities, villages and rural areas of China and Burma—which few Europeans had ever experienced or observed.

From Rangoon, Morrison travelled through India and proceeded to Calcutta where he contracted a severe fever and almost died.

I have no idea how, but Morrison had somehow managed to complete his doctoral thesis sometime in between all his travels and adventures. He decided to recuperate back in Australia and then return to Edinburgh and submit his thesis and gain his Doctor of Medicine, which he subsequently did.

It may astound readers to realise that all I have written about this remarkable Australian so far has been a mere preliminary prologue to what he is mostly remembered for in the sphere of world politics and history. His greatest achievements were yet to come.

Morrison was approached by *The Times* to take up an appointment as a special correspondent in Asia. This was to be a 'secret' commission for two reasons. Firstly, it was the first position of its kind and the newspaper was not certain it would be a permanent one. Secondly, it involved Morrison working for the first time, but certainly not the last, as a secret agent for the British.

Late in 1895 he travelled via Saigon into Indo-China as far as Bangkok, reporting on French activities in Cambodia. His superiors at *The Times* and the British Foreign Office praised his public and secret reports, and his position was soon made permanent.

In March 1897 he was stationed in Peking (Beijing) as the first official China correspondent of *The Times.* Peking would be Morrison's home base for the next twenty years. In that time he would become the world's leading expert on the politics of China and the region and survive the Boxer Rebellion, in which he helped save countless lives and after which he wrote the most reliable and definitive history of the crisis. He would be credited with precipitating the Russo–Japanese War, be chief adviser to the ruler of China, bring about China's entry into World War I and be part of the Chinese advisory team for the Peace Conference at Versailles after the declaration of peace. He would even read his own obituary!

During the Boxer Rebellion of 1899–1900, all ex-patriot and diplomatic foreigners were blockaded in the diplomatic enclave in Peking for 55 days. The refuge was besieged not only by the Boxers, but by elements of the Chinese Imperial Army loyal to the Dowager Empress Cixi, who had decided to support the Boxers and taken power from her nephew, the emperor.

Morrison acted with his customary bravery throughout the siege, plotting and scheming with elements of the Chinese army who supported negotiation, and fighting his way in and out of the blockade to rescue Christian Chinese and European families who were being attacked.

At one point, Morrison led a party of twenty British troops and a few Americans to a church where Christian converts were being tortured and slaughtered by Boxers. He reported that they found 46 Chinese Christians dead with their hands tied and a gang of Boxers about to kill another hundred. Morrison's patrol saved more than a hundred and he reported casually: 'All the Boxers were killed, only one dared to face us, I myself killed at least six.'

Those rescued joined a thousand more in a safe area, a palace called 'The Fu', and Morrison and others made many daring journeys between the besieged legation and The Fu to make sure the refugees were safe and to tend to the wounded.

On one such occasion Morrison was badly wounded as they made their way to The Fu with some Japanese military who were also trapped in the siege. In the same exchange of gunfire, his friend Captain Strouts was shot dead beside him. Morrison, in his usual objective fashion, wrote about his wounding and the subsequent removal of the bullet fragments:

> Another bullet had splintered and some fragments struck me ... When they were cut out I fainted again and then vomited, the pain being intense, though I have no reason to believe it was one half as great as other pain I have suffered.

The following day a false report, posted by another newspaper but carried by *The Times*, reported that the Boxers had butchered all Europeans in Peking. *The Times* then ran an obituary of Morrison, praising him for being the most accurate and reliable reporter in China whose reports were always days ahead of any other news or official bulletins.

Had the newspaper waited it would have received a more accurate account of the situation from the man whose praises it was singing in print, supposedly posthumously. As it was, Morrison became one of the few people in history who ever read his own official obituary in a newspaper.

The frightened besieged diplomats and their families saw the tall handsome Australian as a saviour, though in fact he was often dishevelled and untidy. One American woman, quoted in L.C. Thompson's *William Scott Ament and the Boxer Rebellion*, wrote:

> Not a foreign man on the place to protect us ... we waited ... and our reward came when we saw down the valley a dusty figure ambling along on a dusty Chinese pony, crossing from the direction of Fengtai ... it was Dr Morrison.

When the siege was lifted with the arrival of British, German, Russian and French troops, the situation was reversed with suspected Boxers beheaded and many innocent Chinese slaughtered by rampaging troops, mostly Russian.

Morrison's next plan involved getting rid of the Russians in China. Russia was a threat to Britain's influence in China and therefore her empire states of India and Burma. When it became apparent that Russia, through demands and intimidation (about which Morrison had inside information), had taken over the Chinese warm weather port of Port Arthur, Morrison declared, 'There must be war, there *shall* be war!'

There was war. Britain could not oppose another foreign power like Russia directly, so the Machiavellian Morrison decided the Japanese should take on the role of China's protector. He helped engineer the surprise attack on the Russian navy by Japanese troops at Port Arthur and rode into the captured city with the Japanese general who led the attack. Morrison was described as 'the author of the Russo-Japanese War'. Tsar Nicholas's determination to continue this unwinnable war was one of the factors that led to the Russian Revolution.

The influence on world affairs exerted by this doctor from Geelong would, however, grow to even greater dimensions. When the Manchu Dynasty finally ended with the abdication of the last emperor in 1912, the military power broker Yuan Shikai become the President of All China. In 1915 he declared himself emperor. Morrison was his chief adviser, virtually the foreign secretary of China.

Although Morrison was a supporter of Japan, in order to prevent

Russian pressures on China from escalating, and actually precipitated the war between Japan and Russia in 1904, he later saw Japan as a similar threat and warned Australian prime ministers Deakin and Hughes about Japanese expansionism. He was involved in negotiating the Japanese relationship with China and convinced the Japanese to water down their infamous Twenty-One Demands made to China in 1915.

Morrison also campaigned for conscription in Australia in World War I, was instrumental in changing British policy on the opium trade in India, and considered taking the position of British Minister in China. *The Times* in London offered him the post of Foreign Editor, but he turned it down.

That is really just a brief outline of the life and times of George Ernest 'Chinese' Morrison. Whole books have been written about him and his name occurs many thousands of times in accounts of the complex history and politics of China, Japan and South-East Asia in the decades leading up to World War I but, oddly, he is hardly known by Australians today.

Morrison's private life was also fascinating and his romantic and erotic adventures were recorded in his diaries in similar detail to his political and social observations. He married his New Zealand–born secretary, Jennie Robin, in 1912. He was 50 and she was 22. They had three sons who all graduated from Cambridge University. Their eldest son Ian was killed while reporting on the Korean War for *The Times*.

George did not live to see his sons graduate, his health began to deteriorate in 1919 and he realised he had little time left, so he retired to England where he died on 30 May 1920.

Banjo Paterson, in his role as a war correspondent, visited China to report on the Boxer Rebellion. Commenting on world political figures, he once wrote that he had met and spoken with Winston Churchill, Cecil Rhodes and George Morrison and, in his opinion, George Morrison was the 'most impressive' of the three.

Banjo noted that:

> Morrison had gone into China on a small salary for *The Times* and had outclassed the smartest political agents in the world—men with untold money at the back of them.

So, if at any time someone asks you to name the most influential Australian that ever lived, don't hesitate to answer. You will certainly surprise them.

Just say, 'George Morrison, ever heard of him?'

2

THE ECCENTRIC MUSICAL GENIUS

ECCENTRICITY AND GENIUS

The term *eccentric* entered the English language around 1500, but originally it had nothing to do with human behaviour. It was a term first used in astronomy and geometry.

Derived from two Greek words, *ek*, meaning 'out' and *kentron*, meaning 'centre', the Latin version was literally *ex-centros*. Thus, in medieval Latin texts on astronomy, orbits not perfectly circular were referred to as *eccentricus* i.e. not properly centred.

Sometime in the 17th century the term was applied to human behaviour which seemed 'off centre' or 'out of kilter' with the rest of society and didn't conform to what was considered 'the norm'. By 1700 the term had entered the language as an adjective, and odd behaviour was known as 'eccentric'. It became a noun, applied to a person—an eccentric—during the 19th century, and the first written evidence of the word used in this manner occurred in the 1830s.

It was certainly a well-recognised characteristic in British society by 1860 when John Stuart Mill complained that there was not enough of it. He commented: 'The amount of eccentricity in a society has generally been proportional to the amount of genius, mental vigour, and moral courage which it contained.' He then went on to say that social conformity and lack of eccentricity was 'the chief danger of the time'.

This British acceptance of eccentricity, especially among wealthy or titled members of society, developed rapidly. Dame Edith Sitwell commented in the 1930s that eccentrics were a boon to social, artistic and technological advancement because, 'they are entirely unafraid of and uninfluenced by the opinions and vagaries of the crowd'.

In recent times the term has been used rather loosely, as a label for flamboyant behaviour, excessively egotistical behaviour, certain forms of mental illness and even syndromes such as Asperger's and autism. Oddly, there has been very little psychological or behavioural research and study done on the phenomenon of eccentricity, although many of history's greatest leaders, monarchs and artistic and scientific geniuses and innovators have displayed eccentric behaviour.

I have seen lists of supposed eccentrics which include people like Oscar Wilde and Howard Hughes, neither of whom was eccentric. Oscar Wilde was flamboyant and creative, while Howard Hughes, who suffered obsessive-compulsive disorder, was obviously mentally ill.

Psychologist Dr David Weeks, one of the few people to actually make a study of eccentricity, published in 1995, believes that true eccentrics are less likely than anyone else to suffer from mental illness. He concluded that, while they may be aware that their behaviour is unconventional, the fact certainly doesn't cause them any stress or worry. In other words, they do not 'suffer' from their eccentricity.

Dr Weeks believes there are certain distinctive characteristics that differentiate an eccentric person from a 'normally centred' person, or, indeed, one with a mental illness. Several of these are universally common to truly eccentric people. Firstly, their nonconformity, once it begins, is enduring and permanent, you cannot be a true eccentric merely on weekends, or when the whim takes you.

Secondly, all true eccentrics are excessively inquisitive and display creative or exploratory behaviour and curiosity about certain things, or even many things. They understand that they are different from other people, but are not worried by the fact and they are mostly not competitive with anyone but themselves and require no approval or assurance from others. They are, however, mostly idealistic and are often driven to achieve at a high level in order to, as they see it, make the world a better place or show people things that they believe to be true.

As well as these universal characteristics, there are other traits that true eccentrics *usually* display. They are not usually interested in the opinions of others and are not particularly interested in socialising and do not have a large circle of friends. Usually they have between one and six 'interests' or hobbies that they are happily obsessed with and about which they are extremely knowledgeable.

Then there are life situations, character traits and behaviours that are *often* found in eccentric individuals. They are often single and the only child in the family, or the eldest. They often have unusual living arrangements, eating habits and daily or domestic routines.

Not all true eccentrics also display 'genius', although the human quality of genius is far more common in eccentric people than in the general population.

As with the word 'eccentric', the word 'genius' was originally not applied as a human characteristic. It originally meant, in Latin, the 'spirit' of anything; that is, the inherent individuality or originality of a particular place or object. So, applied to a person, it would simply be your spirit of individuality, the thing that made you, *you*.

It was the philosopher Immanuel Kant who redefined 'genius' to mean a 'rare capacity' to independently understand concepts or demonstrate skills that would normally have to be taught to us by another, more experienced, person.

Genius, defined in this way, came to mean something other than 'talent'. While talent could be taught, practised and gained through learning and experience, 'genius' was used to describe a superior and exceptional form of understanding only inherent in certain individuals. The classic 20th century example is, of course, Albert Einstein. However, as the word is also used to describe people with extraordinary inherent artistic and creative abilities, it can be applied, with equal certainty, to Percy Grainger, who also qualifies as a true eccentric.

PERCY GRAINGER

Percy Grainger was an eccentric Australian creative genius who was born on 8 July 1882, in the very respectable Melbourne suburb of Brighton.

Much has been made of Percy's relationship with his mother, Rose, the daughter of wealthy Adelaide hotelier George Aldridge. Her family was prominent in Adelaide affairs. Her brother Jim was a well-known sportsman, hotelier and pioneer racehorse-breeder who had taken a herd of cattle into the Northern Territory as a young man, owned hotels and established the successful Richmond Stud in Adelaide. Another brother, George, was president of the Adelaide Stock Exchange. Both brothers had been members of the Goyder expedition to explore the Northern Territory in 1868.

Rose separated from her husband when Percy was eight years old, and devoted the rest of her life to her son. Percy's relationship with his mother was so intense and obsessive that the influence of his father in his life is often neglected in biographies, but his father's influence was substantial.

John Harry Grainger, Percy's English-born father, came from a family of builders, architects and engineers, although John's own father was a master tailor. He grew up surrounded by music, art and poetry, in the home of a wealthy opera-loving uncle who was a personal friend of the great theologian and poet Cardinal Newman. For several years John was educated at a monastery school in France before starting his engineering training when he was fifteen. He studied architecture and bridge-building and travelled to Spain, Italy and France, before emigrating to Australia in 1877, aged 22, to take up a position with the South Australian Department of Public Works. Just over a year later he resigned, after winning a competition to design the Albert Bridge in Adelaide, and he set himself up in private practice as an architect.

John Grainger was a competent amateur musician and water-colourist and, in 1878, established Adelaide's first string quartet. In 1879 he successfully tendered designs for two bridges in Victoria, the swing bridge at Sale and the Princes Bridge across the Yarra River in Melbourne. In 1880 he married Rose Annie Aldridge and, by 1882, when Percy was born, they were established in Melbourne and John was supervising the construction of both bridges.

The couple had a circle of influential artistic and music-loving friends, including, among many others, successful Melbourne builder David Mitchell, who built the Melbourne Exhibition Building and St Patrick's Cathedral. Mitchell's daughter, Helen, would become world famous as Dame Nellie Melba. John Grainger would later design a home for Nellie Melba, on the eastern fringe of Melbourne at Coldstream.

In partnership with an old friend, Charles D'Ebro, with whom he had emigrated from England, John designed many notable buildings in Melbourne, and also the Fremantle Town Hall in Western Australia and the Auckland Art Gallery in New Zealand.

As well as being a skilled architect, competent artist and music lover, John Grainger was, unfortunately, also an alcoholic and promiscuous adulterer who had, unknown to Rose, fathered a child before leaving England. The couple finally separated in 1890 and John returned to England, having lost most of his fortune speculating in mining companies. At some point in his life John had contracted syphilis, which he had passed on to Rose, after Percy's birth.

The history of syphilis (*Treponema pallidum*) is complicated and open to speculation. It is a venereal (i.e. sexually transmitted) bacterial infection which affects the skin, bone, body organs and brain. Some medical historians believe it originated from the skin disease *Treponema carateum*, known as 'pinta', which transferred from animals to humans in Africa around 15,000 years ago. This mutated into the skin disease 'yaws' (*Treponema pallidum pertenue*) and the more contagious skin and bone disease 'bejel' (*Treponema pallidum endemicum*), which was widely spread by the slave trade. Evidence seems to show, however, that the venereal form of the disease was established in South America in the pre-Columbian era. It certainly spread rapidly across Europe after European contact with the Americas and was an incurable condition affecting millions worldwide until the discovery of antibiotics in the 20th century.

Although venereal syphilis can only be passed on by sexual contact in its secondary phase, some non-sexual forms of *Treponema* may be passed on through skin contact. These things were little understood in 1890 and this explains Rose's advice to Percy that, should he ever meet his father, he must on no account touch him. She also, evidently, refrained from touching her son for many years. While Percy never had the disease, it certainly impacted upon his life.

John returned to Adelaide from Europe and lived for a time with Rose's brother George and his wife Marion, who were a childless couple. He gave up his excessive drinking and met Winifred Falconer, with whom he would spend the rest of his life. The couple moved to Western Australia where John designed many public buildings. They then returned to Melbourne where he helped establish the architectural firm of Grainger, Little and Barlow and continued to work until his retirement in 1915. John continued to support Percy financially after he separated from Rose. He died of tertiary syphilis in 1917.

Until the age of eight, when his father left, Percy, an only child, was privately tutored and home-schooled by both parents and his father's artistic and musical interests had a profound effect on him. Percy was an excellent artist, and his art tutors, who included the renowned painter Frederick McCubbin and Thomas Sisley, the first secretary of the Victorian Artists' Society, believed he could have achieved equal renown in that discipline, had he not chosen music as his main field of study. His mother, who was well educated and an accomplished pianist, had him reading independently by age four and she had begun his daily piano lessons by age six.

Rose organised his music and literary education and sought out Melbourne's best tutors for languages, art and drama. From his earliest schooling, Percy developed a lifelong fascination with language. As an adult he was fluent in at least six European languages, and could manage quite a few more. Percy was fond of literature and always said that reading the Icelandic saga, *The Story of Grettir the Strong* (which was published in translation by Erikir Magnusson and William Morris in 1900), when he was nine, was a life-changing event. His two main subjects, however, were art and music.

Home-schooling and private tutoring were the only forms of education that Percy knew until the age of twelve, when one term spent at a private school resulted in so much teasing and bullying that the young genius was quickly withdrawn. By then he was, in any case, preparing to leave for Europe to further his musical studies.

Percy always seemed to meet the right people at the right time and he was certainly lucky to come under the guidance of Mr Louis Pabst during Pabst's last two years as a piano teacher in Melbourne.

Pabst was born in Königsberg, in what was then Prussia, in 1846. His father was a brilliant musician who had held the title of Music Director to the King of Prussia and later succeeded Richard Wagner to become director and conductor at the Royal Theatre in Riga, the Baltic sea port which was then the third largest city in Russia. Louis took a degree in medicine but then studied the piano with famed Russian pianist Anton Rubinstein at the Moscow Conservatory. He gave his first concert at sixteen and toured throughout Germany before moving to England in 1867. In 1875, he and his father founded the Riga Music School and continued performing, mostly in Germany and Austria. After his father died in 1885, Louis decided, for some reason, to travel to Melbourne, where he established a private music academy in 1887. (Oddly, Europe being constantly changing in the 19th century, Königsberg is now Kaliningrad, in Russia, while Riga is the capital of Latvia!)

Crucially, Louis Pabst taught Percy Grainger piano during the last two years they both lived in Melbourne, from 1892 to 1894. Pabst also arranged for the child prodigy to perform his first public concert, at the Masonic Hall in Melbourne, in July 1894, one day after his twelfth birthday.

Louis Pabst left Melbourne in 1894 and returned to Europe, where he became Professor of the Moscow School of Music in 1899. He held similar university postings in Vienna, Munich and Nuremberg, where he died in 1921.

After Pabst left Melbourne, Percy was tutored by one of Pabst's ex-pupils, Adelaide Burkitt, who organised for the young 'wunderkind' to give a series of concerts at the Melbourne Exhibition Building in the spring of 1894. It is uncertain whether these concerts convinced Rose that Percy must go to Europe, or whether they were actually fundraisers for that eventuality. Whatever the case, after further fundraising concerts in Adelaide and Melbourne, Percy and Rose left for Frankfurt in May 1895. John sent money from Perth, where his business was now thriving, and Rose taught English to make ends meet, while Percy studied for the next five years at the Hoch Conservatory.

Percy's personality became quite defined in his years at Frankfurt. His singularity and quirkiness were evident early. He blossomed as a pianist under the tutelage of James Kwast, but did not take at all to the teaching methods of his composition tutor, Iwan Knorr, so he simply stopped going to lessons and studied instead under the amateur folkloric composer Karl Klimsch. Some of Knorr's radical ideas on composition, however, did appeal to Grainger and he and four British students of the Hoch Conservatory—Cyril Scott, Norman O'Neill, Balfour Gardiner and Roger Quilter—would become known as the 'Frankfurt Group'. Rather than having a common recognisable style to their musical compositions, what they shared was a resistance to the accepted, conservative, British style of composition and a tendency to use new and radical approaches, such as folk and jazz influences and even atonal and diatonic scales. After leaving the Hoch Conservatory, all members of this group would become admirers and followers of the innovative composer Frederick Delius, with whom Percy established a lifelong 'idea sharing' friendship.

Percy said later in life that he became 'sex mad' during his time in Frankfurt. This, of course, is no surprise for any boy in his teenage years, but it seems his sadomasochistic tendencies, said to have been inculcated by his mother's harsh discipline in early childhood, had developed by the age of sixteen. He was stunningly handsome with flaming red hair and bright blue eyes and fell madly in love with James

Kwast's daughter, although he remained a virgin until he was almost twenty. He later wrote candidly about his first sexual experience with a woman, the London socialite Lillith Lowrey, who was an admirer and supporter, and twenty years older than him. He wrote that intercourse felt like 'an overpowering landslide' that made him feel, 'I was about to die. If I remember correctly, I only experienced fear of death. I don't think that any joy entered into it.'

Lillith Lowrey was able to introduce Percy to all the right people, including Queen Alexandra, and he was soon the most popular and admired new musical talent in London.

Rose's health had not been good and, in the last year at Frankfurt, she had been unable to teach. So Percy had given a public recital to end his student days in Frankfurt and also to provide the necessary funds for him and Rose to live in London. On the strength of his newfound popularity, he was able to undertake a series of public recitals around Britain and then toured Australasia and South Africa with the famous Australian contralto Ada Crossley, a Gippsland girl who had made quite a name for herself in Melbourne and later in London, where she had appeared at five command performances before Queen Victoria.

Percy had been writing music since his childhood, his first known composition, 'A Birthday Gift for Mother', was written when he was ten. Back in Europe in 1904, he was working on a number of compositions and orchestral works. At the same time he undertook a busy schedule of recitals throughout Britain and Denmark. Also, inspired by his earlier work with folklorist/composer Karl Klimsch, and the work of folk historian Lucy Broadwood, he embarked on the massive task of collecting and recording, on a primitive cylinder gramophone, more than 300 folk tunes and songs from around Britain. Arrangements and combinations of these tunes for bands, as well as full orchestras, often with strange combinations of instruments, would be among his most popular and melodic compositions.

In May 1906 another serendipitous event occurred in Percy's life, which saw his musical career and reputation take a huge leap forward. Edvard Grieg, the most famous and admired composer of the day, was visiting London for two concerts in Queen's Hall, organised by the Queen's Hall Orchestra and financed by Sir Edgar Speyer. Grieg had heard, through a friend, some of Percy's compositions, and had sent him a short message of congratulations. When Lady Speyer asked Grieg if there was anyone he wanted to meet in London, he evidently replied, 'Yes, there is a young Australian composer I would like to see.'

Percy Grainger, writing reminiscences for the Grainger Museum in 1938, told the story, with typical honesty and objectivity, this way:

> Lady Speyer knew me quite well (I had often played professionally at her parties) and asked me to dinner to meet the Griegs. Grieg at once treated me like an art-brother, on account of my little choruses. Lady Speyer said 'You should hear Percy play your music' and Grieg answered 'I didn't know he is a pianist' and asked me what of his I played. I answered 'Preferably your Norwegian Folksongs, op.66 and the Slaatter, op.72'. Grieg was amazed, as these two volumes had been almost completely neglected by pianists—entirely so by virtuosi-pianists. But he was still more amazed when he heard how I played them.
>
> Not that there was anything wonderful in my interpretation. But I was familiar with folk-music traditions in England (which do not differ very greatly from those in Norway) whereas the other pianists he had heard murder his op.66 and op.72 had known nothing of folk-music anywhere. So I became his beloved young friend . . . He asked me to turn the pages for him at his London chamber concert and he gave me the copies of his songs . . . used in the two London programmes.
>
> When he got back to Copenhagen he said in an interview: 'What is nationality? I have written Norwegian Peasant Dances that none of my own Countrymen can play and here comes this young Australian and plays them as they ought to be played! He is a genius that we Scandinavians cannot do other than love,' whereby I became an international pianist overnight.

Edvard Grieg would live for only another seventeen months after that visit to London. In that time, however, he and Percy became extremely close and the young Australian visited the famous composer at his home in Norway and was introduced to his influential circle of musical friends. Grieg preferred Percy's interpretations of his piano music to those of any other pianist and, after his death, Percy played the 'Concerto in A Minor' at the memorial concerts for Grieg in both England and Copenhagen.

After an extensive concert tour throughout Britain and Europe, Percy embarked upon another Australasian tour with Ada Crossley and took the opportunity to record many cylinders of Maori and Polynesian music. His passion for collecting and studying folk tunes from all around the globe led to an excessive frenzy of composing, combining melodies and making arrangements of them for all sorts of bands and orchestras, as well as piano. Among the many compositions from this period are some, like 'Shepherds Hey' and 'Molly By The Sea', which have become favourites and are still perennially performed by orchestral college, school and military bands around the world, particularly in the United States.

Percy had, however, decided to establish himself as a concert pianist before attempting to publish and promote his own compositions, and he certainly managed to do so. By 1911 he was, arguably, the world's most famous concert pianist and it was at this point that he began the work of polishing, publishing and recording his own musical works. He also adopted the pen name 'Percy Aldridge Grainger', which appeared for the first time on the sheet music of his works published by Schott and Co. of London.

Throughout 1912 and 1913, with the help of his friend Balfour Gardiner, Percy arranged to perform a series of concerts at the Queen's Hall and the Aeolian Hall in London, which showcased his own original music. These concerts, one of which utilised an orchestra including 30 guitars and mandolins, were, in Percy's own words, 'a sensational success'.

At the outbreak of World War I, Percy made the momentous decision to move to the United States. In later life he would accuse himself of a form of cowardice but, with Rose now gravely ill and with the contribution he felt he could make to the world of music as yet unfulfilled, it seemed the best decision. Percy once honestly explained that he 'wanted to emerge as Australia's first composer of worth, and to have laid himself open to the possibility of being killed would have rendered his goal unattainable'.

Ever the eccentric, Percy always believed quite objectively (and refreshingly free of any hint of hubris) that it was his destiny to contribute significantly to the development of Western music. He once made a list of composers, in the order he felt they deserved to be ranked for their overall contribution to the world of music. The list included a number of famous composers that he did not personally like, in quite prominent positions. He placed himself ninth in the rankings and placed Johann Sebastian Bach on top, because he thought that Bach, had he been alive in the 20th century, would have enthusiastically embraced all forms of music and amalgamated them into his own compositions.

Percy began touring the United States, to great acclaim, in 1915 and later that year applied for American citizenship. He performed concerts in the premier concert halls of New York, Chicago, Pittsburgh and many other American cities, several times with Nellie Melba and once at a command performance for American President Woodrow Wilson. He signed a recording contract with Columbia Records and another with a company that produced pianola rolls. Although he was criticised by some who had supported him in Britain, his move to the less conservative musical marketplace of the USA was a huge success.

But his life was about to change and 1917 was a momentous year for the now 35-year-old Percy. His father died in Perth a week after the United States entered World War I in April 1917 and, in June, Percy enlisted in the US Army and became a saxophonist with the 15th Coastal Artillery Corps Band. As well as his commitments with the band, he gave piano recitals in aid of Red Cross and Liberty Bond fundraising. He became an American citizen in June 1918, and he remained in the army until his honourable discharge in January 1919.

Percy's wartime concerts were exceptionally well received and he took to playing the same relatively short encore to end these performances. It was his piano setting of a folk tune he called 'Country Gardens': a version of the tune had first been noted as early as 1724 and there were various other versions, several of them Morris dance tunes, sometimes called the 'Handkerchief Dance'.

Percy had first encountered the tune, which was to become his 'greatest hit' with the general public, in 1908. It had been given to him by folklorist Cecil Sharp, an Englishman who had spent ten years of his life in Adelaide in a period which coincided with Percy's childhood. Sharp had been conductor of the Adelaide Philharmonic and joint director of the Adelaide College of Music. He left Adelaide to return home to England in 1892, in spite of a petition signed by

300 Adelaide music lovers pleading with him to stay in South Australia. He would go on to be the man credited with the preservation and revival of folk songs throughout the English-speaking world, having spent decades collecting songs and tunes in Britain and the United States, which would otherwise have been lost and forgotten. Sharp and Percy had shared their knowledge and passion for folk tunes after the Graingers moved to London in 1904 and were living at Chelsea.

The massive success of the 'Country Gardens' sheet music, published by Schirmer in 1919, broke records for published piano music in the United States and allowed Percy to establish a career pattern for the next few years. Performing about 120 concerts a year, with a repertoire of his own original work plus pieces by Grieg, Brahms, Chopin, Bach and Delius, he also took temporary teaching positions and gave lectures on piano technique. By 1921 he had enough money to purchase a rather grand house outside New York at White Plains, which would be his permanent residence for the rest of his life although he continued to travel extensively.

In April 1922 Percy, aged 40, suffered the most traumatic event of his entire life. His mother's health had deteriorated rapidly and she was suffering from bouts of madness. While Percy was touring on the West Coast of the United States, Rose went to his agent's office on the eighteenth floor of the Aeolian Building in New York and, having left a letter for her son, she committed suicide by jumping from a window.

It has been suggested that she was worried about rumours that their relationship was incestuous, which it was not. This may be true, but it appears more likely that she was generally concerned that her approaching terminal madness, caused by syphilis, was adversely affecting Percy's career. The letter that she left for her son, although it did ask whether he had ever spoken to anyone of any kind of 'improper love', also included the phrase, 'I am out of my mind and cannot think properly', and was signed, 'Your poor insane mother'.

Percy would carry the letter, and a lock of Rose's hair, in a cylinder that he wore around his neck, for the rest of his life. He also prepared a booklet of photographs, including some taken of her in her coffin, which he distributed to family and friends.

In 1922 Percy returned to Europe and stayed for a year, collecting folk tunes in Denmark and performing concerts in Britain, Norway, the Netherlands and Germany. In Norway he visited his soul-mate Frederick Delius, who, now aged 60, suffered from failing vision. On one occasion Percy carried the composer on his back to a hilltop, to watch the sunset. He continued to tour very successfully and, in the United States, preferred to perform in large cinema theatres and other non-traditional venues, where audiences other than the more educated musical elite could enjoy his music. He made successful trips to perform in Europe in 1925 and 1927 and to Australasia in 1924 and 1926. He continued recording and, in 1927, made pianola rolls of a large part of his original repertoire.

Between the years 1904 and 1912 Percy had holidayed with, and conducted a passionate, though mostly long distance, love affair with Danish music student Karen Holten. They would remain friends and correspond regularly until her death in 1953, although she had married somebody else in 1916. Until Rose's death, there was no permanent place for another woman in Percy's life. After Rose died, however, he felt he was free to marry, and eventually did so.

Towards the end of 1926, while returning by ship from his Australasian tour, he met Danish poet and artist, Ella Ström, and a close friendship developed. They met again while Percy was in Europe the following year and, on 20 March 1928, the *New York Times* reported:

> WHITE PLAINS, N.Y., March 20. Percy Grainger, noted pianist and composer, today announced his engagement to Miss Ella Viola Strom, Swedish poet, painter and music lover, who is traveling in Europe. The marriage will take place after Miss Strom's tour, probably in August.

Honest as always, Percy thought it was necessary to warn his future bride about his rather bizarre sadomasochistic tendencies, and he did so in a letter dated 23 April 1928. Writing quite candidly about his sexual preferences he noted that: 'As far as my taste goes, blows . . . are most thrilling on breasts, bottom, inner thighs, sexparts . . .'

He did, however, hasten to add, in his own odd shorthand spelling style: 'I shall thoroly thoroly understand if you cannot in any way see yr way to follow up this hot wish of mine.'

To what extent Ella shared his 'taste' or enjoyed his 'hot wish', we can only speculate. They were, however, quietly married several days before 9 August 1928, when they repeated the ceremony on the stage of the Hollywood Bowl, at the conclusion of a successful concert given by Percy, which had included the debut performance of a piece written in Ella's honour titled, 'To a Nordic Princess'. The marriage, which appears to have been a perfectly happy one, lasted until Percy's death.

Although Percy several times refused permanent job offers with orchestras and universities, and also always refused offers of honorary degrees, he did take some temporary positions as an educator. The most permanent of these, which lasted for a year, was as Professor of Music at New York University.

In a series of lectures, titled 'A Study of the Manifold Nature of Music', he explored the relationships between seemingly disparate forms of music, both old and modern. In one of these lectures, on 25 October 1932, he discussed the harmonic similarities between the music of Delius and that of the Jazz legend Duke Ellington. Ellington took part in the lecture as an invited guest. Several years later, in 1934 and 1935, Percy adapted the lectures into a series of radio talks which he gave for the ABC in Australia.

Another major obsession evolved in the 1930s.

Percy had always been an avid collector and, in 1932, he had begun to sort, catalogue, arrange and classify many of the musical scores and objects that made up his professional history. This collection included music from the many composers with whom he had formed friendships, or who had been important in his development as a composer and musician. This was, obviously, an important record of the development of music in the early 20th century. At the same time he began recovering letters that he had sent over three decades to friends and collaborators, to include in a collection of correspondence that he had received from them.

The mania for keeping and collection was a thing he shared with his mother, who had kept Percy's personal belongings, drawings and letters from his childhood. Rose also collected, among other things, artworks, old furniture, Arts-and-Crafts metalwork, Meissen porcelain, Ottoman ceramics, japonaiserie, textiles, and African, Pacific and Native American beadwork and shellwork.

Percy had always had the ability to see himself objectively, in the third person so to speak, so it seemed obvious to him to include, as part of his collecting, items from his personal life. These included the towelling clothes that he designed and wore, as well as his collection of whips, blood-stained shirts and revealing photographs of the results of his self-flagellation.

Having always had a fond regard for the city of his birth, where the musical community had encouraged his talent and helped set him on his path as a musician, he approached the University of Melbourne and offered to build a museum which would be a repository for his valuable collection of musical items. Typically, he did not expect anything from the university and offered to raise the money required for the project himself.

The university accepted the offer and, in 1933, Percy was in Australia with Ella, supervising the building work and undertaking a tour for the ABC, which he used to finance the cost of the museum building. To raise the funds for the project, he donated two years of his income to the university.

Percy spent several months in Britain in 1936, performing concerts and making broadcasts for the BBC. Back in the United States in 1937, he composed 'A Lincolnshire Posy', a sixteen-minute original arrangement made up of folk tunes he had collected three decades earlier. It was dedicated to 'the old folksingers who sang so sweetly to me'. The piece was written for the American Band Masters' Association Convention in Milwaukee and was played by the combined bands, many of them made up of employees of the various breweries in that city, as the centrepiece performance of the convention. He returned to Melbourne in 1938 for the opening of the museum as a resource for music students. It was finally open to the public in the 1970s.

During World War II, Percy threw himself into fundraising for the war effort. He and Ella moved to Springfield, Missouri, apparently because Percy feared an invasion on the East Coast. It is estimated that he played more than 270 concerts in US army and air force bases and in public halls during this time. He also composed a series of musical pieces inspired by Rudyard Kipling's popular *Jungle Book* stories.

When the war ended, Percy and Ella returned to the house in White Plains, New York, and then took a long holiday in Europe throughout

1946. Percy, now 64 years old, appeared worn out by his heavy concert schedule and for some time he suffered a form of depression and a feeling of failure. He was offered the chair of music at the Adelaide University but gracefully refused, commenting: 'If I were 40 years younger, and not so crushed by defeat in every branch of music I have essayed, I am sure I would have welcomed such a chance.'

He performed at the London Proms in 1948, playing the piano part in his 'Suite on Danish Folksongs' with the London Symphony Orchestra. In 1953 he underwent his first operation for abdominal cancer and recovered sufficiently to perform for the last time at Carnegie Hall in 1954, at 72 years of age, and was presented with the Saint Olaf Medal by the King of Norway in recognition of his promotion of the music of his friend Edvard Grieg.

In the final years of his life, Percy turned his attention to collaborating with Burnett Cross, a young physics teacher, to invent 'free music machines'. These included a sort of pneumatic giant harmonica he called the 'Estey-reed tone-tool', and another using rolls of paper and a series of oscillators that he called the 'Cross-Grainger Kangaroo-pouch'. The novel avante-garde ideas embodied in these instruments and experiments are in many ways similar to those which would make John Cage famous in the 1960s, and foreshadowed the use of synthesising machines in popular music.

In 1955 Percy spent nine months in Melbourne, cataloguing and arranging the displays in the museum. Before he left, he deposited an envelope containing photographs and details of his sex experiences, with instructions that it should be opened ten years after his death. As his battle with cancer progressed, he made one last trip to Britain in 1958 where he performed for the first time on television. Around this time he changed his will and left his skeleton to the museum. It has even been said that he suggested his bones be used as a wind chime.

In 1959 and 1960 he toured and performed his music across the United States for the last time. Percy had never learned to drive, never owned a car, and disliked air travel, so the tour was undertaken using public transport, by bus and train. His final concert was given on 29 April 1960 at Dartmouth College in New Hampshire.

Percy Grainger died in White Plains Hospital on 20 February 1961, aged 78. Despite suffering failing eyesight and hallucinations, he was attempting to work on a new musical score in the weeks leading up to his death. His wishes regarding his skeleton were ignored and his body was flown to Adelaide where, after a funeral service in Saint Matthew's Church where his parents had married in 1880, his remains were buried with those of his mother, in the Aldridge family vault in the West Terrace Cemetery. The memorial plaque is engraved to Rose as the 'Wise, wonderful, devoted, angelic mother of Percy Grainger' and continues, using Percy's birth name 'George Percy Grainger', to credit him as 'World Famous Composer & Pianist', as well as 'Dearly beloved husband of Ella Grainger'. Ella remarried in 1972, at the age of 83, and died, aged 90, at White Plains in 1979.

Many aspects of Percy Grainger's life were unconventional, to say the least. There is ample evidence of his eccentricity. Among some of the many quoted examples are his odd musical arrangements, which required difficult and expensive combinations of instruments, for example, 27 pianos or 30 guitars and mandolins, and even, on one occasion, two of his friends whistling.

Percy was known to push his favourite piano stool from concert to concert in a wheelbarrow and made his own clothing, which he never ironed, from towelling. He is reputed to have been picked up by the police for vagrancy in New York, when he was actually Professor of Music at the New York University. He was also known to walk or run from one city to the next in order to reach the venue for his next concert performance. He has been accused of racism and certainly believed in the cultural supremacy of the Nordic race and Scandinavian music, yet he fully embraced all genres of music and admired Polynesian, African and Afro-American music—and invited Duke Ellington to join him in his lectures at New York University.

His sexual behaviour was highly unconventional at the time, or at any time for that matter, but he appears to never have been especially promiscuous, or to have promoted his sexual behaviour as acceptable to anyone else.

As a pianist his vigorous style has been called 'quirky', and in later years even 'markedly eccentric'. He was something of a fitness fanatic and would often make his entrance by leaping onto the stage when conducting. He also abstained from alcohol and tobacco and became a vegetarian in middle age but, as he didn't like vegetables very much, he lived mostly on fruit and nuts. He often prefaced playing his most famous work, 'Country Gardens', by informing the audience that English country gardens were mostly vegetable plots and suggesting that, as he played, they might like to think of turnips.

He could be brutally honest about his own talents, calling himself a failure, while at the same time proudly recognising his unique musical skills and abilities. In setting up the museum in Melbourne University, he was certainly driven by a desire to leave an historic record and a valuable collection of the music and ideas of other composers, but he is also on record as having honestly stated that, as an atheist, he wished passionately to be remembered and valued by others after his death.

For several decades following his death, Percy's music and memory faded, although the shorter pieces remained perennially popular with college and school bands. His eccentricities tended to be remembered more than his music. Musicologist John Blacking was of the opinion that Percy's contribution to the world of music would have been much greater had it not been 'undermined by dilettantism and the disastrous influence of his mother'. One is tempted to reply that Percy's entire musical career would not have happened without Rose's influence.

In 1960, lyricist Robert M. Jordan put a set of sugary lyrics to 'Country Gardens' and recordings by Jimmy Rodgers, Nana Mouskouri and many others, even the Muppets, were hugely popular and returned the tune to something like its enormous popularity of the 1920s, 30s and 40s.

A true resurgence in recognition of Percy's contribution to the development of music began in the 1980s and, in 1988, through the marvels of modern technology, Percy made a posthumous appearance at the 'Last Night of the Proms', as a soloist with the BBC Symphony Orchestra, playing Grieg's 'Piano Concerto' in the Royal Albert Hall.

Percy left behind many recordings and more than 80 piano roll performances of his own works and those of other composers. Since the 1990s, there has been quite a revival in the playing and appreciation of Percy's music, including many new CD compilations of his recorded works, many thousands of band performances of his compositions, and a Percy Grainger Festival in Britain, which is now planned to be established as a regular event.

His museum at Melbourne University is open to the public and his home in White Plains is now the Percy Grainger Library which contains historic performance material and is open to musical researchers and visitors. Timothy Reynish, renowned conductor of band music, called Percy, 'the only composer of stature to consider military bands the equal . . . in expressive potential to symphony orchestras'.

Of all the remarkable, strange lives lived by Australians, there are few as bizarre, multifaceted, and just plain weird as that of Percy Grainger. Yet, in spite of all his weirdness, his friends and colleagues universally described him as 'the happiest of people'.

Perhaps Percy should be best remembered not as an eccentric, but as a man who appreciated all forms and genres of music and combined and promoted them to please all kinds of people, not just 'music lovers'.

This attitude was reflected in the last series of ABC Radio broadcasts he gave. He called the series, 'A Commonsense View of All Music'.

3

THE SWIMMING SUPERSTAR

A HISTORY OF SWIMMING

Swimming on ocean beaches in Sydney was banned by local councils until 1902–03, due to concerns about 'public decency'. The bans were only lifted when councils imposed strict rules about clothing. Swimsuits were required, by local council by-law, to be 'neck to knee' for both sexes and men's swimsuits were required to have a 'skirt'. This has led to a common misconception that there was very little public bathing or interest in swimming at all until this time, but nothing could be further from the truth.

Swimming and bathing in the harbour had been part of the Sydney lifestyle long before the arrival of the First Fleet. The swimming stroke favoured by the Indigenous inhabitants was evidently a sort of sidestroke with scissor kick, similar to what was later known as the 'trudgeon'. This would have enabled the swimmer to carry a weapon or utensil and keep a lookout for food (and also keep a lookout for sharks that might be doing the same thing).

By 1806 there were 1800 children of European descent under the age of eighteen living in Sydney. Half of them were illegitimate and many of those, referred to as 'the orphans', were more or less running wild around the colony. There is no doubt in my mind that a certain percentage of European kids were regularly swimming in the bays and inlets of Sydney Harbour, probably with the local Aboriginal children.

By 1810 a beach 'close to the Governor's Domain', probably Woolloomooloo Bay, was a popular public swimming place and, in 1816, the *Sydney Gazette* warned parents of the dangers of letting their children swim there, due to the reports they had received of injuries to children from the vast numbers of oysters and dangerous rocks.

The soldiers of the various regiments assigned to New South Wales had their own bathing-houses in Cockle Bay (Darling Harbour) and, in a 1937 feature on the history of Australian swimming, in the Sydney sporting newspaper *Referee*, Dudley Hellmrich wrote that, in 1810: 'The Imperial soldiers stationed at Sydney are alleged to have held competitive events in the military bathhouse at Cockle Bay.'

He went on to speculate that: 'What must be regarded as the first swimming championship of Australia was held in Woolloomooloo Bay on Saturday, February 14, 1846 . . . the carnival at which it was decided was described in the "Sydney Morning Herald" of February 16.'

And, indeed, it was, reported in the *Sydney Morning Herald* under the headline 'PUBLIC SWIMMING MATCHES':

> The first swimming matches of this season, for which public prizes were advertised by Mr Robinson, of the Sydney Swimming Baths, who sent to England for cups and medals for the purpose, came off on Saturday morning in Woolloomooloo Bay, at 7 o'clock. A very large attendance of subscribers and the public who take an interest in this manly and gallant species of contest took place, and the steep shore of the domain, as well as the floating baths, were covered with spectators.
>
> The first match was open to the whole colony, and we regret that so few besides the subscribers to the baths came forward to contest the prize—a handsome silver cup value £8.08 shillings—and to strive to the honour of wearing the swimming belt for the next twelve months.

There were six entrants and the course for the race was 'upwards of a quarter of a mile' around two buoys set in the bay and 'the start from the surface of the water took place at a quarter past 7'. The *Herald* then goes on to tell us that the eventual winner:

> Mr Redman, junior, took the precaution of adopting the ancient Roman practice of anointing his whole person with oil, just as the

> word was given to strip, and as the morning was boisterous and rather cold, and the bay rough, this must have given him an advantage.

Mr Redman, junior, came in ahead of Mr Alistair MacLean who 'gallantly maintained the struggle' but failed to win the silver cup by a margin of about 10 yards. The winner's father, Mr Redman, senior, was third. Mr Thornton, who came in equal fourth with Mr Green, might have done much better, except that he 'gallantly gave up his chance at the early part of the race to assist Mr Whitbread, who suffered from the boisterous state of the bay, and was exhausted'.

The *Herald* then gave an account of the juvenile race over 100 yards and concluded by saying that, on the following Saturday, there would be 'two swimming, and one diving match, at the baths'.

I assume that the stroke used at this time would have been the breaststroke, although I have no proof of this. It certainly wasn't the trudgeon, as Englishman John Trudgeon would introduce the stroke named after him in the late 1870s, claiming that he learned it from a native tribe in South America.

One of the earliest public bathing pools in the colony was established by Mr Thomas Robinson in 1829: the Gentlemen's Baths in Woolloomooloo Bay, at a site slightly to the south of where the Boy Charlton Pool is now. Sometime later he established a smaller structure for ladies to the south of the Gentlemen's Baths.

For men and children, casual bathing was often done naked, or in some form of rudimentary costume. By the middle of the 19th century a standard swimming costume had developed for men, consisting of a singlet top and thigh-length pants. Ladies tended to bathe in some form of 'normal' clothing. Secluded beaches around the harbour, or beach houses with walls extending into the water, or bathing machines, afforded some form of privacy.

Another way of catering to public decency was to have certain times or days set aside for the two sexes. At Brighton Beach in Melbourne it was the custom to fly a white flag above the beach when ladies were bathing. Gentlemen were expected to stay away when the flag was flying.

There were even some beaches assigned to either male or female bathers. Milk Beach in Sydney's eastern suburbs, for instance, was known as a 'ladies' beach' and it is quite possible that the beach was given its name because it was a haven for nursing mothers. Three years after the tramline reached Coogee in 1883, a tidal pool exclusively for the use of women opened at one end of Coogee Beach. Men could swim at the pool located at the other end of the beach and there was even an indoor swimming pool at the Coogee Aquarium.

While bathing was not an uncommon activity in the first half of the 19th century, it was in the second half of the century that the idea developed that swimming was efficacious and conducive to a healthy lifestyle.

Swimming in Sydney was given an enormous boost with the arrival of Frederick Cavill, a Londoner who pioneered competitive and long-distance swimming in Britain in the 1850s and 1860s and then migrated to Sydney via Melbourne with his family in 1879. Fred was a proponent of healthy diet, outdoor exercise and swimming as the key to a long and happy life. He called himself 'professor of swimming', established swimming baths at Lavender Bay in Sydney Harbour in 1880 and published a popular booklet called 'How to Learn to Swim'.

While Frederick Cavill was visiting Britain in 1888, the shore access to the Lavender Bay baths, which Cavill called a 'natatorium', was resumed by the government to facilitate construction of the North Shore railway line. Upon his return the 'professor' was furious and demanded compensation. The New South Wales government gave him permission to build another natatorium, made of timber slats and iron tanks, at Farm Cove. He and several of his six sons taught swimming, diving and lifesaving there until 1909, when the whole structure was blown across the harbour in a fierce storm and smashed on the rocks.

Fred's sons would all become part of Australian swimming history and legend, breaking records, saving lives, winning medals for bravery and teaching a whole generation of future Australian champions. One of his sons, very appropriately named Sydney, is credited with having invented the butterfly stroke.

While the Cavill family played a pivotal role in the development of Australian swimming and promoted the connection between swimming, fitness and a healthy life, they were not alone in doing so.

One of the earliest champions of swimming as a beneficial activity for a healthy life, especially for women, was the amazing Harriet Elizabeth Rowell, who had migrated from England to Melbourne in 1875 with her female companion, Miss Alice Moon. For two years, Harriet taught ladies, including the governor's daughters, to swim at Captain Kenney's St Kilda Sea Baths. Captain Kenney's first baths or 'Gentlemen's Bathing Ship', as it was known, which operated from 1854, was, indeed, an old wooden sailing ship called the *Nancy* that the enterprising captain had scuttled off the beach, after removing the decks. The 'baths' were inside the frame of the hull. By the time Harriet arrived in 1875, he had built more suitable baths.

After a trip back to Britain, Harriet and Alice returned to Melbourne and opened a ladies' gymnasium in the Queen Victoria Building on Swanston Street and, by 1881, they had 190 gymnastic pupils paying 29 shillings a quarter. They also travelled weekly to Ballarat to give swimming and gymnastic instruction, ran a 20-acre organic farm at Beaconsfield and, in 1888, opened a city restaurant.

By 1892 they were both living in Sydney, although their relationship had ended. Harriet opened a ladies' gymnasium in Liverpool Street and, in 1897, she ran another in Castlereagh Street. She returned to Melbourne in 1899, where she gave lectures on women's health and ran a gymnasium in Collins Street until her death in 1902.

Harriet, who used the name 'Miss Elphinstone Dick' professionally, had been a member of the Brighton Swimming Club as a teenager in England and taught swimming before coming to Australia. At the age of 22 she had won a 10-kilometre ocean race from Shoreham to Brighton, against men, in rough seas. At Captain Kenny's St Kilda Sea Baths, she twice defeated a local male challenger, a certain Mr McGonigal, in match races. The second of these was an endurance race which resulted in Mr McGonigal being dragged exhausted from the water after three and a half hours, while Harriet swam calmly on.

It was partly due to role models like Harriet that, when the 'swimming club boom' hit Sydney in the late 1880s, there were many young women eager to participate and compete.

There are more than 40 substantial manmade tidal pools along the coastline of Sydney, and many of them date from this time. There have also been, over the years, scores of netted pools in the harbour and Botany Bay, many with substantial buildings, jetties, boardwalks and dressing sheds attached.

The Balmain swimming baths were built in 1882 by James Reynolds, and the Balmain Swimming Club was formed in March 1884.

By the 1890s this club was staging 'ladies' bracelet' races over varying distances for women competitors. In 1891 the NSW Amateur Swimming Association was formed by the various men's swimming clubs. In his address at the World Swimming Coaches Clinic in Indianapolis in 2004, however, legendary swimming coach Forbes Carlile claimed that, 'the first NSW men's championships were held in 1889 [two years earlier] in the long-since demolished Sydney Natatorium, an indoor pool near Central Railway Station, which was filled with salt water pumped two miles from the harbour'.

The idea of joining a swimming club and competing against the other members in a safe environment was a very attractive one to many women. Interclub competitions were a source of friendly rivalry and excitement, and also a chance to socialise and meet other like-minded women.

Sydney was, and still is, heaven on Earth for anyone wishing to swim. As well as the tidal baths along the coastline and harbour foreshores, there was the Sydney Natatorium and other suburban swimming pools, like the tidal pool at Ramsgate and the St George Pool in Cleveland Street at Redfern. And there were dozens of clubs. Some were based in particular baths or districts like Balmain, Eastern Suburbs, Mosman, Fort Street, Coogee, Balmoral and Redfern. Others were based on vocation, such as the Police Swimming Club and the Palace Emporium Club, which was set up for employees of Anthony Hordern's famous department store.

The great age of swimming clubs continued until the outbreak of World War I. By that time the surf beaches had been opened up to the public and surf lifesaving clubs had been formed. The breaststroke, sidestroke and trudgeon (favoured by female swimmers as the head was out of the water) had all given way to the Australian crawl, originally brought to Australia by the Solomon Islander Aleck Wickham. Not only was the crawl much faster, it was really the only practical stroke to use if you wanted to catch a wave.

It was truly serendipitous that, while the Cavills were teaching swimming at Farm Cove and the swimming club 'fad' was at its peak, the planets aligned for just a brief time to help create the greatest swimming, diving, dancing show-business phenomenon the world has ever seen. Her name was Annette Kellerman.

ANNETTE KELLERMAN

Annette Kellerman—swimmer, athlete, dancer, diver, actress, vaudeville entertainer, author, designer, fitness expert, model, women's liberator, ruthless self-promoter and movie star—was born in Sydney on 6 July 1886. It's an outstanding list of achievements in any era, but even more so when you consider that Annette spent much of her childhood crippled.

Annette was the second child of Frederick and Alice Kellerman, musicians and music teachers. Her French mother, Alice Ellen Laurentine Charbonnet, was a sophisticated and musically gifted composer and pianist who had arrived in Melbourne at the age of 21, to take part in Australia's first International Exhibition in 1880. Alice's father, Benjamin Amable Charbonnet, was born in New Orleans, Louisiana, and was chief justice of the French overseas colonies, including an appointment as Chief Justice of New Caledonia. His wife Ellen was born in London and the couple had married in Paris. Alice was also born in the United States, in Cincinnati, Ohio, and spent part of her childhood travelling throughout the French Pacific colonies, and living in Noumea, before settling in Paris, where she studied at the Paris Conservatoire under the famous female composer Cecile Chaminade.

As part of France's contribution to the Melbourne Exhibition, the French government sent a collection of French-made pianos and, typically, it was decided that an attractive and extremely talented young female pianist should be sent to demonstrate them. At that time France was the world's leading maker of grand pianos and the Australian colonies were importing more than 2000 French pianos every year.

Among the instruments demonstrated every day by Alice at the exhibition in 1880 were those made by Sébastien Érard, whose customers included Beethoven, Liszt, Haydn, Wagner, Verdi and Ravel, and also those made by Pleyel and Company, which were preferred by Debussy, Saint-Saëns and Stravinsky. In eight months, the exhibition attracted more than 1.3 million visitors, many of whom would have enjoyed Mademoiselle Charbonnet's recitals.

Alice, who was completely at home in the *très chic* music salons of Paris, was much in demand at the rather less sophisticated musical soirées of colonial Melbourne and later in Sydney, which she visited when the exhibition ended. In Melbourne she became close friends with Helen Mitchell, the ambitious daughter of a wealthy family who would achieve fame later in life as Dame Nellie Melba. Alice actually taught Helen to accompany herself on the piano.

In Sydney, where she gave a few private recitals and perhaps also promoted the virtues of French pianos, Alice met a young violinist, Frederick Kellerman, the son of German migrants, whose father ran a successful leather goods store in the city. Frederick was not only a gifted violinist, he also taught singing, harmony and counterpoint, and was rather debonair. It was a match made in heaven.

The two talented musicians married on 18 December 1882 and were living in Darlinghurst when their second child, Annette Marie Sarah, was born. There are conflicting accounts of Annette's birthplace and childhood, some of which are simply the result of poor research being subsequently copied. Annette's penchant for embroidering the facts of her life to make a good story may have also added to the confusion.

Peter Cox, a curator from the Powerhouse Museum in Sydney, probably got as close as is possible to the truth in his notes for the Kellerman Exhibition in 2016:

> Annette's birth certificate shows that she was born in 1886, not at Marrickville but 101 Victoria St, Darlinghurst, an address that today

> we could call Potts Point. The family moved to Marrickville, living at 128 Silver St from 1889 to 1892. The house still stands on the corner [*sic*] Calvert Street. The Kellerman family moved back to Potts Point, then lived at 43 Phillip St Sydney where Annette's mother had a Conservatoire de Musique. The building that housed the conservatorium still stands on the west side of Phillip St between Bridge and Bent St, around the corner from the Museum of Sydney.

Alice and Frederick established their Conservatoire de Musique in a three-storey premises in Phillip Street. The building held six pianos and the Kellerman Tuesday afternoon soirées were so popular that people sat two on a chair and the staircases provided extra seating for the artists, musicians, writers and international visitors who joined the wealthy parents whose sons and daughters were taught by the Kellermans. They also helped establish the Sydney Orchestral Society, the Australian Musical Association and the Sydney Philharmonic.

It was in this colonial oasis of culture that Annette grew up, surrounded by music and talented, creative people, listening to her mother's tales of the South Pacific. Above the two grand pianos in the main salon hung portraits of three of her mother's personal friends. All three were world famous. Two, Cecile Chaminade and Nellie Melba, were recognised as stars in the musical firmament. Annette's favourite portrait by far, however, was that of the famous French actress, Sarah Bernhardt, which was signed, 'with great affection' to the 'charming Alice Charbonnet'.

Annette decided quite early that she was destined for show business. The renowned Shakespearean actor George Rignold spent the last 25 years of his life in Sydney, occasionally acting as well as leasing and managing Her Majesty's Theatre from 1887 to 1894. He was often a guest of the Kellermans and Annette prevailed upon her mother to invite him to watch her playing scenes from *Macbeth*, with Annette as Lady Macbeth and her three siblings performing some very minor supporting roles. The ageing actor apparently said that he'd be 'only too pleased' to oblige. There is no written record of his critical response.

In spite of her parentage, Annette Kellerman would never be well known for her musical abilities, but she would one day dazzle the world with her physical feats and her showmanship. Before that day arrived, however, she would have to overcome many difficulties, and the first of these had already occurred and been conquered when she was performing for George Rignold.

When she started walking Annette's legs bowed and would not take her weight. She was diagnosed as suffering from the disease rickets, caused by vitamin D deficiency, and was forced to wear heavy leg braces until she was seven years old, to prevent her legs from being permanently misshapen. Memories of that aspect of her childhood would lead to a lifelong interest in diet, fitness and health. In one of the many later diverse phases of her life, she toured America and Germany lecturing on health and fitness and she also set up health food stores in San Diego and Long Beach, California. 'When I was a girl I was a cripple from calcium deficiency. So little was known about diet that my parents didn't think it was important to make me drink milk.'

One life-changing result of her being crippled was that a doctor recommended swimming as a beneficial activity to strengthen her legs and her father, keen to assist his daughter's recovery in any way possible, took her swimming. Some sources claim that Annette learned to swim at Lavender Bay, but this is not the case. She learned to swim much closer to home, at Farm Cove, just to the east of where the Opera House is today, at Cavill's Baths in Sydney Harbour. Annette recalled:

> When I was a little Tot about six years old, Dad took me to Cavill's Baths, in Sydney, Australia, to learn to swim. Each day we walked with my brother and sister through the beautiful Botanical Gardens, with its wondrous view of the most famous harbour in the world, to our swimming lesson. I was awfully scared and did not learn quickly, but Mr. Percy Cavill, who was my teacher, never frightened me, so I soon lost all fear . . . Before I was thirteen years old I was like a fish in the water . . . Later, in Melbourne, I was the first girl to swim—two, five and ten miles.

Percy was, of course, a son of Frederick Cavill.

By the time the Cavills' floating natatorium was blown across the harbour and destroyed in 1909, Annette was far away from Sydney, touring the United States and appearing as the headline act in some of that nation's grandest theatres. The road to success had, however, been a rocky one and the Kellerman family fortunes had suffered many 'downs' and very few 'ups' along the way.

During the financial Depression of the 1890s, the Kellermans' Conservatoire de Musique struggled to attract students as the wealthy families of Sydney were forced to tighten their belts. The Federation Drought, which began in 1894 and lasted until 1902, only made things worse for rich Sydney families whose wealth was dependent on rural production.

By the end of the decade, with Federation looming, lingering recession, drought and the Australian colonies involved in the Boer War, a private music teaching business was no longer a viable way to support the Kellerman family. They struggled on, but the Conservatoire de Musique finally closed its doors and, when a solution offered itself, the family split into two groups. Alice was offered a teaching position at a school in Melbourne, where she was still kindly remembered and could command good fees for private tuition outside of school hours.

This school was known as the 'Simpson School', as it was run by two spinster sisters, known as 'the Misses Simpson'—it would later evolve into the Mentone Girls Grammar School. Annette's younger sister, Marcelle, who would remain her companion and support throughout her entire life, was the dux of the school in 1903 and 1904. During Annette's brief time under the tutelage of the Misses Simpson, she seems to be remembered only as 'a rebel'.

Annette, who had been indulged and spoiled by her mother (no doubt due to the disability she suffered in her early childhood), was a wilful and self-obsessed young teenager. She neglected her piano lessons and was such a bad pupil that the headmistress of the school she attended in Sydney suggested to her father that removing his daughter from her establishment might be the best thing for all concerned. Annette was, however, apparently relentless in her dedication to her ballet lessons and practice, and loved swimming. In her unpublished autobiography, *My Story*, she explained:

> Only a cripple can understand the intense joy that I experienced when little by little I found that my legs were growing stronger and taking on the normal shape . . . I'd go swimming anywhere, any time, at the drop of a hat . . . I was more often at the pool than at class.

She also happened to be a gifted and extremely good swimmer, and a faultless and fearless diver. The famous Australian athlete, Olympian, movie star and showman Snowy Baker, and his less famous brother Frank (who would become a champion water polo player), often trained with Annette at Farm Cove. Emily Gibson's biography of Annette quotes Frank as remembering that, 'the first time she tried to copy Snowy diving, she hit the water all wrong'. As soon as she had recovered she climbed the tower again and made a perfect dive. From that day on, according to Frank, 'she never made anything but clean dives'.

The Baker brothers, along with the Cavill brothers, were so impressed with Annette's swimming and diving that they suggested to her father that she should turn professional, as competitive swimming and exhibition diving were extremely popular at the time, and there was money to be made. At first, however, both her parents were opposed to the idea, considering it far too common and vulgar a career for one of their offspring.

Annette stayed on in Sydney with her father for a while, before the family was reunited in Melbourne early in 1903. During that time in Sydney, Frederick Kellerman apparently had a change of heart about his daughter's 'hobby' of competitive swimming. Annette always claimed that what she wanted was to be an actress and dancer, but her father asked her to take up swimming and diving professionally to support the family—despite her mother's objection that it was not a respectable career.

By April 1902 Fred Kellerman, who was finding it increasingly difficult to get any work teaching music, had indeed become, according to the *Sydney Mail*, an 'enthusiastic swimming supporter' and the driving force behind the first ladies' swimming championships in New South Wales.

In reality, what Fred had become was desperately anxious about his family's well-being. What Fred became an 'enthusiastic supporter' of, was a plan to use Annette's talents in the pool to restore the family's wealth. Annette would refer to it, later in life, as 'swimming back the family fortune'.

The *Sydney Mail* reported the inaugural event, using the older spelling of the family name, on 5 April 1902:

> **First Ladies' Swimming Championship**
>
> ... Mr Fred Kellermann, the well-known musician and enthusiastic swimming supporter, organised the first championship ladies' swimming carnival. Mr. Kellermann secured the official support of the New South Wales Amateur Swimming Association ... and the association officials enabled everything to go off smoothly. The chief events were the championship races, both won by Miss Annette Kellermann. In the 100 yards championship there were eight entries from among the best lady swimmers in the State, but only five started ... Miss Kellermann drew away and won easily ... but, as it was won without pressure, only one minute 26 seconds was ticked ... The quarter-mile championship had four entries, but three started ... After the first lap Miss Kellermann drew away easily, and eventually won by some 50 odd yards ... The time was exceptional—7 minutes 48 seconds, and is claimed that it has never been approached by lady swimmers in England. As Miss Kellermann is to visit England next year, she should give a good account of herself.

Surely it will be apparent to even the least cynical modern reader that the 'first ladies' swimming championship' at the Redfern pool was little more than a thinly disguised demonstration of Annette's superiority over a small group of hand-picked local swimmers, organised with the help of a few sympathetic friends. The Kellerman profile-building, publicity machine was beginning to roll.

The Kellermans were well-connected and, as entrepreneurial concert performers and purveyors of sheet music copies of compositions by Alice, were quite experienced at dealing with the world of newspaper publicity, advertising, reporting and promotion.

From this point on in our story, we must take into account the fact that Annette was being 'managed' by her father. She only ever had two managers in her entire life, the other was Jim Sullivan, who would become her husband. She was, however, a very charming and clever self-publicist and everything she said and wrote about herself in her long, colourful and fascinating life needs to be checked carefully, or taken with quite a few grains of salt. It is hard to discover the truth about any celebrity's life by reading their publicity, especially if they were writing it themselves, as Annette often was.

The one element of the event at the Redfern pool that couldn't be contrived, however, was the time. The *Sydney Morning Herald*, reporting that Miss Kellerman had won the 'quarter mile ladies' championship of the state in 7 minutes 48 seconds', commented, 'fast swimming for a lady', and indeed it was—at that time.

(A quarter mile is just 2.336 metres longer than 400 metres and, as I write this 118 years later, the women's 400-metre world record is 3 minutes 54.52 seconds.)

By the end of the summer of 1902–03 Annette was living in Melbourne with the rest of the family and had lowered her time significantly. In an interview with the *New Idea* magazine the reporter asked, 'What are your times, by the way?' And she answered:

> One hundred yards, 1 min. 18sec.; quarter-mile, 7 min. 2sec.; and mile, 32min. 39 sec. These are the best times for Australasian lady swimmers, and as far as I know for English swimmers, too. The only English published records are:—100 yards, 1 min. 26½sec.; and mile, just a shade under 40min. I hope to go to England next season, and do some swimming there.

Part of the Kellerman legend is the story that the Cavill brothers and the Baker boys had to convince Annette's father that she should go to England, and attempt to swim the English Channel in the lead-up to the planned celebration of the 30th anniversary of the first successful crossing by Captain Webb. As her father was, it seems, already talking to the press in April 1902 about Annette going to England, it doesn't seem to me that he needed much convincing. Everything that Annette did, from early 1902 until she left in 1904, was about 'getting to England'.

What they *needed* was money and the way to raise money was through publicity. The plan to visit England did not come to fruition for two more years. In the meantime, the family were all together again in Melbourne, where, in terms of making publicity and building profile, state titles and record times in the pool were not an option.

In Sydney Annette had given diving demonstrations, broken records and swum as a professional at various baths where the public could be charged admission, like Ramsgate and Coogee Aquarium.

There were also opportunities for publicity in fundraising in Melbourne. For some time, Annette swam twice a day (probably on weekends) in a large tank with fish at the Melbourne Aquarium, which was situated in the Exhibition Building, where her mother had delighted audiences by playing French-made pianos some twenty years earlier.

Annette described this as, 'the largest glass tank in the world—sixty feet—with fish swimming all about me'. There is a story that these performances began when her younger sister dared her to do it and then passed the hat around. It is far more likely that David Mitchell, Nellie Melba's father and the man who built the Exhibition Building, arranged for the performances to take place. The tank was also reported to be rather smaller than 'sixty feet'.

Annette also performed at Prince's Court amusement park, near Prince's Bridge on the Yarra River. This was where she first developed the idea of dressing as a mermaid. After displaying herself on a high platform in her glittering costume and plunging down a slide at high speed into the pool, the climax of the act came when Annette would stay underwater for more than two minutes—until the audience was certain something had gone amiss. She would then reappear smiling, arms raised, to thunderous applause.

In June and July 1903, the Bland Holt production *The Breaking Of The Drought* was staged at the Theatre Royal in Melbourne. This was a melodrama written by Arthur Shirley and adapted for the theatre as a series of spectacular tableaux by the actor and impresario Bland Holt, who staged his productions at the Lyceum Theatre in Sydney and the Theatre Royal Melbourne. As the story was set in Australia, which was quite a novelty for theatre productions at that time, and was staged when the Federation Drought was beginning to break, it was a quite successful extravaganza. The *Coburg Leader* of 6 June 1903, two days before the production opened in Melbourne, assured readers that it 'contains many thrilling incidents, both in acting and scenic effects'.

The production had opened in Sydney in December 1902 and had a successful run through to February 1903. The Australian content of the production was considered novel and newsworthy enough for the Brisbane *Courier* of 17 January 1903 to note that:

> In Mr. Bland Holt's sensational drama, 'The Breaking of the Drought', there is a bathing scene representing Little Coogee and the Cavill family give some clever swimming and diving feats.

For the successful Melbourne run of the production, possibly on the recommendation of the Cavills, the 'Kellerman family' replaced the Cavill family. Now, Annette's parents were famous concert musicians and both Annette's brothers were talented violinists, and we know that the three older children had been taken to Cavill's Baths and could swim, but there seems to be no record of any part played, either musical or athletic, in the 'Kellerman Family' tableau, by any Kellerman other than Annette, who performed some of her most spectacular diving and underwater swimming tricks in a huge tank set in the stage. Although the name Kellerman does not appear among the top twenty performers listed on the poster for the production, it was her first taste of the theatre, and she loved it.

The money earned by Annette for her various performances was a help but not enough to provide for her brothers' education and a comfortable lifestyle. Frederick struggled to find work and, around this time, suffered the first of a series of what were either mild heart attacks or serious bouts of angina. It became more important than ever to capitalise on his eldest daughter's unique talents. They needed to get to London.

Annette commenced long-distance training, under her father's supervision, in the Yarra River, which provided further possibilities for publicity. *The Australasian* newspaper reported on 30 April 1904 that:

> A notable feat was accomplished on Saturday by Miss Annette Kellerman . . . who swam 2 miles 21 chains in the Yarra River in the record time of 46 minutes 32.5 seconds.

As the plan was for Annette to attempt an English Channel crossing the following year, the cunning seventeen-year-old made sure to tell the reporter that she now preferred swimming 'the long distances'. She received further publicity for swimming 5 miles in the Yarra and then 10 miles. The Kellermans' clever promotional plan soon became reality.

By the end of 1904, sufficient funds had been raised for Annette and her father to travel second class to London and live there for several months. During the voyage, however, a new problem arose. Annette, now eighteen and free from the discipline of training for several weeks, quickly became the ship's champion at deck quoits and the most popular girl on the dancefloor. A shipboard romance developed with a New Zealand lad and Frederick, seeing all their plans about to go up in the smoke of teenage passion, was forced to disembark with Annette at Naples, and take the unhappy young woman overland to London.

In the early spring of 1905, when Annette and her father arrived in London, they found that the situation for professional athletes in Britain was quite different than it was in Australia. Unlike most Australians of the time, the Kellermans, with their American, French and German backgrounds, had no family connections in Britain and little first-hand knowledge of how English society worked.

Very few people in Britain swam, and those who did were mostly men in exclusive private clubs. The stigma attached to anyone making a living from sporting activity was far greater than it was in Australia. Frederick's health was failing and the money was fast running out, there was only one thing to do. Annette's long-distance swims in the polluted Yarra River had aroused the interest of the press so, dressed in her one-piece bathing suit, she entered the River Thames at Putney on 30 June 1905 and swam 13 miles (21 kilometres) downstream to Blackwall, right through the heart of London.

Only 25 years earlier the Thames had been an open sewer. Just 40 years previously 6000 people living along the river had died of cholera. Conditions had improved by 1905, though much of the raw sewage had been replaced by the garbage, oil and debris of the world's busiest port. 'I shall never forget that swim through the flotsam and jetsam of London,' Annette said, 'dodging tugs and swallowing what seemed like pints of oil.' The swim, of course, caused a sensation and made newspaper headlines. Frederick had no doubt alerted the press in advance.

The *Daily Mirror* was different from other British newspapers. Being the first daily newspaper to make use of photographs (lots of them—as well as illustrations), it appealed to a new kind of reader, the poorly educated, often semi-literate working class. These people could not swim themselves but were very interested in an attractive teenage girl who could do it exceptionally well, better than most male athletes, in fact, while displaying a greater percentage of the female body than most British men had ever seen.

The *Daily Mirror* paid Annette eight guineas a week to swim from beach to beach along the coast from Dover to Margate every week for eight weeks in the summer holiday season. Each weekday she left from and arrived at the holiday beaches of St Margaret's, Deal, Ramsgate and Margate, covering more than 70 kilometres a week. To cap it off she then set a new record for a direct swim from Dover to Ramsgate in 4 hours and 20 minutes. It was, of course, wonderful exposure both for Annette and the *Daily Mirror*, which was sponsoring the great race across the Channel to commemorate the 30th anniversary of the crossing by Captain Webb. The entire eight-week exercise was billed as 'training' for the event, which for Annette it certainly was. For the newspaper it provided snowballing publicity in the lead-up to the cross-Channel race, and it made Annette Kellerman the most famous and photographed woman in Britain.

She was inundated with invitations to give demonstrations at swimming clubs and it was at one of these that she adopted what was to become her trademark swimming apparel. Some minor members of the royal family, the Duke and Duchess of Connaught, were expected to be in the audience at one exclusive private swimming club and Frederick thought it improper for his daughter to appear before them with bare legs, so she attached a pair of ladies' black stockings to the thigh-length legs of the men's style one piece that she wore.

It is hard for us to imagine what novelties diving and swimming were in 1905. Crowds packed the beaches and the headlands day after day and then, naturally, bought copies of the *Daily Mirror* to see the photographs.

Annette secured more sponsorship for her Channel attempt from the Cadbury chocolate company, which involved her testifying in newspaper advertisements that Bourneville Cocoa was the source of her stamina and her favourite drink. The ads featured photographs of the 'Australian Mermaid' in her swimming costume.

In the first week of August, Annette and British swimmer Ted

Heaton attempted a channel swim, which seems to have been a practice for the big race at the end of the month. It is recorded as an official attempt in the lists kept at the Dover Museum and was reported as a Channel attempt by the Australian press. Evidently rough seas ended the attempt and the *National Advocate* newspaper, reporting on 5 August, added a piece of doggerel in a rather feeble attempt to find some humour in the failure:

> Miss Kellerman and Heaton tried,
> But neither proved a winner.
> They both threw up the job and cried,
> And then threw up their dinner.

The big race was held on 25 August 1905. There were five entrants, each of whom was accompanied by a steam tug and a rowboat, which contained the support crew and a *Daily Mirror* reporter. Annette was the only female and was forced to wear a swimming costume, which chafed under the arms, while the men were allowed to swim naked, covered in seal fat. Annette was liberally coated with porpoise oil. Contestants were not allowed to touch the accompanying rowboat, but were handed a sandwich every hour on the end of a pole. As she was obliged to do by her sponsorship agreement, Annette also drank hot chocolate during the rest stops. In her book, *How to Swim*, published in 1919, she recalled:

> A manufacturer had supplied me with a good deal of cocoa . . . but after four hours the chocolate and the chop of the water made me very seasick and from then on for the rest of the swim I was seasick every half hour.

After four hours the weather turned and none of the entrants were able to make much progress. Annette, whose agreement with the newspaper was that she was paid a set fee plus a bonus for every hour she kept going after the first three, struggled on for a total of six and a half hours before being dragged exhausted into the rowboat.

Among the male contestants that day were champion cyclist Montague Holbein, who had set a record of 43 miles in one swim in the Thames in 1899, Scotsman Jabez Wolffe and Yorkshireman Thomas Burgess. Wolffe made 22 attempts to swim the channel, and came within a mile of succeeding on three occasions but never made it. Burgess, who would become the second person to swim the Channel in 1911, would have a part to play in Annette's next great adventure, a race held on the River Seine, through the city of Paris.

La Traversée de Paris was the brainchild of Henri Desgrange, a cyclist and journalist who started the French sporting newspaper *L'Auto* in 1900. This was the newspaper that, in 1903, founded the cycling event that Desgrange named *Le Tour de France.*

The swimming events at the 1900 Paris Olympic Games, held on the Seine, had been a great success, drawing huge crowds of spectators, and Desgrange, having successfully established *Le Tour de France* in 1903, was encouraged by his friend Georges Moëbs to create a swimming version of *'Le Tour'* two years later—in conjunction with the French National Society for the Encouragement of Swimming, of which Georges was president.

Incidentally, Australian Frederick Lane, who had grown up swimming in Sydney Harbour and attended Sydney Grammar School, made history by winning our first ever Olympic gold in the 200 metres swim at the Paris Olympics in 1900. He also won a second event, the swimming obstacle race, which involved clambering over or swimming under a row of small craft placed across the river. Sadly, this race was never held again. The organisers of the 1904 Olympics in St Louis, USA, decided to abandon the event, which makes Fred the one and only Olympic champion of the obstacle swimming race. The organisers of the St Louis Olympics did, however, introduce medals for winners. For his victories in Paris, Fred was awarded a 25-kilogram bronze statue of a horse.

Only eight invited swimmers lined up at the Pont National for the very first *Traversée de Paris*, an 11.6-kilometre race to the d'Auteuil viaduct, on 10 September 1905. There had been an open qualifying race the week previously, but none of the eager aspirants had managed to finish the course. In the *Traversée de Paris* only four of the invited contestants managed to finish. Three of them, Montague Holbein, Thomas Burgess and Annette, had all attempted to swim the English Channel three weeks earlier. The race was won by Frenchman Émile

Paulus, the first French swimmer to give up the breaststroke in favour of an overarm stroke.

The Kellerman version of the event is that Annette's chances were ruined when the French officials, worried that she would drop out, encouraged her by telling her that the finish line was only 2 kilometres away, when it was actually four. This made her sprint and run out of energy and she was about to give up when Thomas Burgess came alongside, cheered her up and swam with her to the finishing line, thus ruining his own chances of victory and finishing in the equal third position with Annette.

The less romantic French version is that Thomas Burgess finished second, Montague Holbein third and Annette fourth.

However, it was Annette who managed to capture all the publicity. A cheering crowd escorted her and Frederick back to their hotel and the teenage Australian swimmer made the front page of most Parisien newspapers the next morning, although she herself admitted that 'not one of them forgot to mention the fact that I was the daughter of a French woman'. She also received telegrams of congratulation from two of the women whose portraits had hung in the Kellermans' salon in Phillip Street, Nellie Melba and Cecile Chaminade. Sadly, though, the event seems to have gone unnoticed by Sarah Bernhardt.

Annette's next adventure was a race down the Danube against Europe's most famous lady swimmer, Walpurga von Isacescu, who had been the first woman to attempt to swim the English Channel in 1900. Although she was known as Baroness Isacescu, Walpurga had been widowed quite early in her marriage to a Romanian nobleman, who seems to have left her nothing but the title. She supported herself by swimming and working as a clerk for the Austrian railways. The Kellerman legend claims that the baroness issued the challenge, but it was very likely that it was Annette, who was some fifteen years younger than Walpurga. The race was to Vienna from the university town of Tulln, a distance of some 45 kilometres, and the swimmers started from different sides of the river. Annette's account of the swim, melodramatic as ever, states that the baroness knew the river well and chose the better side to start. Despite encountering whirlpools and injuring her foot on sharp stones, Annette came in more than half an hour in front of the Viennese champion.

The year Annette turned twenty, 1906, was a big year for the young swimmer. In the summer she made a third and final attempt across the English Channel. She stayed in the water for ten and a half hours before giving up. Annette later admitted that, although she had the stamina, she lacked the brute force necessary to conquer the Channel. Her record for the time spent in the water by a woman was not broken until 1926, when American Gertrude Ederle became the first woman to swim the channel.

The publicity provided by the *Daily Mirror* and her long-distance swims began to produce money-making opportunities in that year. After dozens of diving and swimming exhibitions in private swimming clubs, the 'Australian Mermaid' became the feature attraction at the London Hippodrome. This amazing venue, which still operates today as a casino, was built in 1900. It was designed to present spectacular performances, which were an odd mixture of variety theatre and circus, featuring lions, tigers and other 'wild' animals.

The theatre's remarkable design featured a proscenium arch stage and an arena that could be transformed by hydraulics into a 100,000-gallon water tank, with eight central fountains, and a circle of fountains around the side containing more than 400 tons of water in which polar bears, sea lions and even elephants could perform in aquatic spectacles. Entrances on each side could also be flooded, to allow boats and sea animals to come and go.

Just weeks before her debut at the hippodrome, Annette had badly gashed her head near the hairline when diving into a rather shallow pool at a swimming club demonstration. She suffered quite a severe injury which, when she returned to swimming and diving before the cut had healed properly, became infected and required further treatment. She would carry the scar for the rest of her life and often wore her hair as a fringe, or used a hat to cover it.

It was in the hippodrome, which had an audience capacity of more than 1300, that Annette made a triumphant return to the world of theatre spectaculars, giving her trademark 'Coo-ee' call and performing spectacular dives and water ballet. Her fifteen-minute performance was the climax of the show and she performed it more than 100 times in the later months of 1906. At least one of those performances was a royal command performance, after which she was presented to the wife of Edward VII, Queen Alexandra, who was, according to Annette, 'sitting in an armchair calmly nursing a baby tiger' which had recently been born in the hippodrome's menagerie.

In spite of all this, there was no guarantee of a regular income for Annette and things were still tough for the Kellerman family. Frederick's health had deteriorated further and London winters were grim and cold. Back in Melbourne, Alice and the three other children were surviving on Alice's teacher's wages, supplemented by money from London, and Alice was dreaming of relocating the whole family to Paris. It was around this time that a telegram arrived inviting Annette to come and perform permanently at Chicago's recently established White City Amusement Park. The invitation was eagerly accepted.

Chicago, with a population of more than 2 million in 1907, was large enough to support a permanent outdoor amusement venue, which hosted carnival attractions, dare-devil displays and circus acts in what was essentially an enormous 'sideshow alley'. Annette's 'site' consisted of a glass water tank 14 feet long and 6 feet deep surrounded by seats and enclosed by board and canvas walls. There was no roof, and the snake man was next door. Annette, very aware of her father's poor health and her mother's desire to relocate the family to Paris, performed as many as eighteen times a day when weekend crowds were good. The act consisted of demonstrating the various swimming strokes, a brief water ballet and sixteen backwards, forwards and sideways dives. Advertised as 'The Water Nymph' Annette had to compete with attractions like the 'Educated Flea Circus' and 'Mundy's Trained Wild Animal Arena'. The *Chicago Daily Tribune,* which carried ads for the amusement park featuring photos of Annette in her swimming attire, also informed readers that, 'None should fail to see Miss Kellerman, as she is not only an expert swimmer but a beautiful woman, who is at her best in her bathing suit.'

The act was so successful that, by the middle of the summer of 1907, there was enough money to relocate the Kellerman family to a suitable residence in Paris. By that time, however, Frederick's health had deteriorated to the point where he was on constant medication and often needed a wheelchair. It became apparent that he could no longer manage Annette. Frederick had arranged for his sister Josephine to join them and act as chaperone and companion to his daughter. He had also recruited the services of an assistant manager.

Jimmie Sullivan was just one year older than Annette and was working as a program seller at White City. He took an interest in the Kellermans as soon as they arrived at the park and helped them to settle in and understand how the place worked. He proved to be a loyal and trustworthy addition to the team and was soon managing the day-to-day logistics of the operation. Jimmie did everything from organising the publicity and acting as personal bodyguard, to maintaining the venue and even keeping Aunt Josephine distracted with museum visits, so that Annette could do some discreet flirting and dating and learn to play golf with the more acceptable young men out of the hundreds who clamoured to meet her.

Alice and the other children had settled in Paris by the end of summer and Frederick, now gravely ill, left to join them. He and Alice were reunited for just three months before he passed away on 8 October 1907, aged 47.

Annette was now 21 years old and, although he tolerated some of her flirtations, Jimmie Sullivan, now her manager and press agent, was very aware of the fine line between publicity and scandal. When a wealthy admirer sent a very expensive gold and emerald bracelet, he insisted that Annette return it immediately. In spite of his best efforts, however, she did manage to get herself engaged to a reasonably respectable young doctor. Fortunately, the engagement did not survive the next career step, which was a move to a much bigger amusement park in Boston.

The Wonderland Amusement Park, which claimed to be the biggest in the world, was situated on 25 acres (10 hectares) of land near Revere Beach, Boston. The 1908 season featured Pawnee Bill's Great Wild West Show (with a cast of 70), Manning's Open Air Circus, the Human Laundry, the Scenic Railway, Chiquita 'The Doll Lady', band concerts, a roller-skating rink, a fortune-teller and an on-site hospital where 'incubator babies' could be viewed. (This weird attraction was popular at fairs after the 'child hatchery' at the Berlin Exposition of 1896, designed to demonstrate the new medical technology, proved to be the most popular attraction at the show!)

Above all this, the huge illuminated sign which read, 'The Australian Mermaid', could be seen from anywhere in the park.

Two events, which either did or didn't happen while Annette was performing in Boston, would become part of Kellerman mythology for the next 50 years. The first incident is supposed to have occurred around 1908, while Annette was training for another long-distance publicity swim in Boston Harbor. She is supposed to have appeared in a one-piece swimsuit on Revere Beach, been arrested for indecent exposure, and 'let off' by the judge after she explained that she could not undertake a long ocean swim dressed in the more acceptable swimwear. The problem with this story is that there is absolutely no evidence that it ever occurred. Annette first told this story in the 1930s and wrote about it in the 1950s.

Revere Beach was noted for the strict enforcement of clothing rules around that time and it is possible that some sort of a disturbance occurred when Annette attempted to enter the water, but there are no newspaper articles or court records to substantiate the story. Whether or not the incident ever occurred, Annette was certainly making a name for herself in Boston as an advocate of more sensible swimwear for women.

She gave her opinions in an article titled 'Bathing Suit Must be Cut', which appeared in *The Boston Post* on 7 November 1908 and included the following ditty commenting on the demise of the shapely, corseted, fashionable woman made famous by artist Charles Gibson at the turn of the century. If Annette had her way, the newspaper said:

No more the Gibson bathing girl
Shall grace the Newport summer whirl.
Annette declares her garment's wrong,
At both ends too extremely long.
The Gibson girl may be a peach,
As she perambulates the beach,
But now if in the 'swim' she'd be
She must with sweet Annette agree.
Her heavy skirt she must replace
With filmy raiment for the race.
Think you she will consent to dress
In such approach to nothingness?

The second story emanating from that period involves Annette being named in a divorce case in 1909 in which the wife suing for divorce, a certain Mrs Pattee, claimed that her husband became obsessed with Annette while they were staying at the same boarding house in Boston and would stay up with her 'eating crackers and drinking beer'. There was no direct accusation of any sexual activity and Annette countered by saying that she was constantly chaperoned at the time, certainly never drank beer or any other alcohol, and hardly knew Mr Pattee, although she remembered he and his wife argued a lot.

One thing that certainly did happen, towards the end of 1908, was that the famous vaudeville impresario Benjamin (B.J.) Keith came looking for the Australian Mermaid. Annette's days as a carnival act were over. It was back to the theatre. Keith and his partner Edward Albee had invented 'vaudeville' as a respectable form of 'burlesque' and 'variety' in the last decade of the 19th century, in order to attract middle-class family audiences. The theatres were grand and signs warned male patrons that stamping and whistling were not tolerated as they 'upset the ladies'.

Keith had pioneered the concept of continuous vaudeville in his famous Keith's Theatre in Boston and then formed a partnership with Frederick Proctor who was doing the same thing in New York. Keith and Proctor soon ran one of the most powerful vaudeville circuits in the United States.

On 25 November 1908 the *New York Star* reported:

> There is a new Venus in town. She rises from the sea every afternoon and evening at Keith and Proctors . . . Miss Annette Kellerman is her name. She is as graceful as a mermaid and as daring and as wet when she comes out of the tank after each headlong or footlong dive.

In 1909 there was no need for Annette and Jimmie to look for opportunities for publicity. The opportunities would come to them. Annette was chosen by huge popular vote to be Queen of the Auto Carnival and led the parade down Broadway in a Buick converted into what the *New York Times* on 1 May 1909 called 'an enormous float, surmounted by a dolphin and a large sea shell, with a playing fountain in the foreground'. The parade of 310 motor vehicles was reportedly watched by 200,000 people.

That was nothing, however, compared to the massive publicity that was gained from a court case involving two theatre chains, Keith and Proctors and Morris's. The huge success of 'The Diving Venus' at Keith and Proctor's New York theatre had led to offers from rival theatre owners and, either as a result of inexperience or greed, Jimmie had signed for Annette to appear at different times each day for both promoters. The matter was further complicated when both Morris's *and* Keith and Proctor attempted to prevent a nickelodeon chain from showing short films of Annette diving in their coin-operated viewing machines. It seems that Jimmie had signed a third deal, without realising it conflicted with their theatrical contracts.

The result of the court case was that Annette claimed she didn't know the contents of the contract she signed with Morris's and, although Jimmie disagreed with the decision, she remained with Keith and Proctor for the next three years. According to the *New York Star* of 15 May 1909, Judge Hough, who had to sort out the mess, concluded:

> ... that neither Miss Kellerman nor her manager has the slightest regard for business honor; indeed, they seem incapable of understanding the obligations of contract.

The saying that 'there is no such thing as bad publicity' held true for Annette. The court case, which was reported on by newspapers right across the United States, only made her more famous. B.J. Keith recouped the many thousands he lost in the court case by increasing the amount of money that theatre operators had to pay to stage her show. Newspaper reports of the 'bidding war' for the right to stage her shows mention Annette earning $2500 a week. The figure was actually closer to $1500 a week, which was still an absolute fortune at a time when factory workers in the U.S.A. made $400 per year and dentists and doctors $2500 to $5000 per year.

The costs involved with presenting the show were enormous. A huge glass tank had to be transported from city to city and town to town, along with the orchestra and the cast of mermaids and the support staff required to assemble the tank and the set. Miss Kellerman's personal entourage, which at times included a professional tennis coach among others, meant that the show was the most expensive, as well as the most successful, on the national vaudeville circuit. Annette Kellerman was a star.

Other publicity was built around that symbol of modernity, the motorcar. Annette was given a Buick, which presented the opportunity for another publicity stunt. She advertised for a chauffeur and the newspapers reported that there was a riot when hundreds turned up to apply. She was later fined $100 for speeding down Broadway because she was running late for a show, although her chauffeur was doing the driving. Annette herself was arrested for speeding in San Francisco but a sympathetic judge let her off with a warning. She even accepted an invitation to race at the speedway in Cleveland. The *Atlanta Georgian* reported in March 1911 that she 'drove the 50 horsepower Buick 63 miles per hour and thereby won to the delight of about 5000 spectators'.

When Annette crossed the Atlantic on the ocean liner *Adriatic* in April 1912, to play a season at the Palace Theatre, in London's West End, she was listed as travelling alone. Evidently, she and Jimmie had discussed marriage and also had many rows about 'inappropriate suitors'. Annette said later that Jimmie was not sure he was the right person for her. This was to be proved quite wrong and, after some honest discussions and debates during their two-way crossing of the Atlantic, they married quietly while on tour later that year in Danbury, Connecticut.

Annette always cleverly promoted herself as a champion of healthy lifestyle and a liberator of women from the confines of an old-fashioned regime and restrictive clothing. She knew, however, that the success of her carnival act and theatre show was due in no small part to sexuality and salaciousness. The swimming, diving and the theatrical frills were an excuse to show a very attractive female body in a way that was quite unheard of at the time.

There was, of course, a good deal of truth in what Annette was saying about the role of women and the clothes they wore. She was at the forefront of the movement that would slowly but radically change the role of women in society throughout the 20th century. In the *New York Evening Journal* of 11 May 1912, she declared: 'The corset has done more to make physical cowards of women than any other thing since slavery. You cannot be brave if your diaphragm is squeezed and you can't breathe properly.'

But a prurient interest in the female body was always the 'elephant in the room' in Annette's show business career. There is some wonderfully amusing newsreel footage of Annette, arriving in Australia in 1932, in which she says that she is writing a novel which will never 'see the light of day' because 'nowadays a novel has to have so much sex appeal and I don't know a thing about that'. In the next breath, straight faced, she says that she's going to go camping for four weeks and adds, 'and I'm not going to wear any clothes'.

In her 2011 publication, *Race and the Modern Exotic*, Angela Woollacott, the Manning Clark Professor of History at the Australian National University, summed up the situation well:

> Kellerman sought to balance the shock and titillation of her bodily display with the respectability of her athleticism and career as an expert in physical culture. Kellerman's respectability was shored up by the vegetarianism (by which she meant avoiding red meat) that was part of her physical culture methods. By casting herself as a fitness guru, and a record-winning champion, she repeatedly claimed that her immodest swimsuits were a matter of practicality. Invoking Venus and mermaids placed her bodily exposure in the fanciful realm of mythology, thus claiming an ancient cultural legitimacy.

Addressing the issue of Annette's attitude to what would later be called 'women's liberation', Professor Woollacott notes: 'Though Kellerman's message was one of liberation, as well as modernity, she was . . . not a feminist; for example, her arguments for women to exercise included their need to stay physically attractive to their husbands.'

In giving this advice to wives in her book *Physical Beauty: How to Keep It*, in 1918, Annette typically added, with a literary twinkle in the eye, that the reason wives needed to do this was that, 'our religion and all our morality has failed to keep men good'.

Back in 1910, the concept of the perfect woman would become central to Annette's entire publicity machine, but it was not something she dreamed up herself—it was handed to her on a plate by the Director of the Harvard University Gymnasium, Dr Dudley Sargent.

Sargent had been doing a study of the 'physical proportions' of female students, thousands of them, in order to test the validity of a theory that was common at the time—that the changing role of women in society was making them less feminine and this 'evolution' was measurable. The end result of the study was Sargent's conclusion that, while exercise and diet had changed the shape of female bodies in the past two decades, it had not made them more masculine. Indeed, physical fitness and exercise had the effect of helping the female form return to what he considered the classic Greek ideal of feminine beauty.

The *New York Times* reported that Dr Sargent had not found anyone, male or female, who conformed exactly to his estimation of the perfect proportions of the athletic human body. Sargent based his calculations partly on Greek and Roman statues of athletes and goddesses and, somehow, Annette became involved in the experiment. Kellerman mythology says that Dr Sargent sought her out, but just what part she and Jimmie played in him finding her we will never know. Mind you, it was not difficult to 'find' Annette Kellerman in 1910—by that time she had been performing as the 'Diving Venus' at Keith and Proctor's Fifth Avenue Theatre for months, and was the most talked about woman in New York.

Dr Sargent measured Annette all over and admitted that she was the 'nearest to a perfectly proportioned woman' that he had found. Newspapers printed details of her measurements including her weight (137 pounds), height (64.5 inches), and every 'girth' measurement you could think of—head, neck, chest, ribs, waist, thighs, knees, calves, ankles, feet and instep. To be fair to Dr Sargent, he had taken these measurements from thousands of women, although perhaps not personally. He asked Annette to make a special appearance in a lecture hall filled with Harvard's female students and athletes. He commented that her proportions matched quite closely those of the Venus de Milo, except the arms, of course.

All this, including a chart of measurements comparing Annette to the Venus de Milo, appeared in an article titled 'Modern Woman Getting Nearer the Perfect Figure', in the *New York Times* on 4 December 1910. This was advertising 'gold' for Annette and it would be used in her publicity for shows, movies, talks and books for the rest of her career. The references rather distorted and exaggerated what

Dr Sargent's research had really been about, to the point where it became a story about the professor who had set out to find 'the perfect woman', and found Annette Kellerman.

Because World War I changed the world forever, there is a tendency for us to forget what the world of show business was like in the first fifteen years of the 20th century, before the war, before Hollywood, before radio. I think this is why, by the end of that century, we seem to have forgotten Annette Kellerman. Her iconic status could be best compared, perhaps, to that of Marilyn Monroe in the 1950s and 1960s, except that Annette had far less competition for publicity. The two decades after World War I would see the production of many hundreds of talking movies a year, radios in every home and scores of magazines devoted to publicity. In the first two decades of the century, however, with the film industry in its infancy and the vaudeville circuit in full swing, stars like Charlie Chaplin, Al Jolson and Annette Kellerman were able to achieve levels of publicity which later celebrities could only dream about. Annette wrote books, gave talks and lectures on women's health, had her own line of clothing in department stores, and was consulted by the press on anything to do with women's affairs, clothing, swimming or the ocean.

In 1916, after several fatal shark attacks on New Jersey beaches, *The Washington Post* even commissioned her to write a feature on sharks. Of course, she knew very little about sharks, but she had swum in the ocean and, the paper assured its readers, was familiar with 'the shark-proof inclosures [*sic*] of the Australian bathing beaches'.

In America in the 1920s, 'Kellerman' was a household word for a woman's close-fitting one-piece swimsuit and the girls who wore them were said to dress 'Kellerman style'. A diving catch in baseball was known as 'an Annette Kellerman'.

After B.J. Keith retired to Florida in 1909, his partner Edward Albee had seen off most of the competition and had a virtual monopoly on the main vaudeville circuit. Late in 1912 he called a meeting with Jimmie and Annette to renegotiate their contract. By this time the mermaid spectaculars had reached staggering theatrical proportions, especially with the addition of new elements to keep them fresh and popular. Annette was touring a show she wrote and designed called *Undine—The Water Nymph.* Set in medieval England, it involved Annette dancing and singing. In 1912 she took the show to London and New York and it gradually evolved into *Annette Kellerman, The Perfect Woman, and her Dancing Girls, in 'The Wood Nymph', A Classical Aquatic Entertainment.* Albee informed Jimmie and Annette, who were now Mr and Mrs Sullivan, that he could only keep the shows touring if Annette reduced her fee to $750 dollars a week.

Highly offended, as the shows were still playing to packed houses, Annette stormed out of Albee's office and decided to become a movie star. She had already appeared in six short films shot around New York. These were mostly the typical silent melodramas of the time. One was called *The Bride of Lammermoor: A Tragedy of Bonnie Scotland* and another *Jephthah's Daughter: A Biblical Tragedy*, but two made in 1911, *The Mermaid* and *The Siren of the Sea*, were forerunners of the great project Annette had in mind, *Neptune's Daughter.*

However, in spite of the fact that Annette could be very charming and persuasive, the idea of mythological gods, mermaids, girls diving from cliffs and fighting underwater did not interest any of the film studios. Then a chance meeting over dinner with an English screenwriter named Captain Leslie T. Peacock gave Annette a chance to outline her ideas to him. Peacock went home enthused, wrote a screenplay overnight and arranged a meeting with Carl Laemmle, the boss of Universal Studios, who agreed to make the picture, which would become Universal's most expensive production to date.

There is evidence of the 'Kellerman touch' in a short comedy film titled *The Surf Maidens,* written and directed by Peacock in 1913, and I suspect that Annette was learning the ropes. Here is a synopsis:

> A bevy of chorus girls, at the close of a successful season, decide to go on a spree, to a quiet beach resort. They plan beautiful designs in bathing suits. The country rubes go crazy over them, but the local Spinsters' Club is aroused and the girls are all arrested in their bathing suits. The judge fines them each five dollars. There is no money in their bathing suits. The judge pays their fines himself and later goes to collect the money. The girls give him the time of his life. From being a 'Rube Town' the conditions become altered, but the Spinsters' Club

gets busy and the girls aid the cause; eventually a good moral lesson is given to the community.

I rest my case.

Neptune's Daughter was filmed on the island of Bermuda and a cargo ship was chartered to transport the entire cast, crew and equipment, as there was no passenger service to the island in 1913. The director, Herbert Brenon, although still in his early 30s, had directed more than 40 films and also had a background in vaudeville. He and Annette got along famously and, because he could swim, Brenon also played some of the villain roles which required underwater fighting. During one such scene, the glass tank containing 5000 gallons of water, rocks, seaweed, fish and a turtle, as well as the two actors, shattered, leaving Annette with a badly cut right foot and Brenon requiring 46 stitches.

The plot summary of *Neptune's Daughter* reads like an amalgam of the Old Testament, the legend of Beowulf and the *Perils of Pauline*. The official 'brief synopsis' of the plot runs to almost 1000 words, and includes King Neptune's little daughter dying after being accidentally caught in a fishing net by fishermen from the kingdom of King William. Her older sister, played by Annette, seeks revenge with the help of a sea witch and a magic spell. Changed to human form she meets King William, falls in love, dances for him and is attacked by the evil Count Boris, the lover of William's wicked cheating queen, Olga. Their plan to murder the king is foiled by Annette, then after many fights and dives and dancing and adventures, Olga is turned into an octopus, and Annette quits being a mermaid and marries the king.

Needless to say, the film was a great success. Having cost Universal Studios $35,000 to make, it returned a profit of $1 million and played to packed houses for nineteen weeks, which set a record in some cinema franchises that was not broken until *Cinerama* in 1955.

Annette always maintained that her first love was the theatre and she did not particularly enjoy making movies. This is borne out by the fact that, surprised by the success of *Neptune's Daughter*, she sold her share of the rights in the film back to Universal for $30,000, left the United States for Paris and embarked on a musical project written by Captain Peacock. This was to be a full-scale Broadway musical called *The Mermaid*, in which she would star as a legitimate singer and dancer.

The main reason for heading to Paris, however, was that her mother was ill and Annette joined her siblings at her mother's bedside for the last few days before Alice passed away on 1 June 1914. Annette had planned to stay in Paris taking singing and dancing lessons, in preparation for her planned Broadway success as a singing, dancing theatrical star. But it was not to be.

With her mother gone and the war clouds gathering, she cut short her visit and she and Jimmie returned to New York where two big offers were on the table, in the wake of the success of *Neptune's Daughter.*

Firstly, Edward Albee had apparently had a change of heart and wanted to talk to Jimmie and Annette again. They refused to go but sent their New York agent who gave them the news that the offer was now $2500 a week and complete artistic control.

The other offer was from William Fox, of Fox Studios in New York. He wanted Annette to make another movie with Herbert Brenon, even more swashbuckling and spectacular than *Neptune's Daughter*. It was to be filmed in Jamaica and the title was *Daughter of the Gods.*

The film is reputed to have cost more than US$1 million and one set used, an Arab city constructed of solid timber and complete with a functioning palace, was said to have cost $350,000 and caused the destruction of a rather large area of Jamaican jungle.

The making of the film was certainly a huge boost to the economy of the island of Jamaica, although part of the Kellerman legend is that Annette threatened to walk out on the whole project before filming began when she was refused permission to bring her pet pug Cooee onto the island. The awkward situation was finally resolved when the captain of a merchant ship in the harbour offered to keep the dog on board, and offered Annette and Jimmie a cabin so they could stay on board as well.

Daughter of the Gods was made just one year after *The Birth of a Nation*, the three-hour, twelve-reel W.H. Griffith epic considered to be the first narrative film with a serious storyline. That film was supposedly made for $100,000, so it is hard to imagine *Daughter of the Gods* being the first million-dollar picture ever made. Other estimates put the cost at closer to $600,000. As there are no copies of the film known to exist, it is hard to judge what it might have cost. Publicity photographs and stills do exist, however, which show that no expense was spared with sets or costumes and a cast of thousands. What the stills also show is that, while Annette claimed to have worn a thin body stocking of some kind, the reports by reviewers and others who saw the film that she and other female members of the cast appeared naked are absolutely true.

For all of us who will never have a chance to see the film for ourselves, here, at least, is the plot summary:

> Embittered for many years by the drowning of his little son Omar, the Sultan promises to aid the Witch of Evil in her effort to destroy a mysterious beauty named Anitia if the witch will restore the young prince to life. Nearby, the Arab Sheik plots to seize the Sultan's lands by placing his beautiful but treacherous daughter Zarrah in the palace harem. Prince Omar appears by the seashore as Anitia, abducted from the Sheik by a band of thieves, is taken to the Sultan's harem. Anitia's dancing so arouses the Sultan that Zarrah jealously locks her in a tower, but she escapes by diving into the sea. Finally captured by guards, Anitia is about to be executed when Prince Omar comes to her rescue. Next, Anitia is thrown into the sea, but she reaches safety in Gnomeland, where she learns that Zarrah has killed the Sultan and instigated a revolt against Omar. Anitia leads the gnomes to Omar's defense, but he accidentally slays her. When he rejects Zarrah's advances, she stabs him to death, whereupon his soul is reunited to the spirit of Anitia.

As well as female nudity, the film also apparently had even more swash to be buckled or buckles to be swashed than *Neptune's Daughter*, including dives down 60 foot (18 metre) waterfalls and the burning of the sultan's palace, which spectacularly destroyed the entire set. The most dangerous stunt involved Annette diving into a pool which contained live crocodiles with her hands tied. After experimenting with a dummy, which looked anything but lifelike, she decided to do the stunt herself, after the crocodiles had been well fed and while Jimmie was away from the island for a few days. A ladder strategically placed just out of camera range enabled her to make a hurried exit from the pool, as soon as the stunt was shot. When Jimmie returned he evidently had quite a confrontation with Brenon for allowing Annette to do the stunt.

Filming on location, which had originally been estimated at two to three months, dragged on for more than twice that time and creative and financial tensions culminated in a blazing row between Annette and Herbert Brenon when filming had ended. They never spoke again. The same issues caused Fox to sack Brenon before the movie was released, but Brenon went on to have a successful career in the talkies.

The film received mixed reviews but the enormous publicity campaign around it, with competitions, interviews, appearances and promotions, only added to the fame and star status of its leading lady.

While training for the riding scenes in her next movie, *Queen of the Seas*, Annette was thrown from a horse and severely injured her spine. She was bedridden and it took months of physiotherapy before she was ready to do the filming. This time the plot involved her escaping from the villain by walking a tightrope across a section of Bar Harbor in Maine and then diving from a tower on a headland directly into the sea. She had taught herself tightrope walking several years before and used it as part of the stage act so, as usual, she was able to perform the stunts herself. There is a photograph of her diving from the tower into the ocean but once again, sadly, not one copy of the movie has survived.

With the war effort in full swing, Annette was able to achieve one of her dreams by performing as a serious ballet artist at the Metropolitan Opera House in a huge fundraising extravaganza for the war. She performed 'The Dying Swan', conducted by Toscanini, as a tribute to the great ballerina Pavlova, who she counted as a friend. It was the most artistically satisfying performance of her entire career.

Although the planned Broadway musical *The Mermaid* never did come to fruition, Annette did get to perform in a musical written for her called *The Model Girl*, in which she sang and danced. Reviews were polite and lukewarm, with reviewers finding the plot negligible and the songs rather weak.

She did, however, take up Edward Albee's offer and toured on the Keith circuit again. She was also the star attraction in a spectacular called *The Big Show* at the New York Hippodrome. This venue had seating for more than 5000 people and the stage was reputed to be twelve times bigger than any other in the United States. It boasted an 8000-gallon (30,000 litre) clear glass water tank that could be raised hydraulically from below the stage. Famed producer Charles Dillingham gave Annette a free hand to design her own set when she replaced Pavlova as the star attraction at the hippodrome.

Her last feature film in the United States was the only film she ever made on the West Coast. It was also the only non-fantasy feature film she made and was directed by a woman, Lois Weber. Called *What Women Love* it was the story of an athletic free-minded young woman and satirised the prudish and stuffy attitudes of the day. The most dangerous stunt involved Annette diving from the mast top of a yacht directly into the water. She later recalled that Jimmie was worried, but it all went off perfectly.

Although the film did quite well, Annette missed the theatre so it was decided to return to Australia and show the locals what she had been doing in the theatres of Britain and the United States for the past decade and a half. She had been away from the land of her birth for sixteen years.

Annette appeared as the star of a variety show at the Tivoli Theatre in Sydney. The show was a huge success and was also staged in Melbourne, Adelaide and Hobart. Then Annette and the entire entourage crossed the Tasman and toured New Zealand.

It was in New Zealand that Annette made her last feature film, on the very modest budget of $10,000. It was partly funded by a consortium from Christchurch and filmed around Nelson. The idea was that the film would promote New Zealand. A film crew was brought in from the United States. Jimmie directed and the footage was then sent back to be cut and edited in Hollywood. Unfortunately, New Zealand was pretty much edited out and the 47-minute film, *Venus of the South Seas* was promoted as a story of the South Sea Islands. It is the only one of Annette's feature films which survives complete and today it looks very old-fashioned and amateurish, having been made on a skimpy budget which obviously affected the production values. One reel and some fragments (total 25 minutes) of *Neptune's Daughter* survive, also.

When Mr and Mrs Sullivan returned to the United States, it was apparent that vaudeville was dying; theatres were being turned into cinemas and the once lucrative touring circuits were rapidly shrinking. Work was hard to get and the money required to stage spectacular shows was not there.

Things were different, however, in Britain. There, the variety theatre circuit lasted well into the 1960s, and it was still very much alive and well in the 1920s. Annette played the London Coliseum, which could seat 2500 people. She then had an offer to stage her show at the Scala theatre in Berlin, which involved learning to speak German, or at least enough German to do the show.

Annette learned her entire show dialogue in German by heart and the show was a great success. She then moved on to the Scala in Copenhagen where she did the same thing, learning her entire show in Danish. This was repeated in Stockholm, where she performed the entire show in Swedish. She then took the show to Norway and finally to Rotterdam and The Hague where she found Dutch to be 'a truly horrible language to learn and speak'.

Though Annette claimed to be fluent in quite a few languages, and was of course perfectly bilingual having spoken French all her life, her sister Marcelle said later that, apart from French, all she really knew of other European languages was the script of her show.

Marcelle, and her husband Fred, travelled in Europe and the United States as part of the Kellerman entourage. While Annette and Jimmie stayed in the best hotel in town, paid for by the show's promoter, Marcelle and Fred would be accommodated down the road in some modest hotel. The two couples became great friends and, returning to Australia in 1926 when the general strike meant there was no work in Britain, they stayed at Fred's parents' property near Gympie in Queensland, before spending quite a bit of time on the islands of the Great Barrier Reef near Mackay. After several more years of performances in Britain and Europe, they returned to Australia in 1932.

Annette had a fascination with the Reef and it would become their playground for many years. They even leased an island, Newry Island, and lived there for several years before returning to the United States in 1937.

Jimmie had been filming Annette swimming underwater and was

keen to do something with the footage. Back in the States he discovered that technology had moved on and there were better ways to film and edit. So, he began the process again, filming Annette performing in crystal clear waters in Silver Springs, Florida. The footage still survives and shows a remarkably fit and attractive 51-year-old Annette performing a graceful ballet underwater.

Annette is credited not only with the invention of the close-fitting one-piece bathing suit for women, but also with 'water ballet' and the sport of synchronised swimming. At the exclusive Palm Beach Bath and Tennis Club in Florida in the summer of 1937, she staged an open-air swimming spectacular, which included water ballet involving both synchronised diving and swimming by a team of girls who had been trained and choreographed by Annette. President Franklin Roosevelt and his wife Eleanor were among the invited guests who enjoyed the show.

With the demise of vaudeville in the United States and the war clouds once again gathering in Europe, Annette and Jimmie returned to Australia and embarked upon what was to be one of the most enjoyable and satisfying phases of their varied and amazing lives. Annette had twelve huge crates of her costumes and sets shipped to Australia and set about creating shows to perform for the troops.

There was no government funding so she used her own money to create and stage the shows. Annette was in her element, writing songs and performing with troops of girls from various dancing academies in the towns and cities where the shows were performed, all volunteers who were trained by Annette.

After America entered the war, one million US servicemen passed through Australia at one time or another. Jimmie and Annette worked as volunteers in the army canteens in Sydney and Brisbane, and Annette entertained at army bases and at hospitals for the wounded soldiers. Some of her shows were quite grand, with a cast of more than 50, but mostly they were fairly amateurish. Annette had taught herself to play the piano accordion and wrote songs and choreographed dance routines for the girls.

Most of the songs were quite jolly but Annette is not remembered for her song-writing skills. Here is an example of the lyrics of one song which accompanied a dance routine called the 'Diggers Dip':

> Let's do the Diggers Dip, hi diddle de diddle dee tee dee doo,
> Hump your bluey and hum and holler, hoppity hop like a kangaroo.

The patriotic song 'ANZAC' went like this:

> Who is behind the union Jack? We are.
> Who is behind the Empire? Australia.
> Australia, Australia the land of the Southern Cross.
> Australia, Australia you're free as an albatross.

Annette and Jimmie gave generously of their talents and money to the war effort and enjoyed feeling useful. Annette was always at her best in front of a live audience and had fond memories of those days for the rest of her life. No doubt her theatrical vitality and *chutzpah* lifted the spirits of thousands of soldiers during World War II—and the lyrics hardly mattered!

Annette wrote an autobiography which was never published, but she sent a screenplay version to MGM. Originally called 'The One Piece Bathing Suit', the screenplay was turned into a movie, called *Million-Dollar Mermaid,* in 1952. Swimming in movies had been made popular by Olympians Eleanor Holm and Johnny Weissmuller and Hollywood's glamorous swimming superstar, Esther Williams, who played the part of Annette in the film.

Williams was an American champion swimmer who never became an Olympian due to the cancellation of the 1940 Olympics during World War II. She joined Billy Rose's Aquacade, which had originated as the feature event at the Great Lakes Expo in 1937, the same year as Annette's show in Florida. The Aquacade featured diving, fountains, comedy and formation swimming. Williams had already starred in swimming movies like *Bathing Beauty* in 1944 and *Neptune's Daughter* in 1949. The plot of that movie in no way resembled Annette's 1912 movie of the same name, although some elements of both the Aquacade and Esther Williams's earlier films appear to have been inspired by Annette's theatre shows.

The making of *Million-Dollar Mermaid* in 1952 gave Annette a brief period of recognition, celebrity and fame in Hollywood. She became friendly with Grace Kelly and Lucille Ball and certainly enjoyed the long-deserved recognition for her achievements in the early film industry, including the unveiling of her 'star' on Hollywood Boulevard. Although the film was no doubt profitable for Annette, and she enjoyed the renewed popularity, she was not especially happy with the result. While the swimming spectaculars, designed by famed choreographer Busby Berkeley, were extravagant and inventive, the film's direction lacked vitality and Annette referred to it later as 'namby-pamby'. She thought the choice of Victor Mature to play Jimmie was ridiculous and seemed to have forgotten that film scripts *based* on real life rarely stick accurately to the facts. She even complained that Esther Williams was not Australian although there was, of course, no one else in the film industry who could have played the part. This was rather unkind of Annette, as Esther Williams had been the one who fought to get the movie made. The film received lukewarm reviews although Williams said she was quite proud of the swimming scenes in the movie.

The problem was that, in spite of the renewed recognition and fame, Annette really wanted to be performing. Watching other people perform, especially if they were supposed to be portraying events from her life, was not really her cup of tea.

Although she enjoyed the social life of Hollywood, it was obvious that there would be no opportunity for her to perform. She was 65 years old and her style of entertainment was 'old hat'. She opened a health food store in Long Beach, California, and remained in the United States until 1956. She and Jimmie were back in Australia for the Melbourne Olympic Games, where Prime Minister Bob Menzies introduced Annette to a cheering crowd at the MCG.

Their next trip back to Australia in the 1960s would be a permanent move. They settled at Labrador on Queensland's Gold Coast and lived there quite quietly and modestly. Jimmie was hit rather badly by the Asian flu epidemic in 1970 and passed away several years later. Annette then lived with her sister Marcelle, who was surviving on a war widow's pension after her husband Fred passed away, in a small fibro house with lino on the floors. Annette never really recovered from losing her 'partner for life'. In 60 years of marriage she and Jimmie had only ever been apart for one period of three weeks.

In 1974 newspaper reporters were surprised to discover that Annette Kellerman was still alive, aged 88. She decided to sell her mink coat and a friend placed an ad in the *Sydney Morning Herald* classifieds that read 'Film star, retired to the Gold Coast, no longer has need for mink coat'. The resulting interviews and publicity created renewed interest in Annette's remarkable life and enabled the International Swimming Hall of Fame, in Fort Lauderdale, Florida, to find her. They had been searching for her for quite a while, in order to inform her that she was to be inducted into the Hall of Fame later that year. Not only that, she was to be the star attraction and the film of her underwater ballet from 1937 was to open the event.

Plans were made for the trip but, just one month before she was to leave, Annette tripped and fell onto the concrete patio of the house she shared with her sister, badly injuring her leg. Annette was approaching 90 and her attempts to regain her strength through physical exercise only made the condition worse. Finally, she was admitted to the public ward of the local hospital, where she passed away on 5 November 1975. The pallbearers at her funeral were members of the Southport Surf Lifesaving Club and her ashes were scattered on the Great Barrier Reef.

In his 1992 cult classic book about swimming, *Haunts of the Black Masseur*, Charles Sprawson, having comprehensively discussed virtually every swimmer of note in history, concluded:

> Webb and Kellerman remain the two pivotal figures in swimming's history. As a result of their example swimming became popular and fashionable throughout Europe and America.

Enough said.

PART II

SPIRIT OF ADVENTURE

While it is true that all twelve of the life stories in this collection are, in one way or another, 'adventures', the three individuals whose stories are related in this section all set out to do what they did as true adventurers, rather than having adventures occur while they were striving to achieve certain other things in life.

It is a fascinating fact of human nature that seemingly insignificant events that we experience, such as reading a book or watching birds fly, can have a profound effect on how we end up living our lives, and the things we end up achieving. And it may well be that sometimes, like Matthew Flinders, we only realise the significance of certain childhood experiences when we are old enough to look back and see our lives in retrospect.

Many years ago I happened to read a book called *Us Aussies*, written by the broadcaster Mal Garvin, in which he put forward a very interesting theory that the first Australian-born, ethnically European generation on the Australian continent, the children of the first convict fleets, were markedly different from their parents. This, Garvin argued, was partly due to spending time with the Aboriginal people and partly a result of being what the journals at the time referred to as 'orphans'—they often grew up fatherless, or even parentless.

Being free from many of the colony's social constraints, this generation developed an 'Australianness' that set the trend quite early for what would become known as typical Australian traits: a sense of independence, self-reliance, and a laconic and practical attitude to life.These children, who became known as 'currency lads and lasses' were bold by nature because, in a strange environment in which they were the first European generation who were both 'native born' and free, everything was an adventure.

4

A CURRENCY LAD

A NEW BREED

The first generation of native-born children of migrant settlers and convicts in New South Wales were called 'currency lads' and 'currency lasses', to distinguish them from the non-convict British settlers, who were known as 'sterling' or 'pure sterling'.

The terms used referred to the fact that New South Wales did not use British currency (sterling) until 1822. There were insufficient coins to establish a sterling currency and what coins there were left the colony on every ship that departed. Rum was used as currency until Governor Macquarie ordered 40,000 Spanish dollars for the colony, to be paid for by the British Crown. They arrived in Sydney in November 1812, from the East India Company in Madras, on board HMS *Samarang*.

The convict forger William Henshall then cut the centres out of the coins and counter-stamped both pieces. The 'holey dollar' was worth 5 shillings and the 'dump' was worth 15 pence. The makeshift currency stayed in New South Wales, as it was obviously useless outside the colony.

So the terms 'currency lads' and 'currency lasses' were originally derogatory, that is 'not British born'. They soon, however, became terms of pride for those to whom they referred. The currency lads were also referred to as 'cornstalks' because they were mostly taller than their British counterparts and had a distinct way of talking. It quickly became clear that the currency lads and lasses were quite different from the migrants.

Commissioner John Thomas Bigge reported in 1820 that the children of convicts were generally industrious and surprisingly free of any criminality. He described them as taller, fairer, stronger and healthier than the free settlers who had migrated here. They were also better educated and more literate; in Sydney and Parramatta more than 80 per cent of the men and 75 per cent of the women signed their own name on the marriage register. The currency lads excelled at sport and usually won when running, field sports and boxing contests were organised between 'currency' and 'sterling' athletes.

Captain James Kelly, our first native-born Irish-Australian national hero, was the archetypal currency lad.

JIM KELLY

James 'Jim' Kelly was pure 'currency' and the first Australian-born child to ever become a ship's captain. Sadly, his name is mostly forgotten now, except perhaps in Tasmania, where several places are named after him.

Ask mainland Aussies if they know who James Kelly was and they would probably say, 'Wasn't he Ned's dad?' Well, no, he wasn't; Ned's dad was John Kelly, known as 'Red'. Red Kelly was born in County Tipperary three decades after Jim Kelly's birth at Parramatta and, at the age of 21, Red was transported to Tasmania for the very 'Irish' crime of stealing pigs.

Jim Kelly's mother Catherine Devereaux was also Irish—and was probably from Dublin. She was certainly in Dublin Gaol in 1791, having been sentenced to death for theft. We don't know what she stole, but it probably wasn't a pig.

Eighty-five prisoners from Dublin Gaol left from Cork on the convict transport *Queen*, along with more than a hundred other Irish prisoners. The *Queen* was the first convict ship to ever sail directly from Ireland to New South Wales. Among the 85 prisoners from Dublin Gaol were two women who had originally been condemned to death. One woman, who we know only by her surname of Rositer, had stolen linen. The other was Catherine Devereaux, aged 30.

There is a story that Jim Kelly's father was James Kelly, a cook on the *Queen* who might have taken that job to enable him to travel to Australia with his pregnant, but condemned, girlfriend Catherine Devereaux. It's a good story and might be partly true. Jim Kelly's father was either James Kelly or an English soldier.

What cannot be true is that James Kelly knew Catherine was pregnant. The *Queen* sailed in early April 1791 and arrived in Sydney in September. Catherine's child was born on Christmas Eve, 1791. So, assuming positions aboard the *Queen* were being filled in late March 1791, it is hardly likely that James Kelly applied for a position knowing Catherine was pregnant. Indeed, she might have conceived while on board or just before—and perhaps James Kelly was the father.

What we do know is that the child was christened James Devereaux and later changed his name to Kelly. He may have grown up on a farm at Parramatta where Catherine and James Kelly Senior lived quite happily, but he was already working on sailing ships at the age of twelve.

A month after turning thirteen, having already made several voyages out of Sydney, he was apprenticed to boat-builders and traders Kable and Underwood and sailed on sealing expeditions along Bass Strait until 1807 when, aged sixteen, he sailed to Fiji for sandalwood and, later, as far as India on trading voyages.

Kelly became chief officer of Kable and Underwood's *Campbell Macquarie* and was on watch one night in June 1812 when the vessel became caught on a lee shore in storm and fog off the coast of Macquarie Island, off western Tasmania.

The ship was driven onto rocks and wrecked, but Kelly and the ship's captain managed to get all the men into boats and make it ashore. Four months later they were picked up by the sealer *Perseverance,* which sailed back to Sydney but could not enter the harbour due to a savage storm.

The ship was forced to take refuge in Broken Bay, north of Sydney, and Kelly walked overland to be re-united with his fiancée Elizabeth Griffiths, a 'currency lass' and the daughter of a former marine.

They married later that same year and Jim was given command of the sealing vessel *Brothers*, which left Sydney on 24 December 1812, his 21st birthday, for an expedition to Bass Strait. He returned five months later with more than 7000 seal skins. Soon Kelly's skills as a mariner and sealer were much in demand by merchants and ship owners.

A few months later, in command of William Collins's ship the *Mary and Sally,* he set out on another very successful sealing voyage and, on his return in March 1814, he was employed as captain of the schooner *Henrietta.* She sailed between the various ports of the colony: Sydney, Newcastle, Hawkesbury, and the two settlements in Van Diemen's Land. The *Henrietta* was owned by Thomas Birch and was also used to explore the coast of Van Diemen's Land searching for new seal colonies, those along Bass Strait being almost wiped out by sealers within twenty years of the first settlement at Sydney Cove.

It was around this time that Kelly decided to circumnavigate the island of Tasmania (then Van Diemen's Land), using a whale boat. He borrowed the boat from the magistrate of Pittwater, Major James Gorden, who had named the little boat *Elizabeth* after his wife. Kelly set off on 12 December 1815, with four convicts from Hobart. During the voyage he made the first detailed explorations of Macquarie Harbour and Port Davey.

Kelly wrote a detailed account of the voyage, which was later edited and published by James Calder in 1881 as *The circumnavigations of Van Diemen's Land in 1815 by James Kelly and in 1824 by James Hobbs/ edited from their own accounts.*

Having become very involved in exploring and pioneering whaling in Van Diemen's Land, Kelly decided to move his family to Hobart and, in 1817, they settled in a stone house he built on the banks of the Hobart Town rivulet that runs from Mount Wellington into the Derwent River.

James Kelly's friend and patron, Thomas Birch, had been given a monopoly on huon pine as a reward for the discoveries made by Kelly and their next joint entrepreneurial venture would involve Kelly crossing the Tasman Sea, in the ship *Sophia,* to explore trading possibilities in New Zealand. He was accompanied by his brother-in-law and several friends interested in trade possibilities, including William Tucker, who had previously lived with the Maori in the Otago area.

It seems they sailed into a dispute between tribes and, after an originally friendly greeting, the party separated into two groups, one of which was suddenly attacked a few days later. Tucker, Kelly's brother-in-law and another man were killed and eaten. It seems that previous contact with Europeans had made the Maori distrustful and cautious, but to Kelly it was simply an unprovoked act of treachery, murder and cannibalism.

Kelly's retaliation certainly did little to help relations between Europeans and Maoris. He shot and killed a number of Maori warriors and then set about destroying their canoes and burning the Maori town of Otago, which was reputed to have had 600 houses.

Kelly was evidently a brave man, a fearless opponent and a crack shot with a pistol. On his return to Sydney in 1818 he led an armed detachment, which scoured the islands of Bass Strait searching for escaped convicts. Kelly had earlier reported that sealing and whaling was being made a dangerous business by bands of escaped convicts who attacked parties of sealers or crewmen who went ashore to get water and fresh food.

According to the 'Jim Kelly legend' the young captain had previously fought and killed a few of these desperate escapees, on earlier voyages around the area, with a pair of long-barrelled duelling pistols he always carried.

The hunting party arrived back in Sydney to much celebration and congratulations. Kelly was preparing to leave the ship and visit family at Parramatta when he heard a whisper along the docks that an attempt was to be made by a certain group of convicts to seize a ship and escape. Kelly quite rightly suspected that these convicts had designs on the *Sophia* and knew that he was planning to ride to Parramatta.

He rode away towards Parramatta before doubling back to Sydney. He then went aboard and prepared his crew to defend the ship.

Here is the account of what happened next, as reported in the *Sydney Gazette* on 20 June 1820:

> On Thursday night, or rather at an early hour yesterday morning, a daring attempt was made by a set of ruffians in a boat, to board and carry off the brig Sophia (Mr James Kelly master) from her moorings in Sydney Cove. Happily, owing to a judicious measure of Police some time since adopted in consequence of the frequent

piratical attempts made on the shipping in Port Jackson, the design was completely frustrated and the party well peppered by a brisk discharge o' musketry under the direction of Captain Kelly, who was fully prepared for the occasion, and exerted him self so successfully in repelling the attack, as to leave no doubt that some of the party were severely wounded.

Immediately on the firing being heard on shore, a boat, well-manned, set out under the direction of Mr Williams, His Excellency the Governor's coxswain, in pursuit of the desperadoes, but they were not fortunate enough to fall in with them, though little doubt remains that the vigilance of the Police, combined with the circumstance of one or more of the party being wounded, will quickly lead to the complete discovery of the miscreants, and drag to public punishment a set of monsters who were bent on embruing their hands in the blood of their fellow creatures, the master and crew of the vessel.

The time chosen for effecting their diabolical purpose was when it was supposed Mr Kelly was at Parramatta, whither it was known he had gone in the morning; and this circumstance, which lulled the assailants into a perfect security as to their success, eventually proved the means of their discomfiture, for the whole of their plan was well known to those whose duty it was to repel it.

Viewing the above attempt, and all the circumstances attending it, with its final defeat, and the exposure and punishment awaiting this band of pirates, we have no hesitation in saying that were that constant vigilance observed on the part of the masters and crews of vessels, which the faithful discharge of their duty to their owners and employers demands, and equal intrepidity as that of Captain Kelly, when attempts such as we have now described were made, we would not have to lament the different losses sustained in this way by the merchants and ship owners of New South Wales.

We hold out to public view and admiration the bold spirited faithful conduct of Captain Kelly, which cannot be too highly commended or appreciated; and the masters and crews of the colonial shipping in particular are called on, by every principle of duty, to show an equal zeal and promptitude in defence of the persons and property entrusted to their charge, whereby they will not only secure the good will and favour of their employers, but also render their own persons

> and property safe against the attempts of such midnight assassins, and merit, at least, public good opinion, if not public remuneration.
>
> It is with no little satisfaction, we understand, that it is a contemplation, with the merchants and ship owners of Sydney, to present Captain Kelly with a handsome piece of plate, inscribed with the record of his manly and successful exertions, in repelling a strong and desperate party of sanguinary pirates, in their attempt to seize the brig Sophia under his command, on the morning of the 19th instant; and we hope a liberal consideration, proportioned to their respective situations and exertions, will be also extended to the meritorious crew.

Kelly was duly rewarded for his actions and presented with a commemorative plate. His actions also brought him to the attention of Governor Macquarie, who offered him the position of pilot and harbourmaster in Hobart.

In 1821 he took up the position and the colonial administration also chartered the *Sophia* to transport convicts to the newly established penal station at Macquarie Harbour, which Kelly had discovered in 1815. In 1825 he was engaged to set up the convict settlement on Maria Island.

The former 'currency lad' also became a director of the Derwent and Tamar Fire, Marine and Life Assurance Co. and helped build the Theatre Royal and was on the Regatta Committee. He sent two of his sons to be educated at Bath Grammar School in England.

The swashbuckling Captain Kelly settled down to being a respectable citizen, but fortune was not always kind. In 1831 his wife died and three years later his ship *Australian* was lost and another of his ships, the *Mary and Elizabeth*, was attacked and burnt by Maoris in New Zealand. Then, in 1841, his eldest son was killed while chasing whales and another son drowned in the Derwent River. In fact, seven of his ten children died before he did.

Things went from bad to worse in his business life, too. Apart from shipping losses, Kelly was financially ruined when Depression hit the colonies after transportation ended in the 1840s. He was forced to return to working in a government position and was given the job of assistant harbourmaster for Hobart. Although he had pioneered the whaling trade, others reaped most of the benefits while bad fortune, exacerbated by the Depression, saw all his assets lost to creditors. He died suddenly in 1859, aged 67.

Fame, as well as fortune, can be fleeting. In his day Captain James Kelly was about as famous as you could be in the colonies of what was still called 'New Holland', 'Terra Australis' or just 'New South Wales'. In fact, he was so famous that ballads were written about him. His name was given to the steps at Battery Point in Hobart, which he built, as well as Kelly Island and Kelly Basin at Macquarie Harbour. Kelly Point on Bruny Island was also named after him—but the name was later changed to Dennes Point, as the memory of our first home-grown hero faded.

Footnote:

Not everyone, it seems, forgot James Kelly. Many Tasmanian history buffs have kept his memory alive and, in 1986, author Bern Cuthbertson and four friends recreated the voyage around Tasmania in a replica of the *Elizabeth*, which is now on display in the Bass and Flinders Centre, in George Town. Bern Cuthbertson, like James Kelly, wrote an account of his voyage, called *Around Tasmania in a Whaleboat*.

5
THE PIONEER AVIATOR

AVIATION IN AUSTRALIA

Aussie inventor Lawrence Hargrave can be called the father of the aeroplane. He is credited with being the most important contributor to the development of the powered, heavier-than-air (non-inflated) flying machines and he quite possibly made the world's first powered flight in 1894, when he built the world's first box-kite, hitched four together, lifted himself from the beach at Stanwell Park and flew 5 metres.

After he developed the machine further and published his designs, almost all early experimental aircraft used Hargrave-type box-kite structures. Hargrave opposed the idea of patents and believed in sharing discoveries and ideas. He did not patent or copyright his inventions and designs, but allowed others, such as the Wright brothers in the United States and Alberto Santos-Dumont, Gabriel and Charles Voisin and Louis Bleriot in France, to use them freely. While he is remembered for flying his box-kites and aircraft at Stanwell Park, he also flew them many times over Sydney Harbour, from where he lived at Point Piper. The Wright brothers used Hargrave's ideas, and even patented some of them, and never acknowledged him. He was featured on the Australian $20 note from 1966 to 1994.

The first controlled, heavier-than-air flights in Australia 'officially' recognised occurred at Narrabeen in Sydney, on 5 December 1909. On that day George Augustine Taylor successfully flew a glider he designed and built. His wife Florence and their friend Emma Schultz also flew the glider, which makes them the first Australian women to fly an aircraft. According to aviation historian David Craddock, Florence had to tuck up her skirts in order to make the flight and later commented, 'My dressmaker never realised I was a budding aviatrix.'

As far as our pioneers of powered flight are concerned, there are three conflicting 'claims to fame' as the first person to fly a powered aircraft in Australia.

George Augustine Taylor, the man who made that historic glider flight at Narrabeen and later wrote the official history of Australian aviation for the first edition of *The Australian Encyclopedia*, gave the credit to Ehrich Weiss, who flew his French Voisin biplane at Diggers Rest, near Melbourne, on 18 March 1910. Weiss, who was better known to the world by his stage name Harry Houdini, made a number of flights around Australia at that time.

There is well-documented evidence, however, that on 9 December 1909, just four days after George Taylor made his heavier-than-air flight in the glider at Narrabeen, a young Englishman, Colin Defries, left the ground in a Wright Model A aircraft at Victoria Park racecourse, near Kensington in Sydney. Defries flew the aircraft, named *The Stella* after his wife, 'straight and level' at a height of about 20 feet (6 metres) for a distance of 115 yards (105 metres) in front of a crowd of 150 people. A reporter from the *Sydney Morning Herald* reported that Defries had actually flown 300 yards (274 metres) when his hat blew off and, in his effort to retrieve it, he crash-landed the aircraft, which was badly damaged.

Defries was not mentioned by George Taylor in his official history and it was not until the 1960s that Defries was legitimately recognised as the first man to make a powered controlled flight in Australia. There are three possible reasons why George Taylor did not consider Defries worthy of the honour.

One reason could have been simple professional jealousy, but it may also be true that Taylor did not consider the flight made by Defries to have been 'controlled'. The third reason may be the fact that the flight was made in an aircraft designed by the Wright brothers. Taylor, and many other Australians, resented the fact that the Wright brothers used Lawrence Hargrave's ideas and never acknowledged the fact.

In 1960, aviation journalist Stanley Brogden suggested that the first powered flight in Australia actually occurred in South Australia, at a town called Bolivar, near Salisbury just north of Adelaide, when Fred Custance flew a Bleriot monoplane on 17 March 1910, just one day before Houdini's flight at Diggers Rest.

In 1967, Brogden retracted the claim as there were no independent authorities that witnessed the flight and there was no clear evidence that Custance, who had never flown before, had 'proper control of his machine'. The owner of the property on which it took place, Mr F. Jones, who had imported the Bleriot, and several of his neighbours witnessed the flight. Custance made a second attempt but crashed, damaging the plane. Custance was a skilled mechanic and motoring pioneer who migrated to South Australia with his family from England as a child. With his partner, Gilmore White, he drove from Melbourne to Adelaide in 20 hours 6 minutes in March 1909 and from Melbourne to Sydney in 21 hours 19 minutes in December 1909.

During World War I Fred Custance joined the Royal Flying Corps and flew BE2s in Palestine. BE2s were 'British Experimentals', part of a range of aircraft that were developed quickly during the war. They were known by the men who flew them as 'Bloody Emergencies'. After the war Custance continued his motoring exploits until he perished in the South Australian outback after a car breakdown. He was just 33 years old.

In 1909 the new Australian government, carried away by all the excitement about flying, offered a prize of £5000 to anyone who could invent 'a flying machine suitable for use in war'. There were more than 40 entries, but none were practical and so the prize was never collected.

The men who developed the Australian aviation industry in the 1920s were almost all survivors of World War I. These were men who learned to fly during the war and survived to develop aviation in Australia. Many of the young men who enlisted in the army in the war saw the chance to join the flying corps as a wonderful piece of luck. They would never have had the opportunity to learn to fly back home on the farm or in their city jobs. The majority of them died, in training, in battle, or just in the normal course of flying. The few who survived mostly wanted the chance to keep flying as civilians.

This small group became the foundation of the emerging aviation industry. They tested new machines and new technology and helped design and develop bigger and better aircraft, and many died doing it.

The list of the men who were members of the Royal Flying Corps in World War I and went on to pioneer our aviation industry includes Charles Kingsford Smith, Keith Smith, Ross Smith, Charles Ulm, Bert Hinkler, Hudson Fysh, Frank McNamara VC, Wally Shiers, Hubert Wilkins, Fred Custance, Raymond Parer, Jim Bennett, Francis Briggs and John McIntosh. When you consider that the life expectancy of a new pilot on the Western Front in 1917 was five weeks, it makes you realise how lucky these men were to survive the war and help build Australia's aviation industry. 'Smithy' always said that being shot through the foot and repatriated to England to be a pilot instructor was the thing that saved his life in World War I. He often commented on the irony of the fact that he was given a medal, as well as having his life saved. Six of the men listed above were killed in aviation accidents within twenty years of the end of the war.

Fortunately for Australian aviation history, one popular and plucky Queensland flyer survived the war and lived long enough to leave a permanent legacy, his name was Bert Hinkler.

BERT HINKLER

Herbert John Louis Hinkler was a short, modest man who spent hours as a boy in his hometown of Bundaberg in Queensland watching ibises fly.

Herbert, born 8 December 1892, was enrolled as 'Bertie Hinkler' at the North Bundaberg State School in 1898 and finished his formal education at age fourteen. He worked in sugar mills and a foundry and became a competent photographer, taking many photographs of ibises in flight.

From early childhood young Bertie had just one ambition: to spend his life flying. As a teenager he built gliders, modelled on the ibis.

There is a story that, when he was a teenager, he left home and headed to Richmond, near Sydney, where he washed down the plane that was making joy-ride flights over Sydney every night in return for just one flight. Unfortunately, his mother followed him from Bundaberg and prevented him from having his first flight.

But nothing could stop Hinkler. He talked his way into a job as mechanic for the American aviator Arthur Burr Stone, who brought his Bleriot monoplane to Bundaberg in 1912. He then accompanied the American flyer on his tour of southern Australia and New Zealand.

There were no flying schools in Australia so Bert worked his passage on a freighter to Germany, when still only twenty, and made his way to London, where he eventually landed a job as a mechanic with the Sopwith aircraft company.

When war came, he joined the Royal Naval Air Service. Hinkler was an excellent rifle shot and became the commanding officer's observer and a petty officer by the end of 1915. He flew on many daytime and night raids in Handley-Page bombers and DH4s and is credited, as a gunner, with destroying six enemy aircraft. He also invented a dual-control system which enabled the gunner to take control of the plane when the pilot was wounded.

By the end of the war he had been awarded the Distinguished Service Medal, gained a commission, and joined the Royal Flying Corps.

After the war Hinkler bought a 35-horsepower Avro Baby and flew from London to Turin over the Alps, a feat for which he was awarded the Britannia Trophy. Mechanical problems prevented him from attempting to fly on to Australia, but he and his plane travelled home by ship and he made a series of pioneering flights around Australia, including the first direct flight from Sydney to Bundaberg.

Returning to England in 1922, he spent four years as chief test pilot for the A.V. Roe (Avro) aviation company in Southampton. One of the aircraft he tested was the Avro Aldershot, the first plane in the world to have an engine capacity greater than 1000 horsepower. During this time, he also won the light aircraft trials in 1923 and the Grosvenor Challenge Cup in 1924, flew his Avro Avian from London to Latvia, was decorated by the Latvian government, and made an unsuccessful attempt on the London to India air record.

Hinkler planned most of his epic solo flights from his home, a cottage named 'Mon Repos' on the Thornhill Estate, in Southampton, near where he worked as a test pilot and where he lived, apparently very happily, for many years with his de facto wife Hannah 'Nance' Jervis. He was a popular character at Avro and had a habit of singing while flying.

In December 1917 the banns for his marriage to Hannah were read in St Giles Church, Camberwell, but the marriage didn't proceed, perhaps because Hannah was previously married with a daughter.

Bert Hinkler flew into history in February 1928, when he piloted an Avro Avian from London to Darwin in fifteen and a half days, smashing the Smith brothers' record of 28 days for the journey. At the time, it was the longest solo flight ever made.

He flew the 1100 miles (1770 kilometres) non-stop from London to Rome, a first leg which demonstrated his determination. He continued flying long stages every day, with a regularity that made it seem inevitable that he would achieve his goal.

From Rome he flew to Malta direct, then crossed the sea to Benghazi the following day and on to the North African coast to Tobruk that afternoon. Three days from England to the continent of Africa was a record at that time.

On 11 February, Hinkler flew from Tobruk to Palestine and the next day he set off for Baghdad but actually made such good time that he kept going on to Basra, covering 950 miles (1529 kilometres) in a non-stop flight of nine and a half hours.

On 14 February, after a flight in beautiful weather down the Persian Gulf, the Avro Avian landed in Karachi, seven days after leaving England. This established a new record: 5000 miles (8047 kilometres) had been flown in seven days at an average of more than 650 miles (1046 kilometres) per day.

The fastest normal travel time from London to the edge of the British Empire at Karachi was then about three weeks, by train and ocean liner. The idea that this could be reduced to less than a week was a source of wonderment to the ex-patriots and colonial officers and civil servants, who suddenly began to think of the possibility of being able to read English newspapers only a week old.

The only problem experienced up to this point was a slight leak in an oil tank, which Hinkler discovered as he flew down the Persian Gulf. This was quickly repaired by RAF mechanics and caused no real delay to the flight schedule.

As Hinkler crossed India in two stages, from Karachi to Cawnpore and from Cawnpore to Calcutta, he passed the halfway point of his journey. It took him just two days to cross the sub-continent.

On the next stage to Rangoon, Hinkler encountered the first really bad flying conditions of the trip when he was forced to fly through two tropical storms and heavy rain. The next stage to Burma was relatively uneventful but, on the next day, on the stretch to Singapore, he again struck several heavy rainstorms and, just before reaching Singapore, he found it necessary to make a wide detour to miss a thick storm belt.

From Singapore, Hinkler flew on to Bandung, in Java, on 20 February, and the next day he brought the Avian to Bima, his last stop before facing the final stage, across the lonely Timor Sea to Darwin.

That night Hinkler tried to get as much sleep as he could in a native hut, but mosquitoes kept him awake and tropical rain pelted down.

At dawn he took off, with just a drink of water for breakfast and no food or water on board. Darwin was still a thousand miles away as he climbed with great difficulty through the trubulent tropical air and over the mountains to the south of Bima.

For most of the stage across the vast ocean, clouds gave him some anxiety, but he maintained an altitude of 2000 feet (610 metres) and a speed of 92 mph (148 kph). Despite no visibility for most of the flight, Hinkler's compass reckoning proved very accurate, and he sighted the coast of Australia at 4 p.m. on 22 February.

Following the coast to Darwin, the pioneer airman came in over the jungle to Darwin and circled the Ross Smith Memorial twice. He landed at Fannie Bay, 3 miles (5 kilometres) from the town, just after 6 p.m. local time.

A rather sunburnt and very tired Bert Hinkler gave a speech that evening at a civic dinner held in his honour. In the speech, a typically modest and unpretentious Hinkler said that the most critical day of the whole trip was the first, when he flew for three hours in darkness before reaching Rome, and his only real moment of anxiety was when fading daylight caused a forced landing in the North African desert and some rather menacing natives approached him, but a gift of cigarettes solved the problem.

King George V sent the following message:

> Please inform Mr. Hinkler that I have received the news of his safe arrival in Australia with great pleasure. I have personally watched the progress of the great flight with great interest and am delighted that it has been successful.

Children sang a nursery rhyme parody:

> Hinkler, Hinkler, little star
> Fifteen days and here you are.

Australia went Hinkler-crazy. The government sent a cruiser to stand by as Hinkler flew his final leg, across the Arafura Sea. Composers wrote songs about him, the nation's hit tune was briefly 'Hustling Hinkler'. People wore Hinkler buttons, girls wore Hinkler flying-helmet-type hats, federal parliament stopped to welcome him, the Queensland government gave him £500 and the Australian government £2000, plus the Air Force Cross and the honorary rank of squadron leader in the Royal Australian Air Force.

Bert Hinkler never used the rank or wore the uniform.

Hinkler's rapid progress and endurance seemed incredible at the time. He was small of stature and quiet and modest by nature, but he was physically strong and was a gifted and expert pilot with thousands of hours experience testing aircraft.

Hinkler returned to England, and Nance, and invested his money in a company making an amphibious aircraft named after the bird he used to study, the ibis. The prototype of this new aircraft proved very successful, but the Wall Street crash and Depression derailed the project commercially.

Undeterred, Hinkler headed off to Canada in 1930 where he acquired a Puss Moth aircraft, which he flew to New York and later to the West Indies and South America. He then flew the Atlantic from east to west, which was considered to be the greatest piece of solo navigation in aviation history.

Times were tough in Britain and Bert's happy days with Nance at Mon Repos were coming to an end. Aged 40 he returned to America where, in May 1932, in Connecticut, he married Katherine Rome about whom little is known except that she was probably originally British and lived in the United States.

On 7 January 1933, Bert took off from London in an attempt to break his own record to Australia. It was the last flight of his career. Hinkler's body and plane were finally found four months later, in a remote part of the Apennine Mountains in Tuscany at the end of April. It is believed that he attempted an emergency landing after losing a propeller blade in flight.

The Aero Club of Florence and the Italian Fascist government gave Hinkler a hero's funeral. He is buried in the English Cemetery in Florence. There is a monument to him near the fatal crash site on Mount Pratomagno in Italy.

His wife Katherine was living in Glasgow when he was killed. She returned to America after his death and died at Long Island in 1976.

Nance continued living in Mon Repos until 1952, when she sold the house and moved to South Africa. Amazingly, in 1953, after Nance had sold the house, Hinkler's log book of his 1928 flight to Australia was found in a wing stub of the Ibis, which was still stored in the shed in the backyard.

Mon Repos now stands proudly in the Queensland city of Bundaberg. The Southampton City Council planned to demolish the house and redevelop the site in 1982, but a request was made and the demolition was put off until June 1983. A group of dedicated Queenslanders took the cottage apart and shipped it to Australia, to be rebuilt in Bundaberg.

On 16 June 1984, Mon Repos was officially opened by Premier Joh Bjelke-Petersen and the former mayor of Southampton, Councillor Dorothy Brown. The project was funded by British Aerospace, the Royal Australian Navy, the Royal Navy, the Royal Dutch Navy, Qantas, Bundaberg's Bicentennial Committee, and the District Tourism and Development Board.

In December 2008, the $7.5 million Hinkler Hall of Aviation was opened to the public in Bundaberg. A federal electorate in Queensland is named after him, as are quite a few streets and parks in that state, along with others in Darwin and in various places in New South Wales.

Songs were written about Hinkler, including 'Hustling Hinkler', recorded by Len Maurice and Fred Monument, and 'Hello! Hinkler' sung by Frederick George. The two poems that follow by C.J. Dennis were written during the last days of his historic solo flight to Australia and, on his landing, they appeared in the Melbourne *Herald* in February and March 1928.

THE SINGING ACE

By C.J. Dennis

Utterly fearless, small, active, and with a schoolboy grin, Hinkler (now crossing the Timor Sea on his final hop) is an ideal long-distance flier. He has unique endurance, enabling him to make a solitary flight for hours, singing as the mood moves him.

London *Daily Mail* (quoted in Melbourne *Herald*) 22 February 1928

There's an Aussie in an Avian high o'er the Timor Sea,
Flying on and singing as he flies
For the honor of his country, for the sake of you and me,
And the spirit, true and bold, that never dies.

He is speeding, he is singing, as the boys in old days sang
When the High Adventure beckoned them along,
Where the frowning cliffs of Anzac to their lilting voices rang,
And the crags of Sari Bair gave back their song.

There's an Aussie in the zenith where the Timor spills its flood.
Alone with sea and sky, he rides the air.
He is homing to his own land with her spirit in his blood,
And only sea-birds mark his passing there.

But he's singing, gaily singing with a heart aflame with hope,
And his eyes fixed on the far horizon's rim
Where tropic skies to tropic seas in azure glory slope
And the nearing shores of Homeland beckon him.

Where the Timor basks in sunlight there's an Aussie all alone—
Alone with sea and sky—a speeding mite,
Who flies o'er Asian seaways as no other man has flown
And finds but true adventure in the flight.

And he's singing—still he's singing, while the nations breathless wait
And count the hours of waiting all too long,
Till he ends his long adventuring beside his mother's gate
And his kinsmen catch the burden of his song.

There's an Aussie in an Avian—a speck within the blue—
Who puts to shame old tales of fabled ships.
For honor of his land he sails, for proof for me and you
Who wait with greeting trembling on the lips.

And he's singing—ever singing as he drops the leagues behind—
The man who ventured half a world to roam,
And thankfulness shall mingle with the welcome he will find
When at last the Singing Ace comes winging home.

OUT OF THE BLUE

By C.J. Dennis

Speaking in welcome of the famous airman, Bert Hinkler, yesterday, the Premier, Mr Hogan, said 'Today Mr Hinkler has come to us out of the blue'.

Melbourne *Herald* 19 March 1928

Out of the blue. A glimmering speck
Draws on while the thousands cheer,
With straining vision, with craning neck,
Each one fearing he yet may wreck,
They gaze as his ship looms near,
Bringing, from half a world away,
Something to each man here today.

More than honor and more than fame,
More than a triumphing song
More than the tale of a well-won name.
More than the title of high acclaim,
Brings he to the clustering throng.
'Tis Vision, and Pride, and a Hope that's new
He brings with him shimmering out of the blue.

Strange, vague promptings of waxing Pride,
Vision for me and you.
Men who yet never may learn to ride

Into the void o'er a whole world wide,
Venturing into the blue—
Yet in the bosom of every one
Comes hope, because of a deed well done.

Is it that we of the age and race
Into which he was born
See for the moment, only trace
Something there of a hidden grace
Salve for a world forlorn?
As a sign and a portent of places new
Comes he thus winging it out of the blue?

Doubly an 'Ace' in that he, alone,
Played for the stake and won.
By such high deeds have the seeds been sown
Out of which Empire and glory have grown:
Thus are new worlds begun.
Was it something of this that we sensed today
When out of the blue he came winging his way?

Comes a new era for men of the earth
That the 'Lone Ace' flies this way?
Cook, Columbus were men of worth,
Drake knew much of the wide world's girth—
But night has followed their day:
A night of blackness that gave men fear,
When the gods of war strode all too near.

'Tis but the Dawn. Yet skies grow clear,
And the new Day breaks full fair.
But, as year follows on glorious year,
And the 'Tale of the Air' is an old tale here,
The name of Hinkler, Pioneer,
Shall shine while the skies are there—
Writ indelibly into the Blue—
'This Boy who had made his dreams come true'.

6

THE BOY WHO READ ROBINSON CRUSOE

THE REAL ROBINSON CRUSOE

In the late 18th century most literate European boys read Daniel Defoe's novel with the rather cumbersome title: *The Life and Strange Surprizing Adventures of Robinson Crusoe, of York, Mariner: Who lived Eight and Twenty Years, all alone in an un-inhabited Island on the Coast of America, near the Mouth of the Great River of Orinoco; Having been cast on Shore by Shipwreck, wherein all the Men perished but himself.*

The book was hugely successful and was Europe's first adventure 'novel', a story devoid of the usual mythology and legends and using contemporary ideas and characters. The hero goes to sea against his parents' wishes, becomes a plantation owner and slave trader, is shipwrecked and survives by his own ingenuity, rescues the intended victims of cannibals, defeats a gang of pirates, returns to civilisation and finds he is wealthy after all.

Alexander Selkirk, the 'real' Robinson Crusoe, was born Alexander Selcraig or Selchcraig, in Lower Largo, Fife, Scotland, in 1676, the seventh son of a tanner and shoe maker. He was, by all accounts, a violent, hot-headed and pugnacious youth and, in 1696, he was ordered to appear before the church elders for causing trouble in church. The church records tell us, however, that the nineteen-year-old failed to appear 'being gone to sea'.

He returned, after two years later at sea, and the records tell us that he was in trouble again, in November 1701, for beating his younger brother Andrew with a wooden staff, which led to an all-in family fight in which Alexander assaulted his father, another brother and a sister-in-law.

It was obviously time for Alexander to go back to sea. Luckily for him, the Spanish War of Succession began that year and England needed sailors. In 1703 he joined an expedition consisting of two ships, the *St George* and the *Cinque Ports*, under the command of William Dampier, who had been granted a Letter of Marque by the admiralty. This was a document which authorised private individuals during time of war to attack and capture enemy ships. These men were known as privateers or corsairs—they were pirates with a licence.

Selkirk was the navigator on the smaller of the two ships, the 120-ton *Cinque Ports.* The ships sailed south, via Madeira, Senegal and Brazil, rounded Cape Horn and entered the Pacific. Two months into the voyage the captain of the *Cinque Ports* died of fever and a 21-year-old lieutenant, Thomas Stradling, took over. There were soon arguments between the young and apparently arrogant captain and his 30-year-old more experienced navigator.

In May 1704 the two ships separated and spent the summer searching for Spanish ships. Selkirk, who had already discovered that the ship's food was contaminated with roaches and rat droppings, now declared that the *Cinque Ports* was unseaworthy and evidently threatened to stage a mutiny while the ship was anchored at the island of Más a Tierra, in the Juan Fernández archipelago, almost 700 kilometres west of the coast of Chile. Although Captain Stradling was unpopular with the crew, none of them chose to join Selkirk's revolt. The result was that he was left on the island with bedding, a cooking pot, musket, pistol, gunpowder, hatchet, knife, tobacco, cheese, jam, a flask of rum and a Bible.

The island had been used for many years by ships taking on freshwater, timber and food, especially lobsters. It had a population of feral goats, descendants of those deliberately left behind by previous mariners. Unfortunately, it was overrun by rats also left behind.

Although he evidently changed his mind and begged Stradling to take him back on board, Selkirk was probably not as concerned about his welfare as we may imagine. He only had to wait until the next friendly ship stopped at the island. Unfortunately, this didn't happen until four years and four months later. Several enemy ships did call in at the island and, on at least one occasion, Selkirk had to run and hide when evidence of his habitation led to Spanish search parties attempting to hunt him down.

The first friendly ship to arrive, in February 1709, was the *Duke*, captained by a privateer, Woodes Rogers, who later wrote about Selkirk in *A Cruising Voyage Round the World*, published in 1712. Also on board the *Duke*, as navigator, was Selkirk's old boss William Dampier. The *Duke* stayed at sea for another two years, during which time they had much success capturing Spanish ships and looting Spanish settlements. Selkirk was made second mate of the *Duke* and later became the sailing master of a captured Spanish ship, in which he returned to Britain after an absence of eight years, having circumnavigated the world and become a wealthy man due to his share of the ill-gotten gains of government-sanctioned piracy.

On his return Selkirk was interviewed by the writer Richard Steel, who wrote an account of his adventures for *The Englishman* newspaper. Alexander was arrested and charged with assault in Bristol and possibly imprisoned before returning to lower Largo where he eloped with a dairymaid before enlisting in the navy and returning to sea. In 1720 he married a widowed innkeeper in Plymouth before sailing on HMS *Weymouth*, ironically on a patrol to hunt down pirates. He died of yellow fever in 1721 and was buried at sea.

Daniel Defoe, a well-known British pamphleteer and author, traveller, merchant and political activist, grew intrigued by Selkirk's story and met with Woodes Rogers. The result, in 1719, was the world's first novel which would go on to be one of the most famous books ever written. To this day it has never been out of print and is second only to the Bible in its number of translations.

Defoe had his hero on an island on the other side of South America for 28 years, but many of the incidents in Selkirk's life—a hot-headed young man who runs away to sea, pirates, an island populated by goats, and return to his homeland as a wealthy man—are mirrored in *Robinson Crusoe*. Defoe also attributed to his protagonist some of Selkirk's techniques of survival, making clothes, hunting goats and finding food. Some reported character and philosophical changes during Alexander's life on the island are also used in *Robinson Crusoe*, such as finding serenity and coming to a better understanding of the world and one's self.

There's no doubt the novel inspired a legion of adventurers and explorers, and at least one of these famously found his way to our shores, and indelibly into the pages of our nation's story.

MATTHEW FLINDERS

Towards the end of Matthew Flinders' life, the editor of the *Naval Chronicle* was preparing an article on the then almost forgotten explorer and navigator. When he enquired about any 'juvenile anecdotes', which might be of interest in the biographical sketch, Flinders replied that he was 'induced to go to sea against the wishes of friends . . . from reading *Robinson Crusoe*'.

Flinders himself was not from York, like the fictional Robinson Crusoe, but the adjoining county of Lincolnshire. As a result of defying his friends and family and 'running away to sea', he would himself survive shipwreck, undertake a perilous journey in an open boat to save the shipwreck survivors, spend seven years trapped on an island against his will, give a name to a nation and become as famous for his adventures as his fictional hero . . . at least in the eyes of most Australians.

When Flinders was four years old, the other great hero of his youth was murdered in Hawaii. James Cook, a Yorkshireman like the fictional Crusoe, was to have an uncanny posthumous influence on the life of Matthew Flinders, through his connections with William Bligh and Joseph Banks.

Flinders should have been a country doctor, a physician like his father, grandfather and great-grandfather, in and around the village of Donington, where he was born in 1774.

Young Matthew grew up in the family house (demolished in 1908), attended St Mary and the Holy Rood Church in Donington, and was educated at Donington Parish School until the age of twelve. He was then sent to nearby Horbling Grammar School for three years where he learned Latin, Greek, the Classics and mathematics and was given a good grounding in writing by the Reverend John Shinglar, who noted Matthew's ability to write 'good clear English'. The geometry he learned in those three years enabled him to master the complex arts of navigation and chart making—in which he was essentially self-taught, like his hero James Cook. His 'good clear English' writing skills would prove invaluable, also.

Unlike Cook, Flinders did not have the benefit of many years sailing and commanding commercial vessels and studying navigation and seamanship at night before joining the navy.

Matthew had an uncle, John, who had served eleven years in the navy and tried to turn the young man away from a life at sea. Uncle John, however, could not compete with James Cook and Robinson Crusoe. When the family refused to sanction his plans, Flinders used a more devious method to achieve his dream.

The enterprising young Matthew had a cousin who was governess to the daughter of Captain Thomas Pasley of the Royal Navy and, at just fourteen years of age, he managed to persuade his cousin to introduce him to the captain.

The first meeting resulted in a long conversation and an overnight stay at the captain's house and, as a result of this friendship, Flinders joined HMS *Alert* as an officer's servant at age fifteen. Seven months later he transferred to Captain Pasley's vessel, HMS *Scipio*.

Two months later Thomas Pasley was promoted to the command of HMS *Bellerophon*, a 74-gun battleship named after a mythological Greek hero and one of the most famous fighting ships of the era. Sixteen-year-old Matthew Flinders soon joined his patron as a midshipman on the *Bellerophon*.

Flinders had decided as a young teenager that his chances of advancement would depend on his abilities as a navigator and explorer, rather than a naval commander of warships. In 1791, aged seventeen, he saw an opportunity to advance his cause.

William Bligh had just returned from losing HMS *Bounty* to

mutineers while on a voyage to gather breadfruit plants and take them to the West Indies, where it was hoped they would prosper and provide a cheap source of food for plantation slaves.

Bligh was much admired by the admiralty and was immediately charged with another voyage to complete the work he had begun, this time with two ships, HMS *Providence* and the tender HMS *Assistant*.

Flinders knew that Bligh had learned his craft as a commander and navigator while serving under Cook, and applied for permission to join the voyage. With Pasley's approval he was 'loaned' to the expedition and joined the *Providence* as a midshipman.

Thus, for the last two and a half years of his teenage life, Flinders sailed the waters of the Pacific Ocean, Asia and the West Indies and many ports in between, under the tutelage of one of the finest navigators of the time. He learned to observe weather and ocean conditions and calculate position and distance. He meticulously kept a journal in which he noted the customs of the people he encountered and the landscapes of the places he visited. In short he developed what he called 'a passion for exploring new countries'. During this voyage Bligh's ships explored Adventure Bay and southeastern Tasmania and sailed through Torres Strait to the north.

When the voyage ended, Flinders again joined the *Bellerophon*, this time as an aide-de-camp to Pasley, who had been promoted to rear-admiral and commanded the van squadron of the channel fleet. As rear-admiral, Pasley remained on the *Bellerophon*, which was now captained by William Hope.

As Britain was at war with France, young Matthew was bound to see action and the *Bellerophon* was involved in a number of minor engagements in the English Channel in late 1793 and early 1794. On 1 June 1794, the warship, known to her less-than-classically educated crew as 'the Billy Ruffian', was involved in the famous Battle of Ushant, afterwards known as 'the Glorious First of June'.

The battle came about when the British fleet attempted to blockade French ports during the French Revolution, during which the French declared war on Britain and the Dutch Republic on 1 February 1793. The French Atlantic fleet engaged the British fleet under Admiral Lord Howe in an attempt to get a convoy of grain ships from America into the French port of Brest.

Twenty-five British ships of the line and 26 French warships fought a pitched battle in the Bay of Biscay, after Lord Howe used the unusual tactic of sailing directly at the French and then attacking ship to ship after breaking their line. Seven French warships were sunk while Howes' fleet returned to port at Plymouth, battered and damaged, without losing a ship.

Although the French claimed a pyrrhic victory due to the grain convoy arriving successfully several days after the conflict, the battle was a triumph for the British navy.

Twenty-year-old Matthew Flinders sat calmly on the deck of the *Bellerophon* throughout the battle, observing and making notes. As chaos reigned around him and the *Bellerophon* took broadside after broadside from the French warships *Eole* and *America* in a pitched gunnery battle, he prepared what was to become the most accurate account of the famous battle, a report that ran to 40 foolscap pages.

The battle was to have a great effect on Flinders' career. While his calmness under fire and his skills of observation and expression impressed his superiors, the really important outcome of the battle for Flinders was the retirement from active command of his first patron, Rear-Admiral Thomas Pasley, who lost a leg to a cannonball in the battle, as his protégé sat on deck making notes.

This left Flinders free to move on to another stage of his naval career, as he was no longer duty bound to serve with his mentor. But he had also lost his greatest supporter. Like James Cook, Flinders was not well connected by birth, and he had no commission, he was not an officer. Like Cook he had to wait until he was needed for a special task, before he was made an officer. Cook was not commissioned 'lieutenant' until he was needed to captain a navy ship. Navy regulations said HMS *Endeavour* required a man with lieutenant's rank, so Cook was commissioned 'lieutenant'. He was 'captain' not by rank, but by command.

Here is a chart of Flinders' naval progression:

Officer's Servant HMS *Alert* (14 gun sloop) 1789
A B Seaman HMS *Scipio* 1790 (Captained by Pasley)
Midshipman 1790 HMS *Bellerophon* (Captained by Pasley)
Midshipman 1791 HMS *Providence* (Captained by Bligh)
Midshipman 1793 HMS *Bellerophon* (Captained by Pasley)

Midshipman 1795 HMS *Reliance* (Captained by Waterhouse)
Lieutenant 1798 HMS *Norfolk* (Captained by Flinders) (Commission recommended by Governors Hunter and Phillip for the task of circumnavigating Van Diemen's Land)
Commander 1801 HMS *Investigator* (Captained by Flinders)

This list of achievements is made even more remarkable by the fact they were all earned by Flinders and not granted to him by virtue of his birth and family name, which was the usual practice of the time.

Following the Battle of Ushant, while the *Bellerophon* was being repaired, her fifth lieutenant, Henry Waterhouse, was appointed captain of HMS *Reliance*. This ship was to deliver the second governor of New South Wales, John Hunter, a First Fleet veteran, as captain of the escort warship HMS *Sirius*, to take up his post. Flinders saw his chance and, using his connection with Waterhouse, he joined the *Reliance* as midshipman and sailed from Plymouth in February 1795, bound for the penal colony, which had been largely forgotten by the admiralty during the tumultuous years of war with the French. On board was another native of Lincolnshire, George Bass, the ship's surgeon.

Bass was three years older than Flinders. A farmer's son, Bass also had a grammar school education after his father died when he was seven years old. He became a surgeon at eighteen, having joined the navy after being apprenticed to a local doctor for five years.

The surgeon had an adventurous spirit and had brought a small boat, 8 feet by 5 feet, on board the *Reliance* with the intention of exploring the waterways of the new colony—he called it *Tom Thumb*. He had also brought a servant boy, William Martin, with him.

Flinders made good use of the voyage out to New South Wales to develop friendships with both Governor Hunter and George Bass and, in October 1795, he and Bass and Martin explored the Georges River in *Tom Thumb*. The young explorers were encouraged and supported by Governor Hunter and their voyage led to the settlement of Bankstown, in south-western Sydney, being established.

In a larger version of *Tom Thumb* they explored and charted Port Hacking and Lake Illawarra, and Bass went on to explore the coast as far as Western Port in southern Victoria in Governor Hunter's whale boat and then make the assertion that Van Diemen's Land was separated from the mainland.

The wreck of the trading vessel *Sydney Cove* on an island off the coast of Van Diemen's Land in 1796, and the subsequent rescue missions to retrieve her crew and cargo, had aroused Bass's interest in the area and his exploration of the southern coast led to his belief that there was a passage north of Van Diemen's Land which would shorten the journey from Britain to New South Wales considerably.

Bass was right and, in 1798, he and Flinders circumnavigated Van Diemen's Land in the *Norfolk*, a sloop of 25 tons that was built on Norfolk Island. Their explorations and charts led to the establishment of Hobart in 1803 and it was Flinders who suggested to Hunter that the strait between the mainland and Van Diemen's Land bear his friend's name, noting in his journal that, 'This was no more than a just tribute to my worthy friend and companion.'

Flinders explored the coast of what today is Queensland in 1799 and he and Bass returned to Britain in 1800. Bass married Elizabeth, sister of Henry Waterhouse, captain of the *Reliance*, in October 1880.

Ten weeks after his marriage Bass sailed his own ship to New South Wales and then embarked upon a series of trading exploits in New Zealand and Hawaii (known then as the Sandwich Islands), which culminated in a secretive and possibly illegal voyage to trade in South America, a trip from which he simply never returned.

George Bass was a remarkable man. Among other things he attempted unsuccessfully to cross the Blue Mountains and was made an honorary member of the Society for Promoting Natural History (which became the famous Linnaean Society) for his paper on the anatomy of the wombat.

Upon his return to Britain, Flinders was keen to advance his opportunities to explore and found a valuable patron in another Lincolnshire man, Captain Cook's old patron and friend Sir Joseph Banks, who was also a friend of Flinders' supporter John Hunter.

Flinders' charts and reputation as an explorer had preceded him and, with the support of Banks and Hunter, his career made remarkable progress between his arrival back in Britain in October 1800 and his promotion to commander in February 1801.

In this short period of four months, his plan for the exploration of Terra Australis was accepted, a ship (the *Investigator*) was commissioned for the purpose and his journals were published.

Flinders described his ship this way:

> The *Investigator* was a north-country-built ship, of three-hundred and thirty-four tons; and, in form, nearly resembled the description of a vessel recommended by Captain Cook as best calculated for voyages of discovery. She had been purchased some years before into His Majesty's service; and having been newly coppered and repaired, was considered to be the best vessel which could, at that time, be spared for the projected voyage to Terra Australis.

Indeed, HMS *Investigator* began life as a shallow draught collier, like the *Endeavour*. Launched as the *Frum* in 1795 she was acquired by the navy during the war with the French in 1798 and used as a 21-gun escort sloop, HMS *Xenophon*. Although refitted at Deptford with extra cabins and storage for scientists, she was not in good condition but she was all that could be spared by a navy preparing for war.

Problems of poor timber would plague *Investigator* and force Flinders to abort his mission in 1803. To make matters worse, she had been 'coppered'.

This process was designed to protect a ship's timber from marine worms and prevent marine growth, which slowed a ship's speed. In spite of it being very expensive, the process of routinely sheathing naval vessels in copper sheeting began in 1781 after failed experiments as early as 1761. The problem was that the copper reacted electrolytically with the iron bolts used in timber ship construction and the resultant corrosion of the bolts meant that the timbers leaked and rotted. Various alloys were tried but, over the following decades, many of His Majesty's ships were actually falling apart as the timbers rotted inside the copper sheathing.

But all that was in the future for young Commander Flinders in February 1801. He had other problems.

Against the advice of his patron Joseph Banks, he married his childhood sweetheart, Ann Chappell, in April 1801 and applied for permission to take her on the voyage. When this was refused, Flinders sailed in July, leaving his bride to live alone for the next nine years.

Flinders reached the southwest tip of Terra Australis, Cape Leeuwin, on 6 December 1801. He spent a month preparing in King George Sound (Albany) and then moved slowly eastward. He charted the south coast to Kangaroo Island meticulously, using the technique he had used in mapping Van Diemen's Land. The ship was kept as close inshore as possible during the day so the shoreline was visible and no river or opening could escape notice. Flinders stood at the masthead with a telescope and constantly checked bearings while the land was in sight. Each night he made his rough chart for the day and his journal of observations, and care was taken to start at the same point next morning at daylight.

When bays and islands were found, Flinders went ashore with the theodolite, and measured, mapped and made topographical notes. Soundings were taken constantly and the rise and fall of the tides observed. Time was given for the naturalists to collect specimens, and for the artist to make drawings.

Flinders found and explored Spencers Gulf, and today Lincolnshire names still abound in that area, including Port Lincoln and Donington.

Before the gulf was explored, however, tragedy struck the expedition. On Sunday, 21 February, the ship's cutter was returning from searching for water. Aboard were the ship's master, John Thistle, a midshipman, William Taylor, and six sailors.

Nobody saw what happened, although the boat was seen leaving shore, but it did not arrive back at the *Investigator*. Next day the boat was found floating upside-down with holes indicating it had been smashed against rocks.

The loss of John Thistle affected Flinders deeply. He wrote:

> Mr. Thistle was truly a valuable man, as a seaman, an officer, and a good member of society. I had known him, and we had mostly served together, from the year 1794. He had been with Mr. Bass in his perilous expedition in the whaleboat, and with me in the voyage round Van Diemen's Land, and in the succeeding expedition to Glass House and Hervey's Bays. From his merit and prudent conduct, he was promoted from before the mast to be a midshipman and afterwards a master

> in His Majesty's service. His zeal for discovery had induced him to join the Investigator when at Spithead and ready to sail, although he had returned to England only three weeks before, after an absence of six years . . . His loss was severely felt by me, and he was lamented by all on board.

Flinders erected a copper plate upon a stone post at the head of Memory Cove, engraved with the names of those who died. Two fragments of the original plate are now in the museum at Adelaide.

Some parts of the southern coast had been charted as far back as 1627, on the voyage undertaken by Dutchman Pieter Van Nuyts. Captain Vancouver in the British ship *Cape Chatham* had explored as far as King George Sound in 1791 and Frenchman D'Entrecasteaux explored further east the following year while on his quest to find tidings of missing French explorer La Pérouse.

In typically sentimental Gallic fashion D'Entrecasteaux's ships were named *L'Esperance* (Hope) and *La Recherche* (Searching) and the town of Esperance takes its name from the former.

Captain James Grant had sailed through Bass Strait in 1800 and charted the coast from the east as far as Western Port in 1801.

While Flinders was slowly mapping the southern coast from west to east and finding and charting, Frenchman Nicolas Baudin was doing the same thing but heading westward. They met at Encounter Bay, off Kangaroo Island, on 8 April 1802.

In 1798 Baudin had presented to the French National Museum of Natural History a plan for a hydrographic survey expedition to the South Seas, which would include a search for fauna and flora that could be brought back for cultivation in France. After considering this extensive proposal, the French government decided to proceed with an expedition confined to a survey of western and southern New Holland and Baudin reached Australia in May 1801 with two ships, *Geographe* and *Naturaliste*. Accompanied by nine zoologists and botanists, he explored and mapped the western coast, and a part of the southern coast, and more than 2500 new species were discovered.

In spite of poor health and dissension among his officers, during a time of uneasy truce between Britain and France, Baudin acted diplomatically and honourably in his relations with the colonists and, during time spent in Sydney, was most grateful for the support of Governor King. He spent two and a half years exploring and charting the Australian coast, collecting flora and fauna and making a close study of the Aboriginal people of Van Diemen's Land. He died from tuberculosis on his way home in 1803, at Mauritius.

Although there were some communication problems due to Flinders' lack of French and Baudin's poor English, the two were able to share the fruits of their discoveries and spent two days in friendly communication in Encounter Bay before parting.

As the entire southern coast was now at least adequately charted, Flinders sailed to Port Jackson, with a stopover to make maps of Port Phillip and Western Port, and prepared the *Investigator* for the task of charting the entire coast of Australia. Baudin arrived some six weeks later, with most of his crew needing medical attention due to scurvy and dysentery.

While Baudin's crew recovered, the two explorers shared more of their discoveries and charts during several weeks encamped together at Port Jackson.

Flinders sailed north in July, finding and exploring places like Port Curtis and Port Bowen, and continuing his detailed survey work, mapping the Queensland coast and the Gulf of Carpentaria.

After passing through Torres Strait, it became apparent that the *Investigator*, which was leaking badly, was so rotten that she might have trouble surviving bad weather. The ship was careened for inspection and the ship's carpenter was of the opinion that she could only remain afloat for another six months.

Flinders could not continue his detailed surveying and charting under those conditions, but he was determined at least to be the first to circumnavigate the continent. He therefore sailed westward, spent some time looking for the mysterious Trial Rocks, which had wrecked the British East Indiaman *Tryall* in 1622, and returned to Port Jackson by way of the western coast and Bass Strait, bringing the barely seaworthy *Investigator* safely into Port Jackson on 9 June 1803.

Flinders, however, was anxious to complete the task he had been assigned by the admiralty, the complete survey of the coast of Terra

Australis. So in August 1803 he sailed as a passenger from Port Jackson in HMS *Porpoise* to secure a suitable ship.

Further adventures still lay ahead for Matthew Flinders, but the completion of the survey was not to be one of them.

The *Porpoise* was seven days out of Sydney, sailing in convoy with the passenger ships *Cato* and *Bridgewater*, when two of the three ships struck an uncharted reef in heavy seas at 9.30 p.m. on the dark moonless night of 17 August 1803.

Wreck Reef, as it is now called, consists of 30 kilometres of reefs and sandy islands 450 kilometres east-north-east of the modern-day town of Gladstone.

Seconds after the lookout man on the forecastle called out 'breakers ahead', the ship was beyond control in heavy surf, and a minute later she struck a coral reef and the heavy sea lifted the vessel and dashed her onto the coral.

With her foremast gone and her bottom stove in, the *Porpoise* was being pounded to pieces while a futile attempt was made to fire a cannon to warn the other two ships. Sadly this could not be done and those clinging desperately to the disintegrating *Porpoise* watched the *Cato* hit the reef 300 metres distant and disappear from view.

The *Bridgewater* seemed likely to suffer a similar fate but a huge swell lifted her and she cleared the reef and stood out to sea.

Flinders immediately took charge and ordered the ship's rowboat to be launched. He told Captain Fowler that he intended to save his charts and journals, although his specimens were all lost.

His plan was to row to the *Bridgewater* and take charge of the rescue of those wrecked on the reef. The rowboat, which it was discovered leaked badly, was at a safe distance from the reef and the wreck, waiting for him as he conveyed his plan to Captain Fowler and, rather than risk losing the rowboat, Flinders swam through the raging waves to board her. He and five others bailed and rowed in pursuit of the *Bridgewater* but found it impossible to reach her.

Rather than attempt to return to the wreck of the *Porpoise* through the breakers in darkness, Flinders kept the rowboat outside the reef until morning, assuming that they would all be rescued by the *Bridgewater* at first light.

At dawn, Flinders climbed back onto what was left of the *Porpoise* and took stock of the situation. About half a mile inside the reef, he saw a dry sandy island and directed all survivors of both vessels to jump overboard and swim through the surf to the island, using planks and spars. All were saved except three young crewmen from the *Cato*, who had perished in the night.

Not only did Flinders organise for all left alive at sunrise to reach the island safely, he also managed to get most of the provisions from the *Porpoise* ashore. Stores were landed, and tents were made from sails. 'On the fourth day,' Flinders wrote, 'each division of officers and men had its private tent, and the public magazine contained sufficient provisions and water to subsist us three months.'

Indeed the stores saved from the wreck and itemised on the tiny island included: 940 pounds of biscuit, 9644 pounds of flour, 1776 four-pound pieces of beef, 592 two-pound pieces of pork, 50 bushels of oatmeal, 1225 pounds of rice, 448 pounds of sugar and molasses, 398 gallons of spirits, wine and port, and 5650 gallons of water.

Also, many of Flinders' specimens and the *Investigator* artist Westall's drawings were salvaged—along with sundry amounts of sauerkraut, malt, vinegar, salt, sails, spars, an anchor, an armourer's forge, canvas, twine, four and a half barrels of gunpowder, two swivel cannons, muskets and pistols, and few sheep, which unfortunately trampled over some of Westall's drawings as they came ashore. Their hoof marks are still visible on one of the drawings, preserved in the Royal Colonial Institute Library.

Once the 94 survivors had been organised, Flinders, determined to preserve discipline, read aloud the articles of war and had one seaman, an ex-convict, publicly flogged for disorderly conduct. He was determined to ensure that all survivors, naval men and merchant seamen from the *Porpoise* and *Cato*, knew where they stood. The island operated in the same manner as a British ship of the line until all were saved three months later.

But just how were they saved? And where was the *Bridgetown*?

The answers to these two questions make for two amazing tales: one of heroism, skill, bravery and salvation; the other of cowardice, treachery, honesty and retribution.

So, let us first return to the *Bridgetown*.

After narrowly avoiding the same fate as the *Porpoise* and *Cato*, the *Bridgetown* stood out to sea and waited for the storm to abate. On his arrival in India, Captain Palmer related his story to a newspaper and sent official correspondence ashore at Thalassery:

> When the day was broke, we had the mortification to perceive the Cato had shared the fate of the Porpoise; the bow and bow sprit of the latter only at intervals appearing through the surf . . . with her bottom exposed to the sea, which broke with tremendous fury over her; not a mast standing.
>
> Finding we could not weather the reef, and that it was too late had it been in our power to give any assistance; and still fearing that we might be embayed or entangled by the supposed chain or patches . . . We therefore determined, while we had the day before us, to run to the westward of the northern reef. At five p.m. we could perceive the wrecks . . . After passing the reef we lay too for the night; and in the morning we lost sight of it, having drifted to the northward.

In other words, Captain Palmer sailed back and forth at a safe distance from the reefs and the wrecks and, fearing his ship was in danger if he approached closer, abandoned the two wrecks and sailed away to India.

As fate would have it, Palmer's false account of the shipwrecks was entrusted to his ship's third mate, Mr Williams, to be taken ashore at Thalassery.

Williams was disgusted at his captain's behaviour—he had noted the sandy island inside the reef and thought, from the position of the wrecks on the reef, that there was every likelihood that there were survivors.

When he was chosen to take the message ashore, Williams made a decision that could have ruined his career, as he put it:

> In executing this service, I did, for the first time to my knowledge, neglect my duty, and gave a contrary account; but for this reason—I was convinced that the crews of those ships were on the reefs, and that this was an erroneous account made by captain Palmer to excuse his own conduct.

Not only did Williams contradict his captain's account, he returned to the ship and informed Palmer that he had done it. This led to him being put ashore by Palmer in Bombay without his pay and some of his belongings.

In a twist of fate that would seem implausible in fiction, the *Bridgetown* was lost at sea with all hands on its voyage back to Britain, while Williams and several others who had left the ship in protest at Bombay lived to tell the true story.

Meanwhile, back on the sandy island, Flinders called a council of officers which resolved that he should take the largest of the *Porpoise*'s two six-oar cutters, with an officer and crew, and make his way to Port Jackson, a risky voyage which would have to be made against prevailing strong southerly winds. In case his mission ended in death or failure, he ordered that two boats should be built by the carpenters from the wreckage, so that all the survivors could attempt to sail back to Sydney.

The cutter was prepared for her long voyage, and appropriately named the *Hope*, was launched on 26 August. With Captain Park of the *Cato* as his assistant officer, and a double set of rowers, fourteen men in all set out with three weeks provisions.

Flinders had flown a large blue ensign upside-down on a masthead as a signal of distress for the *Bridgewater* to see. In a gesture of admiration, a sailor hauled it down and flew it right way up as Flinders and his crew left the tiny island.

'This symbolic expression of contempt for the *Bridgewater* and of confidence in the success of our voyage, I did not see without lively emotion,' said Flinders.

On the evening of 8 September, Governor King and his family had just commenced dinner when a servant announced a visitor and Matthew Flinders, who had not shaved for a month, was ushered into the dining room.

Plans to rescue the shipwrecked men were put in place immediately. Captain Cumming of the *Rolla*, a 438-ton merchant ship, agreed to call at the reef and carry some of the survivors to Canton, while the *Francis* would bring the remainder back to Sydney.

Flinders himself was given command of the *Cumberland*, a 29-ton schooner, and was to sail in her to England with his charts and papers as rapidly as possible. The *Cumberland* was a small ship built in Sydney for local service and her crew consisted of merely a boatswain and ten men, but she was the only boat available.

Although it took just two weeks to prepare the rescue mission, Flinders stated that 'every day seemed a week'. On Friday, 7 October, exactly six weeks after the *Hope* had left Wreck Reef, the lookout on the *Rolla* spotted the blue ensign flying on the flagstaff of the little desert island, and the rescue was completed.

Thus it was that Matthew Flinders, having found himself shipwrecked like his hero Robinson Crusoe, took control, formulated a plan for salvation, swam through mountainous seas to board a leaking rowboat and chase a ship which deserted him, managed to save and get safely to shore all but three of the passengers and crew of two wrecked ships, set up a well-run camp, organised the civilised and orderly storage and distribution of provisions, and sailed more than 1000 kilometres back to Port Jackson in an open boat to organise the rescue.

It was, I believe, his finest and bravest adventure. Robinson Crusoe could have done no better!

Having arranged for the relief and rescue of his wrecked shipmates, Flinders sailed off in the 29-ton schooner *Cumberland*, planning to proceed to England by way of the Torres Strait.

The ship soon proved totally unfit for the task, needing almost constant pumping to keep her afloat as well as being almost impossible to sail on the open sea. Flinders therefore decided to seek assistance at Île-de-France (known before and after French rule as Mauritius) in conformity with his 'French passport'—which was, in those days, a document detailing the peaceful nature of a voyage, in accordance with a joint agreement to allow British vessels safe harbour in French ports. He arrived there on 17 December 1803, three months to the day after his friend Baudin had died there and exactly one day after Baudin's ship, the *Geographe*, had departed for France.

There were two small details that were to make this an unfortunate turn of events.

Firstly, in his haste to leave Port Jackson and return to rescue those on Wreck Reef, Flinders had neglected to change the details on his French passport. He was sailing in a different ship to that for which his papers were valid.

Secondly, he had sailed inadvertently into an enemy port, for France and Britain were once again at war.

The story of Matthew Flinders' imprisonment on Mauritius has been told many times. It was six years and six months before he was released—despite the fact that the French government ordered his release just two years after his arrival.

There are many reasons why things went so badly for Flinders on Mauritius.

The governor of the colony, Charles Decaen, was a brave soldier, a good general in battle and a scrupulously honest man with a brusque manner. He was a protégé of the great French general Jean Moreau and his actions were largely responsible for Moreau's crushing victory against the Austrians in 1800 at Hohenlinden. Decaen had good reason to hate the British and feel suspicious of their actions.

In spite of Napoleon's distrust of Moreau, whom he had dismissed for disloyalty in 1797 but reinstated after he seized power as France's ruler in 1799, Napoleon trusted and confided in Decaen and had great plans for him. (Moreau and his wife became the chief opposition in France and encouraged others to join in turning against Napoleon. They were banished in 1804, went to the United States and collaborated with the enemies of Napoleon until his defeat at Waterloo.)

In February 1803, under the conditions of the Peace of Amiens, a truce between France and Britain, Decaen was chosen to sail to India to govern the French territories that had been taken by the British and were to be returned to France under the terms of the treaty.

Decaen left Brest in February, expecting to arrive in India to find the territories restored to French rule, as agreed. The British, however, had decided not to hand back the colonies and Decaen arrived in the port at Pondicherry in June to find the British still in control and unwilling to negotiate.

Another French ship then arrived with news that war was imminent (it had actually been declared in May while the ship was at sea). Decaen was instructed to return to the much less important colony of Mauritius and take up the post of governor there, which he did, four months before Flinders' arrival.

The British, as Decaen saw it, had stolen French territories, reneged on promises made in a treaty, and robbed him of a valuable career opportunity.

It is little wonder that Decaen was suspicious of Flinders' motives. Although he quickly realised that Flinders had not been aware that France and Britain were at war, he suspected that Flinders might have been sent to do reconnaissance on the island's defences for the British government.

It was quite logical for Decaen to assume that the British merely used the Treaty of Amiens as cover to prepare for an onslaught on the French colonies, because in fact it was true.

Both nations used the treaty as an opportunity to plot and spy and make plans. The French naturalist, François Peron, who was a member of Baudin's expedition and wrote the official account of the voyage after Baudin's death, also prepared a secret report, which shows he operated as a spy while in Port Jackson and advocated a French attack on the colony. Peron had undoubtedly spoken to Decaen about these plans and perhaps filled his mind with doubts about Flinders.

It is ironic that Peron, to whom we owe a huge debt of gratitude for his work in collecting more than 100,000 zoological specimens and making the only detailed study of Tasmanian Aboriginal people before their contact with Europeans destroyed their culture, was also operating as a spy and advocated and planned the downfall of the British settlement in New South Wales.

François Peron was an unusual man. He studied for the priesthood before joining the army. While a prisoner of war after the Battle of Kaiserslaten, in which he lost an eye, he read accounts of voyages and decided to become a naturalist. He was the only one of five naturalists to survive Baudin's voyage and his work was excellent. However, he did not like Baudin and the feeling was mutual. It is doubly ironic that, when Baudin refused to fund Peron's exploration of the outlying areas of the colony during their stay at Port Jackson, Governor King gave him the resources he needed and paid for him to undertake the task!

Whatever the reason for Decaen's original distrust of Flinders, the situation soon became exacerbated by the reactions of the two men to each other.

Even though their nations were at war, there was an expectation of mutual respect between officers and gentlemen and especially so in the case of explorers and men of science, but Decaen was suspicious and Flinders was insulted and annoyed.

Soon it was Decaen's turn to be insulted and annoyed. Having concluded his official business with Flinders, he immediately sent him a message inviting him to dine with his wife and himself.

Flinders refused the invitation, although the officer who delivered it begged him to reconsider, pointing out that conversation over dinner would perhaps serve to solve the misunderstandings between him and the governor.

Refusing an invitation to dine with the one man who could help him, as a fellow officer and gentleman, was a decision Flinders would have plenty of time to regret. Indeed, Flinders soon realised that much of the problem between himself and Decaen was caused by him mistaking Decaen's brusqueness for deliberate rudeness.

Decaen was flabbergasted by the refusal. He felt that Flinders' behaviour at their official interview made his invitation to dine an exceptionally gracious gesture. In his memoirs, Decaen recalled that, 'Although he had given me cause to withhold the invitation on account of his impertinence; but from boorishness, or rather from arrogance, he refused that courteous invitation, which, if accepted, would indubitably have brought about a change favourable to his position, through the conversation which would have taken place.'

Apart from all the other obvious impediments to a successful outcome of the unfortunate circumstance of Flinders arriving at an enemy port, the personality clash between the two men was to set in motion a series of events that led to Flinders spending six and a half years on the island.

Decaen saw it like this: 'Captain Flinders imagined that he would obtain his release by arguing, by arrogance, and especially by impertinence.'

Flinders' version was: 'I believe that the violence of his passion outstrips his judgment and reason . . . he is instantaneous in his directions, and should he do an injustice he must persist in it because it would lower his dignity to retract. His antipathy, moreover, is so great to Englishmen, who are the only nation that could prevent the ambitious designs of France from being put into execution, that immediately the name of one is mentioned he is directly in a rage.'

Flinders, however, thought that Decaen was an honest and honourable man and admitted that, 'He has the credit of having a good heart at the bottom.'

To the credit of Decaen, Flinders was treated with dignity and respect during his enforced stay on Mauritius. His every request was agreed to, except his request to leave. His papers and documents were returned to him, his crew were allowed to leave and he was accommodated in comfort at the expense of the French government in very comfortable accommodation in the hills at Wilhelm's Plains.

Flinders made many friends, worked on his journals, learned to speak excellent French and passable Malay, and reflected on life in general and his own in particular. He later said that in some respects those years were the most serene and pleasant of his entire life.

In a letter to his wife he admitted, 'I am proud, unindulgent, and hasty to take offence, but . . . my mind has been taught a lesson in philosophy, and my judgment has gained an accession of experience that will not soon be forgotten.'

Many requests for release were made to both Decaen and the French government on Flinders' behalf, by respected British citizens (including Governor King, Sir Joseph Banks and the governor of India) and also by French scientists, including Bougainville, and eminent citizens on Mauritius.

Although other British prisoners and captured naval personnel were released or traded for French prisoners of war, Decaen obstinately refused to allow Flinders to leave. This he did despite an order for Flinders' release being signed by Napoleon in March 1806. The release document approved of Decaen's actions but asked that Flinders' ship be restored to him and he be released.

It is true that, due to the successes of the British fleet in the ongoing war, no copy of the release document arrived on Mauritius until mid-1807 but, when it did arrive, Decaen chose to take it as advice that he could release Flinders when he thought it appropriate, rather than a direct order.

It was not until three years later, with Mauritius doomed and blockaded by the British, that Flinders was informed that the emperor's order for his release was to be activated. Flinders was then conveyed to one of the British ships involved in the blockade and returned home via the Cape Colony, which was now under British control, arriving back to greet his wife nine years and three months after his departure.

Why did Decaen persist in keeping Flinders on the island so long?

We can only surmise that, once Flinders had been given relative liberty to roam the island and talk to anyone he chose, Decaen realised he knew far too much about the weakened state of the island's defences, and how easily it could be taken, to let him return to Britain with that information.

The longer Flinders remained, the more he knew. Decaen was well aware that the colony was living on borrowed time as the war swung in favour of Britain. Keeping Flinders on the island prolonged the time he could stave off the inevitable fall of the colony to the British.

Decaen has been pilloried by historians for keeping Flinders in an unfair state of captivity but his priorities were to his country and he managed to keep Mauritius in French hands for far longer than he had imagined possible by a combination of bluff and cunning.

Although the public buildings, wharfs and defences were falling apart and food was scarce at times, Decaen managed to bluff the British out of attacking, although a small force could have easily taken the island at any time from 1804. He held out until 1810.

Decaen knew that Flinders would not violate his 'parole' for two reasons. He had given his word that he would not attempt to escape, although it would have been a simple thing to achieve, and he was offered safe passage by at least one neutral captain and refused the offer. Flinders even kept his word in so far as his letters home never gave any military information.

Apart from having given his word as an officer and a gentleman, Flinders was unwilling to leave without his documents and charts and journals. His mission had been to chart the coast of Terra Australis and write an account of the voyage and he intended to complete the task assigned to him. Escaping from the island without his possessions was never an option. Indeed he spent much of his time on Mauritius planning the completion of his mission to chart and explore the Australian continent, even going so far as to decide who should accompany him and what positions they should hold.

This was, of course, never to be.

Flinders returned to a quite different world to the one he left. The Battle of Trafalgar had changed the state of the play, the navy was expanding and the admiralty had many other concerns to deal with. Flinders was some six years too late to capitalise on his achievements and, although he was well received, his only official task for the next four years was to finalise his report and charts. Sir Joseph Banks organised a dinner in his honour and William Bligh took him to visit the Duke of Clarence, later King William IV, but the admiralty took little interest in his work and left him on half pay, which made his domestic situation difficult and led to the family moving five times in four years. The great joy of his final two years was his daughter.

Also, his health was failing. He had suffered from 'internal complaints' on Mauritius and the disease advanced rapidly, leaving him 'worn to a skeleton' in his wife's words and at the age of 39 he resembled an old man of 70. Although he was never heard to complain, his personal diary notes that he suffered severe pain often.

Flinders laboured hard and diligently to make sure that *A Voyage to Terra Australis* was well produced and accurate in terms of text and charts. It is a monumental work, which was designed not as a popular book, but as an accurate record of his endeavours to fulfil his commission.

He was a severe critic of both his own drafts and the printer's work and laboured over corrections and improvements until the final product met with his approval.

The first copies were delivered on 18 July 1814. His wife Ann laid the volumes on his bed while he slept, but he woke the following day only to whisper his last words, 'my papers', before he closed his eyes and died.

Matthew Flinders was buried in St James's Cemetery, behind St James Chapel, on the Hampstead Road, in Camden Town, north-west London, and was all but forgotten in Britain. His wife struggled to live and raise their daughter on a small post-captain's pension.

Hearing this, the government of New South Wales voted that a pension of £100 per annum be paid to them. Not to be outdone by New South Wales, from which it had recently joyously separated, the new colony of Victoria did the same.

Flinders' widow died in 1852, before she heard of this annuity, but his daughter, Mrs Ann Petrie, was very touched and wrote back to her benefactors late in 1852: 'It would indeed have cheered her last days to know that my father's long-neglected services were at length appreciated . . . and the handsome amount of the pension granted will enable me to educate my young son in a manner worthy of the name he bears.'

That son, born 3 June 1853, a year after the pensions were granted, would become Sir William Matthew Flinders Petrie—the most celebrated and respected archaeologist of his era and the first professor to hold a chair of Egyptology in the United Kingdom. As a child he was tutored in French, Hebrew, Latin and Greek, and after a bout of ill health at the age of eight, he was educated at home. His father, William Petrie, a devout member of the Plymouth Brethren, taught him religion, surveying and archaeological techniques.

Young William Petrie studied local Roman sites as a boy and as a teenager made the first systemic study of Stonehenge. In 1880 he made the first serious study of the construction and geometry of the Great Pyramid at Giza.

A pioneer of systematic methodology in archaeology, he was made a professor at the University College, London. There he served from 1892 to 1933 as the first Edwards Professor of Egyptian Archaeology and Philology—training many of the best archaeologists of the day, including Howard Carter who discovered the tomb of Tutankhamun. His large collection of Egyptian antiquities is housed in the Petrie Museum of Egyptian Archaeology in University College, London. In 1923 Petrie was knighted for services to British archaeology. He died in 1942.

Matthew Flinders' protégé, and nephew by marriage, Sir John Franklin, served with him on the *Investigator* and was wrecked with him on Wreck Reef. He had joined Flinders' old ship HMS *Bellerophon* and was aboard her at Trafalgar. He became governor of Tasmania and a famous polar explorer, and perished looking for the North West Passage in 1847.

The *Bellerophon,* on which Flinders saw action as a young man, became even more famous a year after his death. It was the ship on which Napoleon surrendered and on which he was transported to England.

Matthew Flinders is an iconic name in the history of our nation, remembered everywhere today in the names of geographical features and public institutions like universities, suburbs, parks and streets, although Flinders never once named anything in his own honour.

We even owe him the honour of naming our nation. The name 'Australia' was popularised by Flinders, who wrote in 1804, 'I call the whole island Australia', and he wished to use the name in his published works. 'Had I permitted myself any innovation on the original term,' he wrote, 'it would have been to convert it to Australia; as being more agreeable to the ear, and an assimilation to the names of the other great portions of the earth.'

Unfortunately, he was talked out of using this name in the book's title by his great benefactor and supporter Sir Joseph Banks, who thought the term 'Terra Australis' better known and less likely to confuse scholars already used to the terminology.

However, Governor Macquarie had read Flinders' journals. He liked the idea and began using the term, and the surveyor and explorer Major Thomas Mitchell followed suit when he coined the phrase 'Australia Felix' for the land he discovered south of the Murray River.

'Australia' was in such common use by 1901 that there was no debate about the name that should be used when the colonies federated.

In 1980 a stained-glass window, commemorating Flinders' achievements and showing him and the *Investigator,* flanked by Sir Joseph Banks and George Bass, was installed in St Mary and the Holy Rood Church in Donington—as a gift from the Commonwealth of Australia.

Had he become a village surgeon, like his father, grandfather and great-grandfather, Matthew Flinders' life would have no doubt been much less eventful . . . and probably longer.

As it transpired his short life was one packed with discoveries, adventures, achievements, heroism, hardships, disappointments, suffering and, as it turned out, eternal fame. And it was all because, as a boy, he read *Robinson Crusoe.*

Footnote:

St James's Cemetery was used as a burial ground by the Parish of St James, Piccadilly, between 1789 and 1853. Matthew Flinders was buried there in 1814. In 1887 the cemetery was made into St James Gardens and the gravestones still standing were removed and placed around the perimeter of the park.

In 2017, construction began on the expansion of Euston Station, to accommodate the new HS2, the high-speed railway linking London to Manchester, Birmingham and Leeds. To allow for this expansion, St James Gardens was closed and excavated. Seven hundred more tombstones were found, but none of them belonged to Matthew Flinders' grave and any chance of finding his remains among the estimated 30,000 to 60,000 bodies to be exhumed appeared very remote. But a small miracle occurred.

Two days before Australia Day 2019, the HS2 website announced, 'Our archaeology team have recently discovered the remains of Captain Flinders. They were able to identify his remains by the lead depositum plate [breast plate] that was placed on the top of his coffin.'

In October 2019, the BBC announced that Flinders' remains would be 'reinterred in St Mary and the Holy Rood Church in Donington' following 'a request by his descendants and the local community that he be returned'.

The Reverend Charles Robertson, vicar of St Mary and the Holy Rood, said: 'It is with great honour and joy that we received the good news that the mortal remains of Captain Matthew Flinders will come to Donington. It is a privilege to welcome home this great explorer to rest in peace in his home church.'

He announced that Flinders' remains would take pride of place inside the church in a corner dedicated to the explorer. 'We thought it more appropriate to inter Matthew Flinders inside the church,' Reverend Robertson said, 'where people will be able to visit him whatever the weather.'

PART III
SHAPING A NATION

The three individuals whose life stories are told in this section all contributed manifestly to the Australia we enjoy today. Their names would probably not be known or recognised outside Australia, because their contributions and efforts were aimed towards the betterment and development of our culture, our society and our lifestyle, and that makes them uniquely and specifically Australian.

Within Australia, however, these three people are remembered. They have statues and memorials, airports and football grounds named in their honour, and one has her portrait on our $50 note. Whether this means that many Australians are aware of their achievements and legacies is probably arguable, but at least the fact that these symbols remain to remind us that they lived and are considered worth remembering, may prompt some child to ask, 'Who was she?' or 'Who was he?' And that might prompt some embarrassed parent to go to the internet and find out.

The way in which they achieved the things they did differs enormously, and the areas of our everyday life that were enriched by these three people also vary. Their contributions to Australian culture and society were in areas ranging widely, from football to social reform, from developing our aviation industry to fighting for gender equality.

Their personalities, and the ways in which they went about changing Australia for the better, could hardly be more dissimilar. Edith Cowan worked patiently 'within the system' to advance women's causes, alleviate the stigma of unwanted pregnancy, and deal with unpopular issues like the consequences of veneral disease and prostitution. Tom Wills, at the other extreme, acted spontaneously and compulsively when inventing and then changing AFL football, in order to make it more fun to play, and in developing avenues to enable Indigenous athletes to become involved in organised sport.

Nancy-Bird Walton, the only one of the twelve people in this book that I actually knew, talked with and interviewed, achieved the things she did in her life by 'doing'. Nancy wanted to fly, so she defied her father, left home and went to learn to fly. She was determined to make a career out of flying and, in doing so, she pioneered aviation, communication and medical services in rural Australia.

So let's get to know these three Australians who couldn't be more different but were all influential in making us who we are as a nation.

7

THE WEST'S PIONEER REFORMER

With Jillian Dellit

THE SWAN RIVER COLONY

Throughout the 17th century Dutch sailors, traders and adventurers heading for Batavia landed on the coast of what is now Western Australia. Some explored the river we now know as the Swan. Although the Dutch showed little interest in possession, the land along that coastline appeared on maps as New Holland until 1826.

In 1801 Frenchmen Nicolas Baudin in the *Geographe* and Emmanuel Hamlin in the *Naturaliste* had called in to the river from the south, on their way further north. Hamlin stayed to explore but Baudin continued after only two days. Hamlin's view was unfavourable. The reaction of Phillip Parker King, the British colonial-born explorer, who arrived in 1822 on the *Bathurst* was similar.

It was down to James Stirling, a career British naval officer who had served in the Napoleonic wars and defended British interests in the Caribbean, to argue for a colonial outpost at Swan River. Stirling had spent several years on half pay at his home in Surrey, putting various schemes to the admiralty in the hope of a commission. His chance came in 1826 when the colony of New South Wales was short of coins and the experimental colony on Melville Island was short of food and plagued with scurvy. More important to the admiralty were whispers that France was moving to establish colonies on Terra Australis.

Stirling's lobbying paid off when the admiralty realised he was well placed to deliver goods and gather intelligence.

Arriving in Sydney in December 1826 on the *Success*, Stirling, heard that the French had rejected Swan River as their colonial station. So, he sought permission to explore with a view to establishing a settlement. He left Sydney on 17 January 1827, delivered coins to Hobart and continued on to arrive off the coast of Rottnest Island on 5 March 1827. Two days later Stirling took two sailors and a small boat 5 miles up the Swan River. On his return they emptied the ship to drag it over the shallows into the river. For the next week they explored along the river, encountering local Aboriginal tribes, swamp, a fresh water lagoon and what they decided was arable land.

By 21 March, Stirling was on his way back to Sydney, writing an enthusiastic report to Governor Darling, which was forwarded, with other information, to the Colonial Office in London. Stirling sent a further brief report in August of the same year on the strategic naval value of the place.

Back in England in 1828, Stirling lobbied for a Swan River settlement, putting forward, with his friend Thomas Moody, a proposal to the colonial under-secretary for an association of private capitalists to settle Swan River along the lines of William Penn in Pennsylvania. This had the support of Tory MPs but the proposal was rejected. However, strengthening rumours of French interest in Terra Australis led to the colonial secretary sending HMS *Challenger* under the command of Captain Charles Fremantle to establish a colony, and thus claim the area for Britain. Fremantle was followed by Stirling as lieutenant-governor of the colony, along with a colonial secretary, surveyor-general, harbourmaster, naturalist, surgeon, storekeeper, cooper, blacksmith and boat-builder. These men, along with their families, servants and livestock, left Plymouth in the *Parmelia* along with 100 soldiers, three years of army stores, 10,000 bricks and £1000, arriving at Swan River on 31 May 1829.

During that year 21 ships arrived in the Swan Hill colony. Based on the sketchy survey done by Stirling, land was reserved for the Crown, the clergy and for schools. Regulations were worked out to grant land to settlers.

Reports reaching England late in 1830, however, spoke of starvation and lack of agricultural land, and the colony was slow to grow. Between 1833 and 1834 twelve ships took 1358 settlers away from the colony. The European settler population was 1500 in 1832, when the name was changed to the 'Colony of Western Australia', and James Stirling finally received his formal commission as lieutenant-governor.

Although it had been stated in the original plans that the colony should never be a penal settlement, within a decade authorities realised that there was little choice if it was to survive. The population was only 5886 by 1850, when 100 convicts—British prisoners in the last years of their sentence—were brought to the colony. There would eventually be more than 9000 convicts sent to Western Australia before transportation ended in 1868.

Stirling remained in charge of the colony until 1840 when he was replaced by John Hutt and Stirling once again took command of a Royal Navy ship. He does not appear to have enjoyed, or been especially skilled at, administration on land. His initial cursory survey of the Swan River was a poor basis for settlement decisions. While he had lobbied for the establishment of the Swan River colony, this appears to have been more to create a job to get him back into naval service than a desire to become a settler himself. It was a step in a naval career.

Other settlers, however, retained hopes of a better, permanent, prosperous life for themselves and their children.

Edith Cowan's father, Kenneth Brown, was one of those children.

EDITH COWAN

Edith Cowan was born in the colony of Western Australia in August 1861, 32 years after the first British settlers arrived at the Swan River with high hopes of prosperity. Her father, Kenneth Brown, was born in England and came to Western Australia aged three, eleven years into the colony's establishment, with his parents and younger brother.

By 1861 the colony was beginning to show signs of prosperity. But it had been a much longer, slower road than the first settlers had anticipated.

Edith's paternal grandparents, Thomas and Eliza Brown, were typical. Leaving England in 1840 with tools, furniture, a flat-pack wooden house, eight horses and six servants on board the *Sterling*, their vision was of settling land on which they could grow English crops, raise sheep and horses, feed their growing family and sell their excess. No amount of advice from Dr Samuel Viveash and William Tanner, friends already in the colony, could prepare them for a land with a hot, dry climate—attuned to marsupials, eucalypts and native grasses. This was not a land of predictable, seasonal precipitation, nor was it particularly suited to road building, or being easily ploughed, or raising hoofed animals.

Even before they had left the Thames, seven of their horses had died in the stormy weather. The wooden house, while initially helpful in the colony, kept out neither the heat nor the cold and warped in both. The servants, outside the social and economic structures of England, had more incentive to set up on their own than to serve others.

European farming depended on ready labour. Thomas had been a surveyor in England, working for a turnpike company that made roads and charged for their use. To farm his land in the colony he needed to undertake much of the physical work himself, as did Eliza and their children. They were willing and able. Thomas briefly took a job as a surveyor but couldn't manage his farm and a job. The farm won.

The colony, established on the notion that it would be suited for independent, free settlers, had no formal, structured plan, such as that which established South Australia, and lacked an administrative and decision-making structure. Settlers with some education and experience were pressed into duty. This conflicted with working their land grants, which were spreading out from the administrative centre and needed attention if they were to meet government development requirements, produce a living and be permanent. Land holdings came with obligations to be developed and produce within a given timeframe and could be forfeited if the conditions were not met. Labour was in short supply. It was a constant dilemma for a colony of free settlers.

There were proposals from some, opposed by others, for convict labour. In 1839 agreement was reached to send 30 juvenile male offenders from England to serve as apprentices, and 234 boys under the age of fifteen arrived from Parkhurst Prison between 1842 and 1849. Eventually, convicts were seen as the only solution to the colony's failure to develop as hoped, and the first 75 arrived in 1850. Before transportation ceased in 1868 when British policy discontinued the practice, 9721 convicts arrived in the far-flung fledgling colony. It took many years before the 3158 convicts still under sentence in Western Australia were free. The last living convict, Samuel Speed, died in Perth Old Men's Home in 1938.

Within five years of their arrival, Thomas and son Kenneth had joined other settlers to explore to the north of their original land grant, thus putting pressure on the administration to open new land. They took another grant of land at York, an early settlement with an army barracks 60 miles east of Perth. After Eliza travelled the 300 miles on horseback to check their reports, they also established a residence at Glengarry, near Geraldton. Kenneth took part in these exploratory expeditions from the age of eight—holding his own on a horse for days, even weeks, at a time. At the age of thirteen he rode 108 miles non-stop to get a doctor when his mother's labour went wrong. Thomas wrote to his father-in-law in 1850:

> Another little girl was added to the family yesterday under conditions of some danger but I am happy to say both mother and infant are now well. Viveash had not arrived when the illness occurred. Kenneth went for him, riding one hundred and eight miles without stopping, and he only arrived just in time to save her.[1]

While Thomas Brown had been a willing settler, who entered energetically, physically and fully into colonial life, his wife Eliza had been the driving force. In another letter to his father-in-law on 21 December 1850, Thomas admitted:

> It may be said of many and perhaps justly that the love of change induces them to give up fair prospects and probably the same has been said of me. I will therefore state what I have not done before, namely that I never had a wish to leave prosperity in England where I always felt comfortable and happy for the chance of what might be done in any other country. My sole object in coming hither was for the improvement of Mrs Brown's health and spirits, she was often very miserable and particularly in the winter season and often expressed a wish that I would remove to some warmer climate, and took a particular fancy to Swan River which she has never deviated from, always liking the Colony and seeing better hope than I ever did. Her health and spirits were certainly much benefited which makes me not regret the change although it has plunged me into pecuniary difficulties.[2]

In 1851, with the farm running at a loss, Thomas was enticed into Fremantle to take on a job as a police magistrate. His wife was still attached to their original home in York, although the Browns had acquired the attractive property in Glengarry, but his job now required him to be in Fremantle. The difficulties this brought looked like being resolved in October 1862 when Thomas was appointed to be the magistrate in Geraldton but, in July 1863, Thomas died.

In coming to Western Australia, Eliza Brown had hoped for a healthier environment and opportunity for her children. This is made clear in the letters she wrote regularly to her father, William Busson, a chemist and property investor, who provided most of the funding that his daughter's settler family needed for equipment or stock. Eliza had planned to send her sons back to England for education or to find tutors in the colony to provide the classical education she thought necessary for advancement.

By the time Kenneth was thirteen, however, his grandfather was the one to suggest an English school would not provide the education he needed and that he 'would be better engaged in becoming a settler'. Eliza was forced to agree and put her hopes in her younger children but, in fact, they followed in Kenneth's footsteps. As with most settler families, it was left to the women to provide education—either by teaching their children at home, or by setting up schools for small numbers of children.

This idea of seeing value in education was also strong on the maternal side of Edith Cowan's family. Her mother, Mary Eliza Dircksey Wittenoom, born in 1840, was the daughter of John Burdett Wittenoom, first chaplain to the colony, and his second wife, Mary Watson Helms. John Wittenoom was a widower when he arrived at Swan River in 1830, bringing with him his mother and sister and his five motherless sons. At 40 he was an Oxford graduate who had been a lecturer, a parish priest in Southampton and, for fifteen years, headmaster of a boys' school.

John's new job of colonial chaplain brought an annual salary of £250 (soon raised to £350 with a weekly allowance of 2/6 for feeding and stabling his horse). John Wittenoom began building the first church within a fortnight of arriving. As the only clergyman in the colony, he held services in Fremantle, Perth and York as well as in further-flung outposts like Albany. He still found time, however, to look to providing education in the colony. With the support of James Stirling, he established the 'Classical and British School for Gentlemen' with an attached public grammar school for lower class boys. He was also interested in music and art—as a practitioner as well as a patron. Along with his sons, John Wittenoom laboured building their house, including making his own bricks on site.

In 1839 John Wittenoom married Mary Watson Helms, whose brother had erected his wooden house, brought from England, close to the Wittenooms. Mary Helms had run a small girls' school in Perth and shared her husband's interest in music.

In the same year, John Hutt replaced Stirling as colonial secretary. Hutt needed to make savings in the colonial budget. He saw no value in education in a colony, opposed free education, and removed the subsidies that had kept Wittenoom's schools running. Consequently, the schools closed. Nevertheless, interest in education remained strong in the colony and in 1847 Chaplain Wittenoom was appointed to the newly established Board of Education.

In that year, the board ascertained there were 400 children between the ages of four and twelve in the colony. Of these, ten boys were at the state-run Perth Boys' School, three girls were at Perth Girls' School, 30 boys were in Roman Catholic boys' schools, and 60 girls in Roman Catholic girls' schools, 40 children were in Methodist schools, and six private schools held 30, 20, 20, 7, 6 and 4 students respectively. The four were at the school run by the Misses Cowan in Perth. The remaining 170 children were classified as '70 idle and uneducated' and 100 were 'employed at home'.[3]

Three children were born to Wittenoom's second marriage, of which two girls survived. John Wittenoom died in 1855, overweight and suffering from gout. He was held in high regard and had been a well-known and key figure in making the colony liveable. Four hundred people attended his funeral and all shops in Perth closed. He was 66 years old.

Wittenoom's widow and one of his daughters, Mary Eliza, took over the running of the government girls' school in Perth. The curriculum for schools was based on what the settlers knew from their own schooling—grammar, geography, history, writing and arithmetic, with mathematics added for boys. Girls were offered French and drawing at extra charge, and boys similarly offered Latin and Greek.

Kenneth Brown and Mary Eliza Dircksey Wittenoom married in Geraldton in 1859. She was nineteen and he was 22. They had both contributed to their family's survival, worked physically, accepted responsibility, seen their fathers and siblings die—and still held to the hope, and expectation, that they would one day see a thriving community in Western Australia.

Kenneth and Mary lived at the Browns' Glengarry property when they married and it was here that their children were born. Kenneth had been left in charge of this property, aged around fourteen, when his father's appointment as police magistrate took the rest of the family to Fremantle.

Like most properties in the colony, it struggled to make ends meet. The colony needed an excess of farm produce to export but English farming methods did not transfer easily, and shipping was expensive, unreliable and irregular. There was a promising market for horses in Madras but although many horses were sent, few were able to be broken-in and trained to the level required by the British military. Kenneth shared his family's interest in horses and put energy into their breeding; it was one of many ways in which he tried to support his growing family in the challenging landscape of colonial Western Australia.

Edith Dircksey Brown was born in 1861, the second child of Kenneth and Mary. Their first child, Blanche Mary Elizabeth, had been born the previous year. Sons Mordant and Clarence were born in 1862 and 1864. Two years later, the fifth child, Ernest, died at birth and, in 1868, when Edith was seven, her mother died in childbirth, along with the sixth child.

While there had been no shortages of tragedies in both the Brown and Wittenoom families since their journeys to the colony, none of them had been as disruptive and destabilising as Mary Wittenoom's death. Kenneth, who as a child had guided explorations, managed a large remote property and ridden more than 100 miles to bring a doctor to his mother's birthing emergency, could not prevent his wife dying in similar circumstances, and he could not look after four children under the age of eight as well as run a financially threatened farm.

Kenneth's mother Eliza took charge of the children. Choosing to remain independent after the death of her husband, she had leased a house in Guildford, Perth, but she gave up the lease after Mary's death and moved to Glengarry. The two eldest children, Blanche and Edith, were sent to a boarding school in Perth run by the Misses Cowan, well known to the family from the York community. Eliza cared for the younger two, Mordant and Clarence.

Kenneth put all his energies into raising horses, although he still contributed to local public life. Unfortunately, the area was entering a decade of drought, wheat rust and sheep scab. Glengarry was mortgaged and running at a loss. Kenneth's brothers agreed to buy him out of the family partnership and paid him around $7500 in 1872. This was two years after the colony was granted representative government with a legislative council of eighteen members, twelve elected and six appointed by Britain.

Eliza Brown moved back to Guildford, which became the children's home when they were not at school.

Early in 1873, Kenneth left for Melbourne with three horses. He was, apparently, the first Western Australian to enter the Melbourne Cup, with his mare Victorian in 1873. The race was won by Don Juan, while Victorian finished with four horses behind her.

A month later, Kenneth married Sydney-born Mary Ann Tindall, twelve years his junior. The couple moved to New Zealand where they had two daughters. The marriage was stormy and apparently Kenneth was drinking heavily. He returned to Geraldton with his family in 1875.

On 3 January 1876:

> After a day of argument and drinking, of trivial enough dispute over the necessity to pack and move everything from the rented house to other quarters, the apparently pointless domestic disagreements broke into sudden bitterness and violence. Taking one of the guns over which there had been dispute during the removal, Kenneth Brown shot his wife. There was no question of accident. He refused any explanation or excuse.[4]

Kenneth was arrested for the murder of his wife and tried three times, because juries were unable to reach verdicts. The facts of the case were not in dispute. What jurors found hard to accept was that Kenneth was responsible. He was well known, well liked and respected in the colony as 'one of us'.

The first jury sat for six days. Eleven jurors opted for the verdict 'of unsound mind'. The twelfth was not convinced, but open to persuasion. However, according to the *Gippsland Times* which later featured the story on 29 June 1876:

> ... when the leading spirit among the eleven, in a last attempt to convince him said, 'Don't think of the prisoner, he is a scoundrel; think of the family,' he replied, 'If that is your best argument, I have nothing more to say.' Thus, the first jury was discharged without coming to a decision.

The second jury sat for ten days, with a similar result. Kenneth's brother Maitland gave evidence at length and his mother Eliza 'explained that her own mother had been subject to fits of depression and melancholia that had required hospital treatment'.[5]

The settlers looked for loopholes to avoid a guilty verdict, knowing the impact such a verdict would have on the accused and his family.

Only when the third jury was hastily chosen from bystanders outside the court was the inevitable guilty verdict returned. Using depositions from previously presented evidence, they convicted Kenneth on 29 May.

Kenneth Brown was hanged on 10 June 1876.

Peter Cowan, Edith's grandson, who has written extensively on the family's history, offered the following explanation for Kenneth's changed behaviour after the death of his first wife:

> There may have in part been a physical cause. For many of those who endured the hardships of the early explorations there were delayed and often unguessed at results. From the sun that could ravage and ulcerate their skin, to internal diseases they suffered without hope of proper diagnosis or cure, the cost could be high, often fatal. Skin diseases, varying degrees of blindness, sun stroke, were commonplace. Drinking infected and filthy water, eating food that was rotten and held parasites, had less obvious and later results very seldom diagnosed, often quite unsuspected as definite illness. A result that seems only recently to have been considered was the effect of prolonged

> periods of dehydration coupled with extreme physical exhaustion. This was a commonplace of exploration in Australia in areas of high temperature and lack of water. The simple enough result had often enough been death. The less obvious results were kidney failure and brain damage. Part of the symptoms could be extreme irritability and loss of control. The behaviour of Sturt recorded by Daniel Brock in his long withheld account suggests the strains and the price these men paid for their endurance.[6]

There is some support for this explanation in the evidence given by his family at Kenneth Brown's second trial.

It is unclear if Edith was in contact with her father after he left Glengarry or whether she ever met her stepmother. We know that she visited her father in prison, in the company of her grandmother, and likely, at least once, on her own. Kenneth's mother, brothers and sister visited frequently, and his brother Maitland was present at his hanging.

The murder and trial were widely covered in newspapers. Maitland Brown resigned his membership of the legislative council, creating more press attention when the governor delayed acceptance and replacement.

Peter Cowan explained:

> The trials attracted great publicity, and comment that destroyed personal privacy and feeling. There was press comment on trial by jury, and on juries, and there were suggestions of conflict in social privilege, politics, and personalities, inevitable in the small community. Eliza withdrew from all social life, and from most of her friends, for a period becoming virtually a recluse.[7]

We can only imagine what impact this had on Kenneth's children at school in Perth and in the care of their grandmother, Eliza. It is reasonable to assume that the personal reserve, including the protection of information about her own health, that Edith exhibited throughout her very public life, grew, in part, out of the impact of this family tragedy on a fourteen-year-old girl.

However, the discharged jurymen, so reluctant to hang a man because of the perceived dire effect it would have upon his family, had underestimated the fortitude and resilience of Kenneth's family, especially his daughter Edith.

Three-and-a-half years after her father's death, aged eighteen, Edith married James Cowan, the older brother of the Misses Lilias and Elizabeth Cowan whose school she had attended in Perth. On leaving that school she had been tutored by Reverend Sweeting, in Guildford. Under his guidance she read widely and voraciously, laying the foundation for her later work in bringing libraries and books to Perth.

James was twelve years older than Edith. He was the fifth of fourteen children, the third son of another pioneering family who were well known to Edith's family. James's father Walkinshaw Cowan had come to the colony as private secretary to John Hutt, the second lieutenant-governor of Western Australia. His family, too, struggled and took public service jobs to make ends meet when farming took so long to turn a profit.

James also wanted to be a farmer, but needing a paid job to help support the family, he had been appointed postmaster to the colony at age sixteen. There was little, if any, supporting bureaucracy and the pay was meagre. James took on additional government responsibilities to make a living and get things moving in the colony. Aged 30 at the time of his marriage to Edith, he was registrar and master of the Supreme Court, but it was his appointment as police magistrate in 1890 that gave them the security of both position and income.

Coincidentally, it was in this same year the colony was granted a constitution and self-government by the British parliament, although Britain, concerned about the treatment of Aboriginal people in Western Australia, retained control of Aboriginal affairs for a further seven years.

It was a pivotal time to hold a key public role.

James may have missed life on the land, but Edith thrived on city life. In addition to a shared pioneering background, they appear to have shared common values, a sense of social justice and a commitment to improving their community.

They honeymooned in Melbourne before settling in Perth, where four of their five children were born between 1880 and 1885. Helen, their youngest child, was born in 1891, just after James's appointment as police magistrate.

From this time, Edith began to engage with society, not as a hostess or socialite, but as a mover and shaker—someone who got things done. She began meeting with a group of like-minded women to read widely and discuss issues of the day. Books were not easily available so they formed libraries and lobbied booksellers to provide a wide range of literature.

The meetings were popular and soon developed into a club with sub-groups forming around current topics—law, health and education in particular. This was the beginning of the hugely influential Karrakatta Club. Women would read the latest literature on a subject and then discuss the ideas. Topics discussed included sex education for children, contraception, emancipation, models of government, venereal disease and prostitution. These were the issues of concern to the emerging Women's Movement, as women began to apply new scientific knowledge and technologies to their lives.

Discussion led to action on many fronts. Members became involved in the push for voting rights for women, which was achieved in Western Australia in 1899, five years after it had been achieved in South Australia, three years before New South Wales and 29 years before universal female suffrage was granted in the United Kingdom.

Inevitably, much of the club's focus was on the needs of women and children—which were not insubstantial in colonial, as well as British, society. James Cowan's role as police magistrate would have introduced many legal and social issues into their thinking. Several of his judgments pushed the boundaries of social attitudes in relation to domestic violence, and also theft.

Edith and her friends also understood many of the issues from their own family experiences. Children frequently died. Edith's mother bore six children, two of whom died at birth. Her maternal grandmother bore three and lost one. Her paternal grandmother bore seven, one of whom was killed in an accident aged five. Her mother-in-law bore fourteen children, two of whom died. Edith also saw women, including her own mother, die in childbirth.

The Karrakatta Club members knew many females struggling to establish businesses and to support themselves and their families.

Edith's mother, and her Wittenoom grandmother, had run schools when her grandfather died, and James Cowan's sisters were independent women, running schools as a living. Women, fully occupied with raising children, working on farms and making ends meet, were always the backstop after family breakdowns and disasters, as her grandmother Eliza Brown had been when her son Kenneth was executed.

Although there was now a form of representative government in the colony, the representation did not extend to women—who were, ironically, often better educated than the men.

Edith's grandson Peter Cowan puts it this way:

> But here James and Edith Cowan possessed shared interests, and it seems to have been the wife who sought the kind of knowledge his day's work offered. She wanted to know, and to use the insights she gained in some practical way. Though she was only eighteen at her marriage she seems to have had a fairly clear sense of where she was going. Her conviction of the importance of education, her struggle to attain a wider education than was usually thought necessary for women, was one kind of evidence. The influence of her grandmother, Eliza Brown, counted also. And she knew at first hand, through the lives of her own parents, of the kind of tragedy that could come to women and to men with lack of simple amenities, tragedy and deprivation that would shape and warp a human being out of recognition.[8]

Although transportation had finished in 1868, there were indentured convicts in the colony well into the 1890s. While the issues James and Edith sought to address arose long before transportation, the 9721 convicts who arrived in the eighteen years of transportation to Western Australia added extra pressure for social reform, as did the influx of would-be prospectors to the Kalgoorlie Goldfields.

The Karrakatta Club gave its members experience in gathering information, speaking to groups, forming opinions and presenting arguments. Edith became its first secretary, then vice-president and president. She also served on the North Fremantle Board of Education, and was involved with the House of Mercy for Unmarried Mothers and the Ministering Children's League.

As the move for an Australian Federation grew in strength, the women, of course, discussed and debated the issue. Like many others, Edith opposed Western Australia joining the Federation, arguing that they were still adjusting to self-rule and that the voice of the established community in Perth, Fremantle and Albany would be overwhelmed by those who had flocked from the eastern states to the Western Australian goldfields.

She did not, however, sulk or recriminate when the decision, by a substantial majority, went in favour of Western Australia joining the Federation. Women, after all, had been able to vote. Instead, she became even more active in public life and in ensuring the emerging state was a fit one for women and children, as well as men.

In 1902 Edith and James travelled to London. James had worked long hours for many years, frequently having his two-week annual leave cancelled because of court pressure. He was exhausted and Edith had medical issues that were not, she felt, being adequately addressed in Perth where, at that time, there were no hospitals or medical training offered. Personally very reserved, she did not discuss or reveal these issues outside her most immediate family.

She had also always wanted to travel. It was an expensive venture. Their fares alone cost more than James's annual salary. They stopped on the way in Colombo, where James refused to travel in a rickshaw, horrified at the sight of men doing 'work as horses'. In Britain they visited museums, galleries, concerts, friends and acquaintances. They both seem to have used the journey for a genuine break and Edith received the medical attention she had hoped for.

Back in Perth, reinvigorated, they resumed their work. Edith's health had improved, their three eldest children were working and the younger two managed the home. The Karrakatta Club was expanding and Edith took on the role of president. Ideas were being generated on many fronts. Other states had established taxation systems and were beginning to establish hospitals and medical training. Typhoid outbreaks were common in Perth and in Kalgoorlie, where the goldrush had also seen an influx of venereal disease. Many women took up nursing—but without training, equipment and regulation, it was a dangerous profession.

There was a growing awareness that, in other parts of the world and in other states, advances in medical knowledge were curbing the spread of disease and maternity hospitals were saving the lives of women and children. When Western Australia finally introduced a taxation system in 1907, legislators were still of the view that home was the place for nursing and medical treatment and no training was required. Women saw it differently, and set about changing things.

There were also other battles to be fought. Edith firmly believed that children should not be tried as adults, and became a founding member of the Children's Protection Society in 1906, helping to bring in the *State Children's Act 1907*. This Act was designed to 'make better provision for the Protection, Control, Maintenance, and Reformation of Neglected and Destitute Children . . .'

It replaced the *Industrial Schools Act 1874* and the *Industrial and Reformatory Schools Act 1893*, and established a State Children's Department, to regulate institutions and individuals responsible for children. The Act established the Children's Court of Western Australia and laws to regulate the employment of children and youths, and made way for the provision of child care for working mothers. In 1915 Edith would be appointed to the bench of the Children's Court, where she served for eighteen years.

In 1909 Edith co-founded the Women's Service Guild, whose first major campaign was to build a maternity hospital in Perth. She co-chaired the hospital committee, and was active in lobbying and raising funds. King Edward Memorial Hospital for Women opened in 1916.

Another project of the guild involved amendments to the *Health Act* in relation to venereal disease. This revealed irreconcilable differences within the Women's Service Guild. One group was opposed to making the reporting of venereal disease mandatory, while another group, including Edith, insisted on reporting. The guild split along those lines and Edith's group left the guild in 1911 and continued their (eventually successful) campaigning as the National Council of Women. She was active in this organisation, as president or vice-president, for the rest of her life.

Although Edith was opposed to war, when it was declared, in 1914, she helped establish a Red Cross branch and chaired the Red Cross Appeal Committee throughout World War I. She also helped to organise Soldiers' Welcome Homes and arrange assistance for returning servicemen and women. In 1916 she joined the Anglican Social

Questions Committee as its first female member. She was co-opted to the Anglican synod in 1923.

Edith's constant drive for reform was always founded on knowledge and built on collaboration, drawing on the shared experience, skills and understanding of women. Her methodology was to build knowledge, then speak out, organise, argue and build momentum in any way that presented an opportunity. She participated actively in more committees, boards and groups than seems humanly possible. Within these groups there were inevitably disagreements and philosophical rifts, but she could always work her way through the issues and determine where she stood, even if she could not always resolve the differences.

By 1920 women had the right to sit in the parliaments of the Commonwealth, South Australia, New South Wales and Queensland. None, however, had elected a woman. When the *Parliament (Qualification of Women) Act 1920* passed the Western Australian parliament, Edith Cowan nominated for the state seat of West Perth, which was ironically held by the attorney-general who had introduced the Act to the parliament. She was one of five women candidates in the election of 1921. Aged 59, she stood as a candidate for the Nationalist Party, which had formed in 1917 from members of the Commonwealth Liberal Party and the National Labor Party.

Four political parties contested the election: the Labor Party of Western Australia won seventeen seats, the Nationalist Party sixteen, the Country Party ten and the National Labor Party three. The three National Labor members supported the Nationalists who then took government. Edith narrowly defeated Draper to take the seat. She was the only one of the five women candidates to be elected, and the first woman elected to any parliament in Australia or a British legislature anywhere in the world.

Edith Cowan, however, refused to agree to always vote with the party, arguing that on their establishment during the war the Nationalists had claimed to be a non-party organisation. In her maiden speech, in response to one of several interjections, she said:

> I am a Nationalist, and I belong to no party in this House. I was sent here to uphold law and order and constitutional government, and it will be my desire to assist in carrying out these objects in a proper

> and satisfactory manner; while in the discharge of my duties here I shall be responsible only to my own constituents. That plank was inserted when the fighting platform of the Nationalists was drawn up, and I think the Premier will grant me that he himself was one who helped to draw up that platform. There are too many here to-day who are possessed of the old party spirit which seems ever to exist, but I cannot see why we should drag party into things that concern the whole of the State. We want every member in this House to realise the mistakes of the past in this direction. I think, too, it has been fairly proved in this House to-day that women can and do stand by women, and will stand by women in the future if it is only to help to get rid of some of that painful party spirit so frequently evinced on questions on which it should never be brought to bear. I must also add that, while a Nationalist, and while supporting a Nationalist Government, I shall always reserve to myself the right to criticise suggestively and candidly any legislation brought forward, and will do everything in my power to remedy any mistakes which may seem to me are being made.

She voted sometimes with Labor, sometimes with the Nationalists, which annoyed both. She was a robust and courageous speaker, undaunted by vigorous opposition and demeaning cartoons in newspapers and magazines like the *Bulletin*. Her major legislative achievements were through two private members' bills: the *Women's Legal Status Act 1923* which self-regulated professions to qualified women, and a bill giving inheritance rights to women whose adult children died without having made a will or having living children of their own. She argued continuously for the interests of women and children in all matters, from a conviction that these had been largely overlooked since colonisation and there was a lot to redress.

To realise just how ground breaking, and basic, some of Edith's achievements were, we only need to read the handbill printed for the election of 1924 titled 'Reasons Why Her Committee Consider You Should Give Your First Preference (No 1) To Mrs E.D. Cowan On Election Day'. Among the seventeen reasons listed are:

> 1 BECAUSE she has proved her practical interest by bringing about the establishment of playgrounds in West Perth, also baby health clinics in various metropolitan centres.

> 2 BECAUSE she was instrumental in getting a reduction on the carriage of perambulators on the Railway . . .
> 4 BECAUSE she moved in Parliament, and obtained the concession that the Speakers Gallery be opened to women, thus breaking down a precedent which had existed for over 400 years, and which implied women's inferiority . . .
> 13 BECAUSE she introduced and succeeded in passing a Bill to remove the sex disqualification of women in civil and other professions, thus giving them the opportunity to qualify for the highest positions.

Among the other reasons are things as basic as positioning tram stops, and as far reaching as registration for nurses, children's welfare and changes in inheritance law to include women. The handbill concludes:

> 17 BECAUSE, above all, she has proved, by over 30 years of social service, her fitness to deal with, and assist in all matters pertaining to the welfare of the community.

Edith was, however, defeated in the 1924 election when the business community ran a strong candidate against her and Thomas Davy won the seat for the Nationalists. In 1927, dissatisfied with political parties, she argued against them and stood as a candidate for the Women's Electoral Lobby. Her policies and goals were no different to those she held as a member of the Nationalist Party and she did not engage in the major party tussles. Davy retained the seat for the Nationalists but the Collier Labor government was returned to office. Splits within organisations that Edith Cowan led contributed to the losses, as did the sheer loneliness of being the only woman in the front line of change.

In 1925 she was elected as a Western Australian delegate to the International Women's Conference in Washington DC. Australia sent ten delegates. Although unwell, she delivered three speeches at the conference and engaged in receptions and discussions. She extended her travel to visit New York, Philadelphia, the southern states, California and Vancouver, gathering information about industrial relations, poverty, prohibition and race relations—and even traffic management. While in Vancouver she received the news of the sudden, unexpected death of her son Norman after an operation.

On her return to Australia she gave talks in Perth, Kalgoorlie and the eastern states and, although her health did not improve, worked to establish the Western Australian Historical Society, which came into existence when she proposed the motion on 10 September 1926 at a public meeting held at the Karrakatta Club. Sir James Mitchell, former premier and at the time leader of the opposition, agreed to be president. The society gathered and preserved documents pertaining to the history of the state and led to Edith being part of the committee organising the state's forthcoming centenary celebration. The women's pages of the *West Australian* that year ran a series of profiles of 'centenary personalities'. Its profile of Edith Cowan, on 5 July 1929, listed 24 boards and committees of which she was a member at the time and concluded with her words:

> As the pioneer women of the past century stood shoulder to shoulder with their men, sharing equally in the dangers, privations and blessings that came, so too must we do, now and always, neglecting no opportunity that comes to us, whether spiritual, moral, economic or political. But no longer, as in preceding centuries, may women allow themselves to be regarded merely as ancillary. That view helped to give the world the Great War, and is responsible for much of its troubles today. Let us therefore try and achieve higher ideals as to our common citizenship and mutual responsibilities, then it cannot be said ever of Australia 'that its menace lies not in its swollen fortunes, but in the shrunken souls of those who inherit them.'

Her final reference appears to be a quote from the debate in the United States around Roosevelt's 1906 proposal for inheritance tax.

At the end of that year, Edith and James Cowan celebrated their 50th wedding anniversary. In the view of Peter Cowan:

> To have lived with her over those many years, as James Cowan did, cannot have been simple or straightforward, and she was the last person to claim otherwise. They did hold together, able to follow their own paths, and together they looked back on a long period of the state's history, a state both had served, and a history both had a part in. Their marriage was not the least achievement of either of them.[9]

Still unwell, and finding it harder to maintain the focus on fact, logical argument and tactful avoidance of personal disagreement that had always been a hallmark of her public life, Edith largely hid her illness and continued her organising and committee work until admitted to hospital in April 1932. To the end she appears to have kept all details of her illness private. It is not revealed in her grandson's biography.

She died on 9 June of the same year.

Controversy surrounded her even after death. The National Council for Women met in July 1932 to discuss a memorial. Opinion was divided between a public monument and a practical project, perhaps a hospital. Eventually a committee was formed and a proposal was made to build memorial gates to Kings Park in her honour. This was rejected by the Kings Park Board, which was 'disinclined to favourably view the creation of further memorials other than National ones, with the Kings Park'.

The implied assumption that Edith Cowan was not of national significance understandably offended the committee, which then submitted plans for a memorial clocktower in the centre of the park. The resulting arguments ended up in the Supreme Court, but building went ahead and the memorial was unveiled by James Mitchell, then lieutenant-governor, on 9 June 1934.

Had they been granted a glimpse into the future, those jurors who, in 1876, refused to convict Kenneth Brown for fear of the impact on his family, might have been comforted to find this prominent public memorial in 21st century Perth. They would no doubt also be surprised to find that his daughter Edith, almost 150 years after her father's death by hanging, has a university and a federal electoral district named after her, and her portrait appears on the Australian $50 note.

References:

1 Cowan, Peter, *A Unique Position*, University of Western Australia Press, 1978, p. 7.
2 ibid., p. 4.
3 ibid., p. 40.
4 Cowan, Peter, *Maitland Brown*, Fremantle Arts Centre Press, 1988, p. 231.
5 ibid., p. 232.
6 Cowan, 1978, op. cit. p. 45.
7 ibid., p. 232.
8 ibid., p. 90.
9 ibid., p. 279.

8

FOOTBALL'S TRAGIC HERO

A BRIEF HISTORY OF FOOTBALL

The origin of all modern codes of football is lost in the mists of time. There are reports of a game played in ancient Greece where the ball was stuffed with hair, and balls filled with air have been reported from as early as the 7th century.

In Britain the game was certainly around in the 12th century, the idea being to get some sort of stuffed leather ball, or inflated pig's bladder, from one town to another. It seems there were no rules about numbers and, in order to win, you had to kick the ball into the other town's church yard. The games, which were conducted on official religious holidays like Shrovetide, were quite dangerous events and were eventually banned in 1349 by a royal decree of King Edward III.

The king was perhaps a little worried about the damage being caused to his subjects but his real reason for banning football was related to the defence of the kingdom. He was keen for all fit men in the kingdom to practise their archery, and it appears that football had been distracting them from the task.

The strength of Britain's army, raised in time of need, depended on its famous archers. The army had already been knocked around somewhat by the Black Death, so it was important that those left alive could at least shoot a few arrows.

Evidently the ban was not particularly successful, because Edward issued another one, in 1363:

> We ordain that you prohibit under penalty of imprisonment all and sundry from such stone, wood and iron throwing; handball, football, or hockey; coursing and cockfighting, or other such idle games.

As early as 1314 his dad, Edward II, had banned football from the streets of London. By the 17th century the young men of London seem to have forgotten this and played rather rowdy versions of the game until 1835, when playing any form of the game in the streets was outlawed. By then, however, quite diverse versions of the game had become popular in the great schools of England.

The version of the game that developed at the famous Rugby School was, not surprisingly, called rugby, and it was an ex-pupil of this school who set up the first official code of football in Australia but, oddly enough, it wasn't rugby.

It all began with a letter published in July 1858 in the quaintly and clumsily titled publication known as *Bell's Life in Victoria and Sporting Chronicle*. This enthusiastic old boy of Rugby School had written a letter expounding his ideas on cricket under the heading 'Winter Practice':

> Now that cricket has been put aside for some few months to come, and cricketers have assumed somewhat of the chrysalis nature (for a time only 'tis true), but at length will again burst forth in all their varied hues, rather than allow this state of torpor to creep over them, and stifle their new supple limbs, why can they not, I say, form a foot-ball club, and form a committee of three or more to draw up a code of laws?

It appears that this enthusiastic gentleman spoke to various headmasters about the idea and he and his friend, publican and cricketer Jerry Bryant, attempted to organise a 'scratch game' in the 'Richmond paddock' adjacent to the Melbourne Cricket Ground. The event was certainly advertised but no one's quite sure whether or not it occurred. The gentleman did, however, help umpire a football game played over three consecutive Saturdays on the same site, between Melbourne Grammar School and the Scotch College. The first game was held on 7 August 1858, and a game between the two schools has been an annual event ever since.

A 'scratch match' was played at the end of the cricket season the following year and the Melbourne Football Club came into existence on 14 May 1859. Three days later the ex-Rugbian met with three other men at Jerry Bryant's Parade Hotel near the MCG to frame a list of rules.

By the 19th century each school in England had its own version of football that had derived from the customs of the schools, the number of boys available to play, and the individual ideas and notions of the masters who supervised them. The four men who met that day examined and discussed the way the game was played in four different English schools, keeping in mind that what they wanted was a game designed to keep cricket players fit and healthy through the winter. Practices such as attacking a player's legs and hacking at the shins were rejected, as was the game played at Rugby. Having experienced that form of football, the ex-student was adamant: 'Rugby was not a game for us, we wanted a winter pastime but men could be harmed if thrown on the ground.'

A gathering at Cambridge in 1848 had attempted to reach an agreement on the rules of what we in Australia today call soccer, but it wasn't until 1863, in London, that the Football Association was formed and a set of rules was agreed upon. In the Parade Hotel in 1859, however, the group of men came up with a simple list of ten rules and, in doing so, made Australian rules football the first codified form of football in the world. There is no doubt that it is the oldest officially codified form of football.

Three of the men were Thomas Smith, the sporting master at Scotch College, and two cricket playing journalists J.B. Thompson and William Hammersley. The fourth man, whose idea it was, would go on to be the best footballer in the colony of Victoria, but that would be merely a minor achievement in the span of his tumultuous and tragic life.

His name was Tom Wills.

TOM WILLS

Thomas Wentworth Wills was born on 19 December 1835 at Molonglo Plains, near Gundagai in New South Wales. He was the eldest son of Horatio Wills, a pioneering pastoralist and politician whose convict father was transported for highway robbery. Horatio was always on the lookout to improve his lot by developing new grazing country and the family moved to western Victoria when Tom was a child and developed a 510-square kilometre property called Lexington, in the Ararat district. Tom and his parents lived in tents while the property was developed.

Tom's middle name was derived from his father's friend, the famous statesman and politician William Charles Wentworth, who was a mentor to Tom and whose father D'Arcy Wentworth was also, coincidentally, transported for being a highwayman.

Tom had no siblings until he was aged seven and spent his early childhood playing with the local Aboriginal boys. He learned their language and customs and often played a game with them that they called 'marn grook'. The game involved kicking and catching and keeping off the ground a circular 'ball' made from a basket of intertwined twigs and possum skin.

For three years from 1846 young Tom attended William Brickwood's

School and played cricket for both the school and the Melbourne Cricket Club, where William Brickwood, was club vice-president.

Back at Lexington things had changed, the house had been built and the number of his siblings had increased to four. But his life was about to change more dramatically than he could imagine.

After just over a year back home, in 1850 when he was fourteen, Tom was sent on a five-month sea voyage to attend the famous Rugby School in Britain. It must have been like entering a new world for the boy from the bush, but he quickly adapted, no doubt due to his sporting abilities.

Tom played the early version of rugby, became the school's best bowler and was in the school's First XI, aged sixteen, when they played against the MCC at Lords where he took twelve wickets. In 1855 he took over as captain of the First XI, which was the most prestigious position at the school. He was invited to play for an All England XI, but couldn't leave his studies to play.

Although Tom Wills was athletic from an early age, he was prone to illness, odd as it may seem, and once, when he was ill for months as a four-year-old in 1839, his parents, according to an account in Greg de Moore's 2011 biography, 'almost despaired of his recovery'.

In a very amusing young man's letter to his father back home, he wrote, 'I know that if I [study] too hard I will become quite ill. We hardly get any play during school time.' The rest of the letter, written on enormous broadsheet-sized pages, is filled with accounts of cricket games and lists of his scores.

Tom's room at Rugby was decorated with Aboriginal weapons and he seems to have been very homesick at times. His father wrote to tell him that his Aboriginal friends missed him and had 'told me to send you up to them as soon as you came back'.

In June 1855, aged nineteen and a half, he finished school and, armed with a regular supply of money from home, wandered around Britain playing cricket. He played against his old school in June 1856 as a member of a team representing the MCC. The team also included members of the royal family and a future governor of Tasmania, Charles du Cane.

It had been intended that Tom would go on to Magdalene College, Cambridge, in 1856, but he did not pass the required matriculation exams. With the permission of Oxford University, however, he played cricket in the Cambridge XI in the inter-varsity match of that year.

This gracious, sportsmanlike gesture was due to the fact that Tom had, by then, become the most notable amateur cricketer in England, playing for both Kent and the Marylebone Club and, on one occasion, after spending time playing in Ireland, for a United Ireland XI.

It's astounding how a kid who grew up speaking the Djab Warrung language and running around the wilds of the Grampians with Aboriginal boys managed the transition to the upper-class English atmosphere of cricket so successfully that he was granted an exemption to be allowed to play in the most prestigious cricket game on the yearly calendar.

Tom was described as 'one of the most promising cricketers in the kingdom'. He had deep blue eyes and hair that was 'impossibly wavy' and it was written of him in the press that 'few athletes can boast of a more muscular and well-developed frame'.

His six years in England had made him a great cricketer and given him many wonderful contacts and experiences, but there was a dark side. Once he left school he fell into a dissolute way of life that was part of the world of cricket in the 1850s, only drinking, spending and playing mattered. He had no interest in anything academic or career-related and his father despaired.

Tom arrived home two days before Christmas in 1856. Once again it was like entering a new world for the 22-year-old, everything had changed.

Melbourne was booming from the goldrushes, his father was now a member of the Victorian parliament, and the family was living on a property near Geelong. Tom took a position with a law firm in Melbourne, but showed no interest in the law, which he never studied and never practised. Cricket was all the rage in Melbourne and he played constantly, mostly for the Melbourne Cricket Club.

It is hard to imagine the bitter rivalry that existed between Victoria and the parent colony of New South Wales in those days. After New South Wales won the first inter-colonial match at the MCG in 1856, it became an obsession for Victoria to beat them.

The hatred ran so deep that when touring sides came from England later to play what might be called 'test matches', as they did from 1876–77, some cricketers refused to play in the same team as their rivals from other colonies. Fred Spofforth refused to bowl to the Victorian wicketkeeper and didn't play in 1876–77 matches, and several others from both colonies also declined to be part of the team.

After a trial game at the MCG, Tom Wills was chosen to captain Victoria against New South Wales in 1858. He was to be their 'Great White Hope'.

Melbourne came to a standstill for the January match between Victoria and New South Wales at the MCG in 1858. Tom Wills took eight wickets, the most for Victoria. On the second day he was knocked unconscious by a ball that rose sharply from a crack in the pitch but came around, played on for two hours, and made 49 not out, which won the game.

The jubilant crowd carried him from the field and the celebrations lasted for several days throughout Victoria, where the newspapers proclaimed him to be 'the greatest cricketer in the land'.

In the midst of this public adulation, however, the darker and more chaotic elements of Tom's character were making themselves manifest in his relationship with the Melbourne Cricket Club, of which he had become secretary in 1857.

He was hardly suited to the role. Outside of sport Tom's life was undisciplined, chaotic and disorganised. His 'continued non-attendance' at meetings and poor administrative skills were blamed when the club fell into debt and his response to the criticism was to dump the club's books into the garbage and quit. To this present day, the only minute book missing from the club's archives is the one from his time as secretary.

Horatio Wills, now a member of the Victorian parliament, was a strident supporter of an Australian republic and campaigner for the rights of the emancipated convicts—in short, a supporter of the ideas of pioneering statesman William Charles Wentworth—and had written and spoken extensively about his ideas and beliefs. His son inherited his capacity to propound ideas and wrote almost daily letters to the newspapers, but his diatribes were mostly concerning cricket, or sport in general.

Of course, the main reason that Tom Wills is remembered today is that he is credited as being the man who 'invented' Australian rules football. As we know, he was the one who called for a winter sport to keep cricketers fit and organised the meeting at the Parade Hotel in 1859 that set down the code's rules.

It is hardly surprising that Tom Wills soon became the best footballer in the colony. He had the longest kick and, being much in demand, played for various clubs and institutions, as well as one he had founded, the Melbourne Football Club.

It was even Tom who insisted on using an oval ball, in a game in which he was captain of the team called Richmond, playing *against* the club he founded, Melbourne. This 'Richmond' was not the team we know today but an earlier band of players who wore jerseys designed by Tom, their club secretary and captain. The jerseys were white with a red sash—later to be the colours of the South Melbourne Club, which subsequently became the Sydney Swans.

Tom was never short of ideas and continued to write prolifically about both cricket and football. His thoughts and suggestions helped the new code to evolve into the unique and much-loved sport it is today. Here he is suggesting, in a letter to *Bell's Life*, that the game should not be restricted by any notions of 'offside':

> I think the ground should be free to all, so that the captain of each side could dispose of his forces in any position he likes; and when this is done, and the ball is carried on from one end of the ground to the other, by a succession of good, well-directed kicks, to the hands of those that the ball was intended for . . . it has a very pretty effect, and is the result of some skill.

In cricket, Tom led Victoria to victory over New South Wales again in January 1859 in a game played at the Domain in Sydney, in which he dislocated a finger on the first day, top-scored in the first innings and took 5/24 and 6/25.

At the MCG in February 1860, 25,000 people saw him bowl unchanged in both innings (taking 6/23 and 3/16) and top-score with 20 not out as he led Victoria to yet another win over New South Wales.

Even the Sydney media, ever keen to remind readers that he was born in New South Wales, lavished praise upon the freakish athlete:

> Tall, muscular, and slender, Mr. Wills seems moulded by nature to excel in every branch of the noble game, and with the ball at the wicket, and on the field we find him the admiration of the ground, while in the combination of his successes, his noble eleven recognise with pride the still more arduous duties of an unwearied and most discreet captain.

Within the game of cricket, and the Melbourne establishment, however, Tom was not particularly well liked. After he walked out on the Melbourne Cricket Club, he joined the Richmond Cricket Club and became vice-president there. Later he switched to Collingwood Cricket Club where he became president.

His willingness to play as a hired hand or guest with any team that invited him caused consternation among the 'sporting gentlemen' of Melbourne, as it often distorted the outcome of matches and greatly affected betting. Tom's lack of loyalty to one club or team was regarded with contempt by the more 'respectable' elements of Melbourne society. His alcoholism didn't enhance his reputation much either.

At the end of 1860 Tom Wills shocked the sporting world of Australia and precipitated another of the massive lifestyle changes that were to be a trademark of his life. The 25-year-old announced his retirement from sport and his intention to leave Victoria to set up a new family property at Cullin-la-ringo, in the outback of Queensland, on the Nogoa River.

Tom spent six months in country Victoria, visiting properties, studying sheep farming methods and preparing for his new life as a pioneer grazier in Queensland. Part of his motivation was the ultimatum given to him by his father. If Tom was found 'misconducting himself' or quit the enterprise, he was to be removed from Horatio's will!

It appeared that Tom was, at last, about to make an attempt to become the kind of son Horatio had always wanted. He would give up the dissolute and disreputable lifestyle that had caused his father so much anguish and show his true mettle as a proud son of a hard-working, pioneering and nation-building family.

What happened at Cullin-la-ringo, however, would not go down in Australian history as an example of nation building. Cullin-la-ringo would be forever remembered for other, very different, reasons.

In January 1861, Tom, Horatio and a party of their family and employees, numbering 25 in total, arrived in Brisbane by steamer, acquired supplies and trekked through the outback of the new colony, which was just eighteen months old.

At times during the journey they had to hunt to stay alive and the first death occurred when a man was drowned near Toowoomba. They collected 10,000 sheep on the Darling Downs and arrived at Cullin-la-ringo, near modern-day Emerald, on Kairi Aboriginal land, in October, after an eight-month, 1300-kilometre trek.

Horatio Wills had always managed to maintain good relationships with Aboriginal people and used them as workers on his other properties. Although wary, he allowed local Aborigines into the camp, which was merely a ring of tents, and gave them sheep to slaughter as a display of friendship.

Two weeks after Wills had set up camp, Aborigines began entering the Cullin-la-ringo locality in small parties until their numbers were estimated at two hundred by the morning of 17 October 1861.

At around 2 p.m. that day they suddenly attacked and six children, two women and five men were clubbed to death within minutes. Another six men working just outside the camp were also killed.

Horatio, who kept all the party's firearms out of sight in his tent, was the only one to attempt a defence. He fired one shot before he was overwhelmed and killed.

John Moore, the cook, who was resting after lunch in the shade of the bush several hundred metres away, heard the shot, witnessed the massacre and ran 50 kilometres through the bush to Rainworth Station, the nearest white settlement.

Tom and three others, who were making a week-long round trip to Albinia Station to pick up stores, arrived back two days after the massacre. A rescue party from Rainworth had already buried the dead and was attempting to round up the 10,000 sheep. Most of the party's equipment had been taken and the firearms had been thrown into the campfire.

Cullin-la-ringo was the largest massacre of white settlers in Australia's history.

When the news reached the cities, the press produced the usual mass of misinformation. Tom was at first reported dead and Horatio was accused of ignoring warnings about the local Aboriginal people.

Tom publicly defended his father but admitted privately, 'If we had used common precaution all would have been well.'

Reprisals were swift and tragic, with much of the local Aboriginal population being slaughtered in the aftermath of the attack.

Tom, who never took part in any reprisals, believed the massacre at Cullin-la-ringo was an act of revenge for an attack made on local Aboriginals by squatter Jesse Gregson. He told a cousin, 'If the truth is ever known, you will find that it was through Gregson shooting those blacks; that was the cause of the murder.'

For the rest of his life Tom suffered from nightmares and flashbacks. He slept poorly and drank even more than previously. Sadly, there were many more scandals and tragedies yet ahead for Tom Wills.

Tom, who was now head of the family, vowed to stay and fulfil his father's dreams at Cullin-la-ringo. He is said to have slept only three hours a night, with a rifle beside the bed, until his uncle, William Roope, who was a shareholder in the operation, arrived to help run the property in December. Tom and his uncle soon fell out and Roope departed. Tom struggled on in isolation for twelve months, and even went blind for a short time after contracting 'sandy blight'.

He made the long trip to Sydney to captain Victoria at the Domain in January 1863. The match turned into a riot over the dismissal of a local batsmen by a Victorian umpire. Tom was hit in the face by a rock and two of the Victorian players fled from Sydney, but Tom and the eight other Victorians continued the game. New South Wales were victorious and Tom, who took eight wickets and top-scored in both innings, commented later, 'I for one do not think that Victoria will ever send an Eleven up here again.'

The Melbourne press blamed Tom for the defeat, saying he should never have played on with nine men and even accusing him of treachery because, starved of cricket and out of practice, he had played several games for New South Wales in the lead-up to the match.

He then travelled on to visit his mother at Geelong, where he became engaged to Julie Anderson, a family friend from a respectable farming family. He upset his family, who had a lot of money invested in Cullin-la-ringo, by delaying his return to Queensland in order to play football for Geelong.

On his return to the property in May, having been made a Justice of the Peace, he wrote letters to the Brisbane press reporting Aboriginal attacks on white settlers and attacking the attitude of city-dwellers towards the plight of the Queensland Aboriginal people.

At the start of the next cricket season, Tom agreed to captain Queensland against New South Wales and then made a dash to Melbourne to captain the Victorian team against George Parr's visiting All England XI, only arriving (to thunderous applause) on the final day of the match. He then continued on with the English team as they toured Victoria.

The Wills family was becoming fed up with Tom and accused him of squandering the family fortune on travel, women and alcohol and running up huge debts at Cullin-la-ringo. They were outraged when he broke off his engagement to Julie Anderson, although it was common knowledge that Tom was a notorious womaniser and had a long-term affair with Sarah Barbor, a married woman he called his 'housekeeper'.

Tom's answer to the criticism was to leave with George Parr's English team on a one-month tour of New Zealand.

On his return he was dismissed by the trustees of the Cullin-la-ringo project, who included his mother and most of his family, and resumed his affair with Sarah Barbor and his dissolute life as a hard-drinking cricketer and footballer.

In those days football games were played as a series of invitations, rather than in an organised competition and, during the 1865 season, Tom often captained Melbourne and Geelong, two of the game's most powerful clubs. This resulted in arguments and eventually he moved to Geelong for the remainder of his career.

Professionalism in sport was a huge issue back then and Tom, who always maintained his amateur status, was often accused of all manner of ungentlemanly conduct, including being a 'sham amateur'.

His bowling action came under scrutiny and he was accused many times of 'chucking'.

Intercolonial cricket resumed at the MCG on Boxing Day 1865, nearly three years since the Sydney riot. Most of Victoria's professionals had been involved in a pay dispute with the Melbourne Cricket Club and defected to the New South Wales team, which was captained by Englishman Charles Lawrence. Tom led the weakened Victorian side, took six wickets and scored the first half-century in Australian first-class cricket—and Victoria won.

Tom's transition to 'professional' sportsman involved, remarkably, his management and promotion of the first-ever all-Aboriginal cricket team.

In May 1866, he promoted a cricket match between the Melbourne Cricket Club and an Aboriginal team from the Western Districts of Victoria, which he coached. The players were mostly Jardwadjarli men who shared a common language with the neighbouring Djab Wurrung people, which enabled Tom to speak to them, using the Aboriginal language he learned as a child.

Eight thousand spectators attended the Boxing Day match at the MCG and the team, with Tom as captain, lost to Melbourne, who Tom accused of cheating during the game.

Many people were shocked that Tom would associate with Aborigines after Cullin-la-ringo but others saw him as a champion of the Victorian Aboriginal people. One journalist wrote, in *The Empire* magazine:

> Although you may not be fully aware of the fact, allow me to tell you that you have rendered a greater service to the aboriginal races of this country and to humanity, than any man who has hitherto attempted to uphold the title of the blacks to rank amongst men.

Members of Tom's family, however, were once again shocked by his behaviour when he took the Aboriginal team to the family property to meet his mother, without giving her any advance warning.

As usual, things would end badly for Tom's new venture. The team went to Sydney in February ahead of a planned overseas tour and Charles Lawrence, who could see the financial potential of the venture, accommodated the team at his Manly hotel.

During the first match in Sydney, however, the police stopped play and Tom was arrested and gaoled over a breach of contract dispute involving himself and W.E.B. Gurnett, a con man who was trying to take over as manager. The team was left stranded and broke, with all the money saved for the overseas tour gone.

Charles Lawrence set up a benefit match, and worked his way into the team, replacing Tom as captain. The team returned to Victoria in May and Tom resumed playing football for Geelong and ended his association with the team.

It was later claimed that he was a bad influence and encouraged drinking among the Aboriginal players, four of whom died over the course of the tour; at least one death was officially linked to alcohol.

The surviving members formed part of the famous Aboriginal team which Lawrence later took to England as the first-ever representative Australian cricket team. Tom was deeply upset at being left out and always resented Lawrence for reviving the team without him.

With limited resources and skills apart from sport, Tom joined the Melbourne Cricket Club as a professional in 1867. The club gave him the title 'tutor' so he could maintain some semblance of the prestige of his amateur past and he captained Victoria to win over New South Wales in 1867.

After his old colleague William Hammersley wrote in his sporting column that Tom, as a paid servant of a cricket club, should not have 'moral ascendancy' over amateur players, the captaincy of Victoria was given to Dick Wardill on the eve of the March 1869 match against New South Wales, the last ever played at the Domain in Sydney.

At first Tom refused to play, but relented and took seven wickets to guide the Victorians to a win. Wardill was out for a duck from the first ball of the Victorian innings.

Tom said that he would never play cricket for Victoria again (this declaration didn't last long) and announced that he would return to Cullin-la-ringo, but his mother ordered him to stay away from the property.

He continued as a 'tutor' playing for the Melbourne Cricket Club, but played football for Geelong. When Geelong played Melbourne at football he was banned from playing, but Geelong was allowed an extra five men to make up for the loss.

In February 1870, Tom was back captaining Victoria in a 265-run win over New South Wales at the MCG. The next crisis in his career occurred when controversy erupted over his bowling style and he was accused by many critics of 'chucking'. William Hammersley went further and said he was ruining the game.

Tom's response didn't help matters. He wrote in *The Australasian:* 'If I cannot hit your wicket or make you give a chance soon, I'll hit you and hurt you if I can. I'll frighten you out.'

In the intercolonial match in Sydney in March 1871 he top-scored with 39 in Victoria's win but was visibly drunk on the field and wouldn't bowl for fear of being called for throwing.

It was the beginning of the end for Tom, but a series of superb club cricket performances saw him play for Victoria in the next intercolonial match against New South Wales in March 1872 on the MCG.

As a result of the controversy over his bowling action, however, representatives from both sides met and signed an agreement that he would be 'called' for any suspect balls. Thus, when he opened the bowling, Tom became the first cricketer called for throwing in a major Australian match and, after more balls were ruled as throws in two overs, he did not bowl again in the match. He was again no-balled when he captained a Victorian side against a combined team from other colonies in 1872.

He accused Hammersley, now his bitter enemy, of a plot to promote English-born cricketers and denigrate native-born Australian players.

Hammersley replied in print:

> You are played out now, the cricketing machine is rusty and useless, all respect for it is gone. You will never be captain of a Victorian Eleven again . . . Eschew colonial beer, and take the pledge and in time your failings may be forgotten, and only your talents as a cricketer remembered. Farewell, Tommy Wills.

Tom sank further into alcoholism but was desperate to play for Victoria against a side led by the legendary W.G. Grace. However, Hammersley was a selector and Tom had no chance of being picked. He toured with Grace's team instead, playing against them in regional matches, which annoyed Grace who later referred to him as the 'old Rugbeian has-been' but neglected to mention that, in the final match of the tour in the remote South Australian mining town of Kadina, Tom bowled him out and ended with 6/28.

Desperation in the light of poor performances caused Tom to be recalled as Victorian captain to lead the team against New South Wales in Sydney in February 1876. He was out for 0 and 4 and failed to get a wicket in spite of bowling the bulk of the overs. Naturally he was blamed for Victoria's 195-run loss.

Tom's career as a serious cricketer petered out into local matches and disputes about his bowling style and finally ended in 1878, when he was 42 years old. He continued to play football and was a favourite at Geelong. After his retirement from football he umpired, was Geelong Football Club's vice-president from 1873 to 1876, and also donated many trophies, as well as money, for football competitions. He was one of Geelong's delegates at the 1877 formation of the Victorian Football League (VFL).

He was broke and in serious debt when he sold his properties in Geelong and moved with Sarah Barbor to South Melbourne in 1878. While there he convinced South Melbourne Cricket Club to start playing football in winter and it was his idea, instituted at both Geelong and South Melbourne, for football clubs to use an oval-shaped playing field, so that the cricket field became the football field in winter.

In 1879, shunned by his family, he and Sarah moved to Heidelberg, then a village outside Melbourne, and he sank into alcoholism, although he did coach the local cricket team, for which, on 13 March 1880, he played his last recorded game.

Contrary to a much-believed myth, Tom was never an inmate of a lunatic asylum but he became, in the words of cricket historian David Frith, 'a complete and dangerous and apparently incurable alcoholic'.

By late April 1880, Tom, aged 44, was suffering from continual delirium tremens and paranoid delusions. On 1 May Sarah admitted him to Melbourne Hospital where he was 'kept under restraint' but managed to free himself and return home. The next day he committed suicide by stabbing a pair of scissors into his heart three times.

Tom was buried the following day in an unmarked grave in

Heidelberg Cemetery at a private funeral attended by six people. Although his sister was one of the six, his death certificate reads 'parents unknown' and his mother is said to have claimed in her later life that he never existed.

The Melbourne Cricket Club erected a monument over his unmarked gravesite on the centenary of his death. The inscription reads, 'Founder of Australian football and champion cricketer of his time'.

Tom Wills was inducted into the Sport Australia Hall of Fame in 1989, and into the Australian football Hall of Fame in 1996. The International Cricket Hall of Fame, in Bowral, New South Wales, contains an exhibition celebrating his life. The Tom Wills Room at the MCG is the venue for important corporate functions.

A statue showing Tom umpiring the famous football match between Melbourne Grammar and Scotch College in 1858 was erected outside the MCG in 2001. Melbourne's busiest freeway junction is known as the Tom Wills interchange and Tom Wills Oval, at Olympic Park in Sydney, is the training base for the GWS Australian rules football club.

In the entire history of Australian sport there has never been a more remarkable, controversial, triumphant, troubled, tragic and multi-faceted character than Tom Wills.

9

THE FEISTY FEMALE FLYER

With Jillian Dellit

WOMEN IN THE SKY

The lives of most aviation pioneers make for amazing reading, especially in Australia where the challenges of flying were exacerbated by challenges of distance and isolation.

Most of the pioneers of the Australian aviation industry were men who had flown in World War I and survived. After the war, many of the pilots who had learned to fly in the Royal Flying Corps were keen to keep flying and found opportunities to do so.

As usual, it was different for women.

In Australia women were not granted pilots' licences until 1927, which was about seventeen years after most other English-speaking countries. Hilda McMaugh, an Australian nursing sister who worked in Britain during World War I, passed her flying test in Britain in 1919. She was the only female among 400 who received their wings that year yet, when she returned to Australia, she was not allowed to fly.

Millicent Bryant was the first woman to hold a pilot's licence in Australia when she was granted licence number 71 in March 1927. Sadly Millicent, who was 49 years old when she was given her licence to fly, died just eight months later, along with 39 others, when the ferry *Greycliffe* was cut in half by the steamer *Tahiti* on Sydney Harbour.

By 1930 eighteen women had gained pilots' licences in Australia and the arrival of Amy Johnson in May 1930 inspired another ten to do so within months. In 1934 Freda Thompson became the first Australian female, and the first woman in the British Empire, to become a flying instructor.

Maude Bonney, who was married to a cousin of Bert Hinkler, is reputed to have taken flying lessons when her husband refused to let her drive a car. Legend has it that the local milkman drove her in secret to Eagle Farm airport to take lessons. Her husband, Henry, a wealthy Brisbane businessman who owned a leather manufacturing business, became far more supportive once he realised what his wife had achieved. He bought her a DH60 Gipsy Moth, which she named *My Little Ship*. She went on to be the first woman to fly from Australia to Britain, and made the first flight from Australia to South Africa in 1937. She also circumnavigated Australia and set a record for the longest one-day flight by a woman when she flew 1600 kilometres from Brisbane to Wangaratta in 1931. Her Gipsy Moth was requisitioned by the defence forces during World War II and scrapped after the war.

While it is true that the majority of early women flyers in Australia came from relatively privileged backgrounds and had the time and money to pursue their interest in aviation, this was certainly not true in the case of Nancy-Bird Walton.

NANCY-BIRD WALTON

Nancy-Bird Walton, the first woman to work in commercial aviation in Australia, once said: 'Other women who flew were women of independent means. But I had to do something with it.'

She was born in Kew, on the New South Wales north coast, in 1915, a year all Australians recognise as the year of the Gallipoli landing. Later in her life, however, Nancy marked 1915 as the year that the Australian military became airborne, in response to a request from the Indian government for air support in the Middle East. She also noted that, at the time, the Australian military flying school had two aeroplanes and a box-kite.

Reminiscing in 2004, Nancy described a childhood that foretold her love of flying:

> My mother told me that when I was a four-year-old I was climbing the fence, jumping off and calling myself an 'eppyplane' . . . I bought books on aeroplanes, I followed everything in the newspapers about aeroplanes. Amy Johnson flew to Australia in 1930—why couldn't I do something like that?

Most of Nancy's contemporaries were content to wait for the benefits of travel and communication that the new form of transport would bring to them. She, however, chose to put her energy behind the fledgling industry, helping it to gain momentum. Her life mirrors aviation's struggle and achievement in Australia.

By the time Nancy was four Billy Hughes, with his interest in aviation, was prime minister and her imagination was fuelled by media stories of aviators as they pioneered the England to Australia and United States to Australia air routes. Billy Hughes understood the potential of aviation to connect Australia to European markets and his government looked for ways to open up the air route.

Nancy's mother took her six children to Sydney so they could get a city education while Nancy's father and his brother stayed on the mid north coast of New South Wales, running the general store at Mount George, near Wingham. In 1928, as the Depression hit, Nancy, thirteen and the eldest, was taken out of school to keep house and 'do the books' for the two men in Mount George.

The Depression made it harder for everyone and its impact was felt in every part of Australian life. The books that Nancy kept told the story of deprivation, long-term debt and hard times. The steady stream of itinerants needing sustenance told a further story of insecurity and poverty.

A few enterprising ex-servicemen were trying to feed their families and their thirst for flying by putting on air pageants in larger country towns. On race or show day, go-ahead country towns would clear a paddock next to the racecourse or showground for any pilot who would come and offer joy rides.

Pilots soon learned they could plot a circuit around the country following the races and shows. 'Barnstorming' kept them in the air and at least paid for petrol and maintenance. Pilots who could purchase, borrow or hire a plane would descend on a country town and entertain locals with aerobatics, sign-writing and fly-pasts before selling five-minute joy rides. It was a hazardous way of making a living, given the costs of petrol and maintenance, and especially so in the Depression when few people had money for luxuries and entertainment.

Nancy's father paid her £1 a week. On her half-day a week off, she managed to get into Wingham on an air pageant day and took a joy ride. She then took a second flight and conned the pilot into aerobatics for an extra £1.

She got herself a copy of *Learning to Fly* by Frank Swoffer. It didn't turn her into a pilot, but it fuelled her ambition, confirmed her commitment and increased her saving zeal. By the age of fifteen she had enough money to take a trial instructional flight while in Sydney visiting her mother.

Every new step Nancy took was towards her goal and every step strengthened her ambition. At the end of that flight, she had enough money left to buy goggles, helmet and jacket . . . although she had to ask the instructor where to buy them.

She took inspiration from flyers like Amy Johnson and, when the German aviatrix Elly Beinhorn visited Sydney in 1932 to promote her book, Nancy made sure she was in Grace Bros department store to see her.

When Charles Kingsford Smith brought a team of pilots to Wingham the next year and offered joy rides, Nancy and two girlfriends went along. It was there she learned from Smithy himself that he was about to open a flying school in Sydney. No wonder he suggested she enrol—she was wearing her goggles, helmet and jacket.

By 1933 she had saved £200. So, at seventeen, she defied her father, whose business now relied on her, and moved to the family home at Manly. The other five children could take their turn at supporting the family store—Nancy was learning to fly.

The Depression was ending. Governments were seeking ways to link Australia more effectively to Europe and everywhere ordinary people wanted their lives to improve.

There were a few people, both men and women, with sufficient money and enthusiasm to learn to fly for sport. They created a small demand for flying instruction and opportunities to fly. Thanks to the persistence of a few World War I veterans, Australia had a small network of experienced, mostly male, pilots who were trying to make a living by meeting this demand, hoping to develop an aviation industry. Nancy was determined to join this network.

Every day she caught the ferry to Circular Quay, got the Botany tram to Mascot and walked the mile from the post office tram stop to the airport. When Kingsford Smith was in Sydney, he might pick her up at Manly and drive her all the way. He didn't approve of women flying, but they paid good money and he respected a client. Much of his time, however, was spent away, attempting long-distance records or pursuing charter work.

He had set up his flying school in a hangar that housed the *Southern Cross* at Mascot. From here he gave Nancy her first two lessons before he again headed overseas and other instructors took over the job.

Nancy ignored the views about women flyers held by most of the men in the hangar. When she asked to learn engineering, she was given the dirtiest jobs to put her off . . . and she ignored that too. She took the lessons, listened to the talk in the hangar and at the Aero Club, watched others fly, and went up with anyone who would take her.

Many fellow students were wealthy, flying for sport or daring. Jobs were scarce in aviation. The dream of reducing time and distance was tantalising, but making it affordable was a challenge.

Any job that kept planes in the air and pilots in work was important. Although businesses could see possibilities in using aviation, initially they were cautious and held back by costs. For example, newspapers grasped the advantage of merging the new photographic technology with flight. For special events such as royal visits or the Melbourne Cup, they chartered planes to get stories and photos to press, but they didn't do this for daily reporting. Air mail routes were beginning to develop but they weren't frequent or regular.

The prizes offered by state governments in air races to their cities were important incentives and, around the fringes, pilots scraped a living from charter work and air pageants.

The Dutch had air services from Holland to Java and the English from London to Singapore. Both advertised for tenders for an Australian extension of their service and Qantas won the Singapore tender against a bid from Kingsford Smith.

In 1934, while still a student, Nancy teamed with a New Zealander, Jean Batten, to offer joy rides at the Cootamundra Air Pageant. In the same year Jean Batten was the commentator for the MacRobertson Air Race. Jean held the England-to-Australia record for a woman and, in 1935, she set the world record for any plane flying England to Brazil. In 1936, against all advice, she successfully flew solo from England to Auckland.

Although the opportunities, records and events kept would-be pilots motivated, there was plenty to discourage them. Many early aviation companies went into liquidation. Crashes were so routine that students checked for them every morning around the periphery of the aerodrome at Mascot, and in those years it was not unusual for planes, and the bodies of their occupants, to be dragged from Botany Bay and the Georges River.

None of this discouraged Nancy Bird. In 1935, at the age of twenty, she had a licence to 'fly for hire or reward' and had to make her own way. No one was going to give her a job; to sell her services she needed a plane . . . and she had no money.

But flying was what she had to do. She convinced an aunt to give her £200 instead of money in her will and went to her father for another £200. With this money she bought a Gipsy Moth aircraft from the estate of the late Reg Annabel. Reg was the pilot who had taken her up on her first flight, as a fifteen year old, at the Wingham air show. Reg had rebuilt the Gipsy Moth from a wreck. He had also been killed in it.

Nancy then asked Peg MacKillop from her flying class to go barnstorming with her. Peg wanted to fly, had independent means and didn't need to be paid. Armed with an agreement to use Shell petrol and a list of country shows and races obtained from a newspaper, they set off for Tamworth and billed themselves as the 'First Ladies' Flying Tour'.

Tamworth had an aero club with no planes and a gliding club with one crashed glider; the mayor gave the 'First Ladies' a civic reception. It was there in Tamworth that Eric Baume of Sydney radio fame paid Nancy £10 to sign-write 'Woman' on the undercarriage of her plane, in order to advertise the new women's magazine of that name.

At Inverell, their second stop, it was the first race day after fourteen years of drought and a local farmer paid for all the kids to be taken up for joy rides.

On their two barnstorming tours, the 'First Ladies' dealt with all their own mechanical troubles and often had problems starting the engines. The tyre they blew had to be replaced from Sydney since there was no local supply.

It was an expensive and unreliable business, but they were independent and they were getting plenty of customers. Even if they were just paying the bills and scraping along, they were making plenty of friends in the towns and on the outback stations.

Many of those they met were looking for new ways of improving the lives and opportunities of those who lived in the country. Nancy knew that aviation could help.

In Narromine they met Tom Perry who had given land for an aerodrome and financed Western and Southern Airlines. He chartered the Moth to inspect land at Dubbo. He gave Nancy a lot of encouragement along with the idea of a larger plane.

At Dubbo they had met Stanley Drummond, founder of the Far West Children's Health Scheme. Since 1924 he had been bringing children with trachoma to Sydney for treatment and organising city holidays for country kids. He had recently begun taking children's health clinics to the far west in railway carriages, which were shunted to sidings to serve as local clinics. He was trying to send nurses by car to those families who lived beyond the reach of the railways. Drummond saw the potential for improving these services and saving time by flying the nurses to distant stations, and he offered the 'First Ladies' the opportunity to trial a flight service from Bourke.

Nancy and Peg fitted this trial in between their two hectic barnstorming tours and winning second prize in the Closed Circuit Aerial Derby at the Narromine Air Pageant of 1935.

So, on her twentieth birthday, Nancy Bird was working an air charter for the Far West Children's Health Scheme, ferrying Sister Webb to homes beyond Bourke for basic preventative medicine clinics, playing her part in influencing a new generation of mothers away from the bread-and-dripping survival techniques of the Depression. Landing in rough, uncharted paddocks around the junction of New South Wales, Queensland and South Australia, and with a road as the only landmark for flying, they took the service to places where fruit and vegetables were luxuries and women regularly died in childbirth.

Flight was making a difference; it was helping reduce ignorance and isolation, improving the health of outback women and children—and saving lives.

The trial ended in an offer of a contract. Stanley Drummond would contract Nancy Bird for six months on a £200 retainer with a guarantee of another £200 work. Stationed in Bourke, she was free to supplement this income with charter work.

Nancy immediately sold the Gipsy Moth and went into debt to buy a £1700 Leopard Moth, which doubled her carrying capacity from one to two passengers. At twenty years of age, she had become the first woman to own and operate a commercial air service in Australia. More importantly, she had the courage to try to make a living by providing a service that changed lives.

For three years Nancy pioneered services to outback stations, first from Bourke and then from Charleville and Cunnamulla. She wore practical, 'outlandish' clothes; shorts and a pith helmet to keep cool in summer and trousers for warmth in winter.

In addition to transporting nurses to clinics, she acted as an aerial ambulance, organised Father Christmas for outback kids, and took stock agents to visit properties when the drought broke. She either performed her own maintenance or engaged the services of the auto-engineer in Bourke.

When she got lost, she landed at homesteads and asked the way.

On their pioneering journey from England to Australia, Keith and Ross Smith had had the services of 200 convicts in Surabaya to clear tree stumps from an airfield. Nancy had stationhands or families hastily take down fences and she asked women to spread sheets over the worst stumps and holes. She navigated with a compass, her watch and a ruler, using landmarks such as dead horses, fresh droppings or the 'dog fence'. She had no landing instruments, no lights for night flying, no radio and little if any back-up. No service tracked her whereabouts and her plane was frequently overloaded to get the job done.

On short notice she went wherever the work took her. It might be local, it might be Adelaide. Often, in bad weather, she could not land at Bourke and would fly on to Narromine's better airstrip. Sometimes she would chase a train to the next station in order to outstrip the weather for a charter client. There are people today who remember helping to load or unload the sick from her plane and there are also many who owe their lives to her service.

Although a determined doctor in Darwin had become a 'flying doctor' in the mid-1920s, and the Australian Inland Mission had established its Flying Doctor bases in Cloncurry and Broken Hill by the mid-1930s, there were still very few inland medical services in 1936. Nancy's work was pioneering and remarkable.

In 1936 she entered the South Australian government's air race from Brisbane to Adelaide via Sydney. The air race was won by a Victorian, Hamilton garage owner Reg Ansett. Flying solo, Nancy won the ladies trophy and set the record between Melbourne and Adelaide. This experience brought her back into the company of other aviators, including Jean Batten and four other women competitors. Although it reduced her feelings of loneliness, it also highlighted her isolation.

In the same year, the Commonwealth government withdrew its subsidy for the Far West Children's Health Scheme. With no need to stay in Bourke, and in need of replacement business and better aviation support, Nancy moved her base to Charleville and tried convincing the Queensland government to set up a similar health scheme.

Charleville was the lunch stop on the Qantas route from Sydney to Singapore and it had an aeronautical engineer. The engineering and hangar costs, however, proved too expensive for Nancy and the Queensland government rejected her idea.

She moved again in 1937, this time to Cunnamulla. Many of her clients remained loyal and continued to utilise her services, so she was often doing long flights, starting early to beat the heat. Amelia Earhart came to Australia in that year, landing in Darwin. Nancy wanted to fly to meet her but couldn't afford the petrol from Cunnamulla. From Darwin, Amelia went on to New Guinea and was subsequently lost over the Pacific.

It was not just the three years of flying alone in hard conditions that took their toll and led to Nancy's decision to give up flying in 1937. In what might today be termed 'burn out' she also seems to have been worn down by the negative messages of influential people and the fact that she never had enough money to do what she knew was needed.

Kingsford Smith, the aviator she most admired, had seen no place for women in the industry; governments were slow and unreliable in subsidising medical and social services to the far west; and even John Flynn, whom she respected, had begged her to give up when he passed through Cunnamulla, telling her that the work was too much for a woman.

At the end of a trip to Sydney, she called it quits . . . for the time being.

Before long, Nancy had another idea.

The newspapers and women's magazines had written about her and her name and story were well known. This led KPM, the Dutch shipping company with airline interests, to invite her to be its guest on one of the first KLM flights from Australia to Java, connecting up with their onward service to Europe.

Nancy, always looking for other possibilities in the aviation industry, saw this as an opportunity to study ground organisation in Europe.

First, however, she went, as part of a National Council of Women's delegation, to see the prime minister, Joe Lyons, in a last-ditch attempt to have the Far West Children's Health Scheme subsidy reinstated. When this failed she accepted the KPM invitation.

She told the *Sydney Morning Herald*:

> I will concentrate on the study of commercial ground organization from the passenger's point of view. If possible I want to obtain a job at some of the airports in Holland, England and America, to learn first-hand everything I can—about passenger and traffic management in civil aviation.

It was a far-sighted decision. In The Hague, seeing her publicity value, KLM organised free travel for her throughout Europe. Nancy provided articles for the *Sydney Morning Herald*. She travelled on the new KLM Amsterdam-to-Manchester route and gave the company even more good publicity. She did a broadcast for the BBC.

In thirteen months, Nancy travelled 45,000 miles and visited 25 countries. She met Lord Wakefield, who had provided Amy Johnson's fuel, and she was received at Buckingham Palace.

Nancy's later accounts of this event suggest she was underestimated by the Australian social set at Buckingham Palace that day. On the other hand, many influential, enterprising, and in some cases wealthy, aviation industry leaders of Europe recognised her kindred spirit and she felt at home in their company. They shared her vision and commitment. She was drawn to the Dutch and German experiences. The British, she felt, were far slower than the Dutch to understand the possibilities of aviation.

Nancy took German lessons so she could converse with the leading German pilots. She spent time with Anthony Fokker and other greats of the aviation industry. She formed a lasting friendship with Elly Beinhorn who she had met at that book signing in Sydney all those years before. She even flew to the 1938 Paris Air Show as Elly's navigator in a Messerschmitt 108.

As she travelled Nancy collected many items, including models of planes not yet seen in Australia, for a planned exhibition on aviation when she returned to her homeland.

She finished her travels in the United States where she met women from the 'Ninety Nines', the Women Pilots' Association of the United States. She joined the organisation as an overseas member and learned about their annual 'Powder Puff Derby'. She then flew to Washington in the newly released DC9.

In 1939 Nancy returned to Australia by ship. It was on this voyage that she met her future husband, Charles Walton. They were married in Sydney by Reverend John Flynn in August 1939, after her aviation exhibition had been successfully staged in both Sydney and Melbourne.

Nancy Bird had done remarkable things. From struggling to provide a regional pioneering service in outback Australia, she had made the leap to understanding how the whole industry might work across the world in the future. When she had been flattened, exhausted and discouraged, she had widened her horizons and set out to learn more, taking an industry view of aviation.

With her wide knowledge and experience she was able to contribute to the development of the Australian Women's Flying Club as it went on to a war footing, training its members in aircraft maintenance, navigation and meteorology.

In 1940 each state formed a branch of the Women's Air Training Corps and, in 1941, the Women's Australian Auxiliary Air Force was authorised by the Commonwealth government. Nancy was commandant of the NSW Women's Air Training Corps throughout the war and she, along with other female aviators, remained doggedly critical of the Australian government's failure to follow the lead of the British and US governments and use women to ferry planes to where they were needed as part of the war effort.

After the war she took a few years off to raise her family, but remained active in community life, even going to the far west as a dental nurse with the Far West Children's Health Scheme in 1950.

Nancy took out a student pilot licence in 1951, which enabled her to fly as co-pilot to her friend Mae Casey, something she continued to do even after Mae's husband became governor-general in 1965.

She maintained links with her friends around the world, including her German friends, many of whom she visited after the war. In 1958 she renewed her full pilot's licence for a trip to the United States. As she would be there for the American All Women's Transcontinental Air Race, the 'Powder Puff Derby', she filled out the forms before she even had a sponsor, plane or co-pilot. Hers was the first ever overseas entry and her gamble, of course, paid off. She hired a Cessna 172 and learned to fly it while friends in the States found her a co-pilot. They came fifth and won $200.

Nancy flew in three more Powder Puff Derbies, and she was the only original competitor to fly in the 1966 re-enactment of the 1936 Brisbane to Adelaide race. She also flew with Dick and Ian Smith in the Perth to Sydney Air Race in the early 1970s.

Nancy's commitment to making sure the benefits of aviation reached the whole community continued throughout her long life and she maintained her links with the international network of women pilots and supported Australian women who wanted to fly. Nancy spent much of her time promoting the idea of air services for rural communities, and speaking about Australian aviation—in books, talks, interviews, articles and film.

In 2000, aged 85, Nancy was on board the 747 round trip flight from Sydney to Wollongong to celebrate Sydney Airport Corporation's 80th anniversary. Accounts of the event note that she took as much interest in the people around her as she did in the aeronautics. She was present on 18 July 2005 at the launch of *Sydney Airport: 85 years as the Gateway to Australia*, a book celebrating the airport's anniversary and, on 16 October 2005, at her 90th birthday dinner, Qantas announced that its first A380 aircraft was to be called 'Nancy-Bird Walton'.

When we were writing a book on Australia's aviation history in 2005, we wanted to include an account of Nancy's amazing life. Jillian wrote a first draft and we wanted to check the facts. So I telephoned Nancy to check the details of the story.

She was in her 90s at the time but answered the phone and chatted happily to me, a complete stranger, for about an hour. She shared stories and laughed about how shocked people were when she was picked up at Circular Quay and driven to Mascot Airport each day by Charles Kingsford Smith, who taught her to fly and was divorced at the time. Nancy's exact words were, 'And didn't people *talk*!'

She graciously agreed to be my guest on a radio program and concluded the conversation by saying, 'Just send the article over to me and I'll proofread it for you.'

She was a very down-to-earth person who once said about herself: 'I don't know why I get the publicity, perhaps my greatest achievement is that I've been a survivor.'

She was also a wonderful, positive, feisty, fun-loving lady, who often said: 'You know it doesn't matter how black the sky is or how bad the storm clouds may be, the sun is always shining up top.'

Nancy-Bird Walton AO, OBE, DStJ passed away on 13 January 2009. She was 94 years old. Her state funeral at St Andrew's Cathedral on 20 January was preceded by a low flight over the city of Sydney and the cathedral by the Qantas A380 aircraft named 'Nancy-Bird Walton'. A large contingent of the Australian Women Pilots' Association members attended wearing pink dresses and pearls—as Nancy had requested. New South Wales Governor Marie Bashir gave her address wearing a pink hat. After the service, three Tiger Moth aircraft flew low over Sydney Harbour.

In 2019 Prime Minister Scott Morrison announced that Sydney's new airport at Badgery's Creek would be officially named the 'Western Sydney International (Nancy-Bird Walton) Airport'.

PART IV

TRANSPORTED

There are 162,000 convict stories, and probably every single one of them would be worth telling. Whether they were victims of circumstance, unwilling, innocent victims of a society in which they were 'surplus to requirements', or simply victims of their own wickedness, selfishness and lawlessness, every convict would have a life story that would be interesting to investigate and know about.

Of all those stories these are three that have always fascinated me. That men could have the skill, ingenuity and presence of mind to achieve the sort of things that Thomas Barrett and William Walker managed to accomplish, and yet still be despised as convicted criminals and sentenced to death, fills me with a sense of wonder and puzzlement about the world they inhabited and the way British society could have evolved to a point where such seemingly absurd contradictions were possible.

On the other hand, it has always been apparent to me that the convict system, which resulted in those 162,000 people being dumped, unwanted, on the shores of this continent, also inadvertently created a society in which many of the obvious distinctions of class, and the age-old prejudices regarding ancestry and background, were removed and replaced by a sense of egalitarianism and opportunity that was certainly rare in British society at the time.

The story of James Squire has always been of special interest to me, for several reasons. For one thing his Romani heritage had been rather neglected until recent times, and yet it explains so much about the skills and ingenuity that led to his success, once he was free of the prejudice that went with it. Secondly, most Australians are only aware of him because his life story has been reduced to a number of clichés and a certain amount of historical fantasy, in order to promote a brand of beer. The truth, as usual, is far more interesting. Another less important, but nonetheless relevant, factor in my curiosity about the way his gypsy heritage enabled him to so successfully make the transition from criminality to respectability, is the fact that one branch on my own family tree appears to have grown from a similar source.

The other 161,997 convict stories will have to wait until I have a little more time. Two others that especially fascinate me, Mary Reibey and William Westwood, who almost made it into this collection, are top of the list.

10

THE FIRST MAN HANGED

THE 'BLOODY CODE'

In the century from 1730 to 1830, 70–75 per cent of all death sentences handed down in British courts were commuted to life imprisonment, or transportation to the American colonies, or later to New South Wales. This occurred either because the jury recommended mercy, or on appeal to the King's Council. Around 50,000 convicted criminals were sentenced to death in this time.

How had Britain found itself in this situation, where so many criminals were condemned to death and such a large percentage, almost three in every four, were then reprieved?

Historically, the British system of criminal justice that led to this situation, which came to be generally known as the 'bloody code', was a result of the dominance of the Whig party in British parliament from 1715 through to the 1750s. In general political terms, the Whig party was made up of conservative Protestant gentry and landowners. As the 18th century unfolded, it also came to include those from the 'upper middle' classes, made wealthy by the Industrial Revolution.

These men, who controlled the British parliament for the first half of the 18th century, were keen to pass laws that protected them and their property from the ever-growing numbers of disenfranchised poor. Their philosophy is perhaps best summed up in the words of one of the earliest supporters of the 'bloody code', George Savile,

First Marquess of Halifax: 'Men are not hanged for stealing horses, but that horses may not be stolen.'

Jacobite uprisings against the Protestant monarchy in 1715, 1719 and 1745, supported by the French and the Spanish, also led to Whig paranoia about criminal activities against property, and parliament passed law after law extending the death penalty to cover crimes such as poaching, highway robbery, arson and theft. These were known as the 'Black Acts', due to the fact that several of these laws were passed in response to large groups of poachers with blackened faces conducting organised raids on large estates in order to kill and carry off deer. The first 'Black Act' was passed in 1723.

The process of widening the scope of the death penalty continued into the 1770s when the Enclosure Acts began taking away the common land, which the poorer classes used for subsistence farming and grazing animals, and granting it to those who already owned land. 'Enclosure' meant land could be added to estates and properties already 'fenced in', ostensibly to make it more productive.

Historian Joseph Stromberg, from the Independent Institute in California, summed up the situation in his essay 'English Enclosures and Soviet Collectivization: Two Instances of an Anti-Peasant Mode of Development': 'The political dominance of large landowners determined the course of enclosure . . . their power in Parliament and as local Justices of the Peace . . . enabled them to redistribute the land in their own favour.'

A folk rhyme from the period put it more succinctly:

They hang the man, and flog the woman,
That steals the goose from off the common;
But let the greater villain loose,
Who steals the common from the goose.

These Acts removed the prior rights of local people to rural land they had used for generations. Rural labourers and seasonal farm workers depended on open fields and forests to fend off starvation. Disenfranchised rural workers were forced to move to the overcrowded cities and join the vast numbers competing for low paid work under harsh conditions in factories, as the Industrial Revolution gathered pace.

In 1700 there were about 50 crimes punishable by death, mostly involving treason, murder, rape or other crimes of violence. In 1810 the number of crimes punishable by hanging peaked at 222. In 1823 Prime Minister Robert Peel drastically reduced that number by removing from the list most of the crimes against property, leaving murder, treason, arson and piracy as the main hanging offences.

During the century from 1725 to 1825, approximately 10,000 people were hanged in Britain. More than 3000 were hanged at Tyburn, London's main place of execution in the period from 1700 to 1783, when the gallows moved to Newgate, where 560 people were hanged between 1783 and 1800.

These numbers, however, represent only about 30 per cent of those who were condemned to die, and there is a good reason for this. Judges, magistrates and juries were often reluctant to send people to their death. Recommendations for mercy by juries, and petitions to magistrates for clemency, or to the King's Council for remission, led to more than two-thirds of those condemned to die having their sentences reduced to life in prison or transportation.

Juries were also given the power to assess the value of stolen goods and could thus avoid sentencing to death those accused of stealing, by valuing the stolen property to be less than that which required a death sentence.

This subtle subverting of the harsh death penalty laws, by magistrates, judges and juries all over Britain, only led, however, to another problem. What was to be done with these hundreds of thousands of convicted criminals?

Prisons became so overcrowded that the old unseaworthy naval and merchant ships were used to house criminals. Often they were moored near naval dockyards or in the Thames Estuary, where the convicted felons could be used as cheap labour. Not even this form of imprisonment, however, could cope with the numbers being convicted. Fortunately, another solution was found—forced migration.

Until the outbreak of the American War of Independence in 1775, transportation had been a common criminal punishment. More than a thousand convicts were transported each year to the American colonies and, although the death rate in transit was about 15 per cent, approximately 50,000 British criminals were successfully transported from 1718 to 1775. Most were sent to Maryland and Virginia, where they were auctioned to plantation owners as indentured workers, to work in the fields beside black African slaves. While the African slave trade provided approximately 47 per cent of the migration to the American colonies in the 18th century, the transportation of convicted criminals contributed a not insubstantial 9 per cent of migrants.

When transportation to American colonies was halted by the war in 1775, the hulks quickly become overcrowded and unsanitary. After the war Britain attempted to resume the practice and convict transports were sent to several former colonies.

The American government soon put a stop to the practice and Thomas Jefferson, speaking in 1786, was keen to deny that criminal transportation had made any real genetic impact on the American population, by blatantly lying about the numbers that had been sent:

> Malefactors sent to America were not sufficient in number to merit enumeration as one class out of three which peopled America. It was at a late period of their history that the practice began. I have no book by me which enables me to point out the date of its commencement. But I do not think the whole number sent would amount to 2000 & being principally men eaten up with disease, they married seldom & propagated little. I do not suppose that themselves & their descendants are at present 4000, which is little more than one thousandth part of the whole inhabitants.

We now know that Jefferson and his ilk were misguided. Transportation undoubtedly affected the character of the colonial population and here, in Australia, the result was at times quite the opposite of what the 'mother country' Britain intended—egalitarianism, opportunity and ultimately even pride in our convict ancestry.

THOMAS BARRETT

Barrett was a petty thief, amateur engraver and counterfeiter, born in London around 1758. Nothing is known of his childhood, but he first came to the notice of the law in his mid-twenties, when he appeared in the Old Bailey, in July 1782, accused of stealing some silver mugs, trays, cutlery and a wine strainer from the home of a certain William Lewis. The verdict was 'not guilty', even though three witnesses said they saw Barrett leave the house just after the robbery.

In September 1782, Thomas was not so lucky. He and another man were seen running from the London house of a lady named Ann Milton, from which a silver watch and chain and some shirts (total value of 72 shillings) had been stolen. The alarm was raised and Barrett was apprehended and found to have the watch in his possession. His rather feeble defence—that he met the other man allegedly involved in the robbery, a complete stranger to him, in the street, and this stranger handed him the watch and ran off—was not believed by anyone in court, including the jury, and he was sentenced to death.

Just after the American War of Independence finished in March 1784, Thomas Barrett, and 178 other convicted felons, left the port of Dover aboard the transport *Mercury*, bound for the colony of Georgia. After just a few days sailing, however, Barrett was apparently one of the ringleaders of a mutiny in which the convicts took charge of the vessel and attempted to sail to Ireland.

Adverse weather caused them to abort their plan and they then returned to the Port of Torbay, in Devon, where many of them managed to abscond from the vessel before they could be apprehended. Most of the runaways were rounded up and tried for crimes including mutiny and being 'criminally at-large'. Of the 108 rearrested, two were hanged and a further 24, Thomas Barrett among them, were tried for mutiny.

Barrett was again sentenced to death but reprieved after evidence was tendered to the court that he had intervened to save the life of the ship's steward and had also prevented the captain's ear from being taken off with a pair of scissors by other mutineers. He spent four years on the prison hulk *Dunkirk* at Plymouth before joining the convict transport *Charlotte*, as part of the First Fleet 'bound for Botany Bay'.

There were 67 convicts from the *Mercury* mutiny on the First Fleet.

Barrett spent his time on the voyage to Rio engraving buttons and small coins that had been rubbed flat to be used as love tokens. These were sold to fellow convicts to give to the female convicts aboard the *Charlotte*.

When the fleet arrived at Rio, it became apparent that Barrett had been able to make more than a few love tokens. Surgeon General John White, also a passenger on board the *Charlotte*, noted in his journal:

> 5th August. Still calm. This morning a boat came alongside, in which were three Portuguese and six slaves, from whom we purchased some oranges, plantains, and bread.
>
> In trafficking with these people, we discovered that one Thomas Barrett, a convict, had, with great ingenuity and address, passed some quarter dollars which he, assisted by two others, had coined out of old buckles, buttons belonging to the marines, and pewter spoons, during their passage from Teneriffe.
>
> The impression, milling, character, in a word, the whole was so inimitably executed that had their metal been a little better the fraud, I am convinced, would have passed undetected. A strict and careful search was made for the apparatus wherewith this was done, but in vain; not the smallest trace or vestige of any thing of the kind was to be found among them.

Barrett had managed the forgery while under the constant scrutiny of marines, and apparently without access to any kind of a furnace.

Arthur Phillip was somewhat of a celebrity in Rio, having served with distinction for many years in the Portuguese navy, and it was obviously a rather embarrassing affair, as White explained:

> The officers of marines, the master of the ship, and myself fully explained to the injured Portuguese what villains they were who had imposed upon them. We were not without apprehensions that they might entertain an unfavourable opinion of Englishmen in general from the conduct of these rascals; we therefore thought it necessary to acquaint them that the perpetrators of the fraud were felons doomed to transportation, by the laws of their country, for having committed similar offences there.

Surgeon John White was obviously impressed by Barrett's skill and, on arriving at Botany Bay, gave the convicted amateur engraver a commission. White gave Barrett a silver kidney dish from his personal medical equipment and asked the convict to create a medallion commemorating the voyage of the *Charlotte.*

Barrett, over the following week, skilfully produced a silver medal, about 3 inches (7.5 centimetres) in diameter, that shows the *Charlotte* at anchor in Botany Bay on one side and has the following inscription neatly engraved on the other:

> Sailed, the Charlotte from Spit Head the 13 of May 1787. Bound for Botany Bay in th Island of New Holland. Arriv'd at Teneriff th 4 of June in Lat 28.13 N long 16.23 W. Depart'd it 10 D. Arriv'd Rio Janiero 6 of Aug in Lat 22.54 S Long 42.38 W. Depart'd it th 5 of Sepr, arriv'd at the Cape of Good Hope the 14 Octr in Lat 34.29 S Long 18.29 E, Depart'd it th 13 of Novr and made the South Cape of New Holland the 8 Jan'y 1788 in Lat 43.32 S Long 146.56 E. Arriv'd at Botany Bay the 20 of Jany. The Charlotte in Co in Lat 34.00 South Long 151.00 East. Distance from Great Britan miles 13106.

At an auction held by the coin and medal dealers Noble Numismatics in 2008, the Australian National Maritime Museum acquired the medal with a bid of $750,000. When the buyer's premium was added, the medal actually cost $1 million. It was good news for retired Melbourne dentist Dr John Chapman, who had purchased it for $15,000 in 1981. A copper version of the medal, also made by Barrett for John White's servant William Broughton, was sold privately in 2013, also by Noble Numismatics, having failed to reach the auction estimate of $500,000.

Barrett could have done with $1.5 million in 1788.

Just over a month after arriving at Sydney Cove, four convicts, driven by hunger no doubt, robbed the government food store, taking an amount of 'beef, butter and pease'. On 27 February 1788, three of them were sentenced to death—the sentence to be carried out later that day, at 6 p.m.

Joseph Ryan, the youngest, was sentenced to 300 lashes and forced to give evidence against the other three. Then, due to the fact that Major Ross, the argumentative and pedantic commander of the marines (who often made Arthur Phillip's life as difficult as possible), refused to let any of his men act as executioner, that task also was assigned to Ryan.

Governor Phillip, it seems, had reluctantly concluded that an example must be made. There was, however, some thought that a hanging might give the convicts an opportunity to attempt mutiny. Eyewitness Arthur Bowes, ship's surgeon from the transport *Lady Penrhyn*, recorded in his journal that:

> A large party of marines were drawn up opposite the gallows and all the convicts were summoned to see the deserved end of the companions.

At the last minute, two of the men, Henry Lovell and Joseph Hall, were given a stay of execution for 24 hours. They were later sentenced to be 'banished to some uninhabited place', but were pardoned several months later, after apparently spending some weeks on Pinchgut Island in Sydney Harbour. Lovell, who was, apart from James Squire, the only other gypsy on the First Fleet, was later sent to Norfolk Island.

According to Arthur Bowes, it took some time before Ryan 'could be prevailed upon to execute his office, nor would he at last have complied, if he had not been severely threatened by the Provost Marshall, Mr Brewer'.

Brewer, who had been Arthur Phillip's personal secretary for many years and was made provost marshall when the First Fleet arrived at Sydney Cove, eventually mounted the ladder and arranged the noose himself, but Ryan did not perform the grisly task of execution until, according to Bowes, 'Major Ross threatened to give orders to the marines to shoot him', at which point the reluctant executioner finally performed the task at gunpoint.

The fourth food thief, the first European executed on Australia's east coast, was described by another eyewitness, Lieutenant-Captain Watkin Tench, as 'an old and desperate offender, who died with that hardy spirit which too often is found in the worst and most abandoned class of men'.

No prizes for guessing his identity—it was Thomas Barrett, and he was barely 30 years old.

Surgeon White noted in his journal that the prisoner was 'taken to the fatal tree' and there:

> Barrett was launched into eternity, after having confessed to the Rev Mr Johnson, who attended him, that he was guilty of the crime, and had long merited the ignominious death which he was about to suffer, and to which he said he had been brought by bad company and evil example.

Thus Thomas Barrett, designer and engraver of artworks worth $1.5 million, gained a further permanent distinction in our history—as the first man hanged in the colony of New South Wales.

The place where that hanging tree once stood is now the corner of Harrington and Essex Streets in The Rocks area of Sydney. A plaque placed there by the Royal Australian Historical Society reads: 'Thomas Barrett, a First Fleet convict, was hanged near this place on 27 February 1788 for stealing provisions and was buried nearby.'

If you are sentenced to death three times, I suppose that you might consider yourself lucky to be hanged only once.

11

THE GYPSY WHO MADE GOOD

GYPSIES

DNA testing has shown that the Roma people (gypsies) are members of a distinct ethnic race that originated in the Punjab region of northern India. They are a nomadic people who made their way into Europe around the 9th century AD. The term 'gypsies' derives from the word 'Egyptian'. This is due to the fact that, in Europe, there was a popular misconception that they came from Egypt. There are distinct groups of Roma, usually thought of as 'tribes' or even 'nations', spread throughout Western Asia, the Middle East and North Africa, as well as Europe.

The Roma are traditionally illiterate and their great skills are in the areas of music, herbs and medicines, metalwork, lacemaking and jewellery, and horses.

To understand the persecution of the Roma, it is necessary to remember that medieval Europe was run on strictly Christian lines. Because of their cultural practice of fortune-telling Roma were seen as evil by medieval Christian church law—'wizards . . . who are inspired satanically and pretend to predict the unknown'. Similarly, in the Islamic Ottoman Empire, Roma were seen as unclean infidels by sultanate law, 'having no visible permanent professional affiliation', and were placed on the lowest possible position on the social ladder.

The religious leaders of the Holy Roman Empire met periodically in the German town of Augsburg to determine uniform doctrine. In

1545, at one of these 'diets', as they were called, the declaration was made that, 'whosoever kills a gypsy [Romani], will be guilty of no murder'. This pronouncement led to a wave of slaughter throughout the empire that later necessitated a law to 'forbid the drowning of Romani women and children'.

In areas of Eastern Europe that are today Romania and Moldova, the Romani were constitutionally enslaved for centuries to work in Orthodox Christian monastries. In 1538, Ferdinand I, who was King of Bohemia and Hungary and also Holy Roman Emperor, ordered that all Romani in his realm be expelled.

The problem for Christian and Islamic societies was that gypsies did not live their lives in accordance with religious law, which at the time was the law of the land. Because they never settled, they were also seen as difficult to control and dangerous—outsiders who did not fit into the strict hierarchical social order.

Centuries later very little had changed. In World War ll it is estimated that the Nazis murdered 250,000 gypsies in death camps, thought to be one-quarter of the Romani population living in Europe at the time. European nations like Denmark still had anti-gypsy legislation until well into the 1950s.

In England, the *Egyptian Act of 1530* banned Romani from entering the country and ordered those living in the kingdom to leave within two weeks or risk confiscation of their property, imprisonment or deportation. This was followed up by a second act in 1554, in which they were ordered to 'abandon their naughty, idle and ungodly life and company' and settle down to a sedentary existence. This Act was generally understood to permit execution of any Romani who failed to comply, as 'a warning to others'.

Those first two *Egyptian Acts*, which banned gypsies from the realm and then ordered them to quit their traditional lifestyle, effectively denied them any rights if they continued to live in England and continue their cultural practices.

Five more similar acts were passed in the following 70 years and the persecution of gypsies, accompanied by fear, distrust and paranoia, continued unabated for the next 400 years. The Romani continued living a modified form of their nomadic lifestyle and became an itinerant workforce, associated particularly with hop picking and other seasonal agricultural activities, as well as mending household items, herbalism and trading in horses.

The Canning Case, in February 1753, was a landmark legal case in the history of the British justice system, in which public outrage and prejudice against gypsies contributed to a major miscarriage of justice.

Susannah Wells (also known as 'Mother Wells') was accused of abducting a young domestic servant, Elizabeth Canning, and keeping her imprisoned for a month in a large house, or barn, at Enfield Wash, southwest of London. She was also accused of 'keeping a disorderly house', which meant running a brothel. Susannah was found guilty, branded on the hand and imprisoned for six months, although she was later exonerated when the maid, Elizabeth Canning, was convicted of perjury.

Mary Squires was accused of taking part in the assault and the theft of Elizabeth Canning's corsets, which she was alleged to have 'forcibly removed'. Mary was sentenced to death for stealing the corsets, but King George II, acting on information presented by the trial judge, ordered a stay of execution and she was later pardoned by the monarch.

Those supporting Elizabeth Canning, who became known as 'Canningites', saw the case as a *cause célèbre* for the rights of the lower classes to have access to the court system and obtain justice. The Canningite faction also attracted many followers whose motivation was to use the case to justify discrimination against, and persecution of, gypsies.

The man who led the case against the gypsies was Henry Fielding, London's chief magistrate and the author of the novels *Tom Jones* and *Amelia*. Fielding was an interesting character who had caused a scandal by marrying his deceased wife's pregnant maid servant. He was regarded as a champion of the lower classes, was a heavy drinker, and suffered from asthma, gout and cirrhosis of the liver. He led the Canningite case throughout the first trial but, being terminally ill, took little part in the debate that occurred during the perjury trial in early 1754 and died in October of that year, aged 47.

The case against Susannah Wells and Mary Squires came to court before a very distinguished panel of five judges, presided over by Sir Crisp Gascoygne, who also happened to be the Lord Mayor of London. Gascoygne and his fellow judge Nathaniel Gundry (Justice of the Common Pleas) were both unhappy with the jury's verdict of guilty and disgusted by the behaviour of the Canningite mob, which had gathered outside the court. This mob had prevented defence witnesses from entering the courthouse, and had badly beaten three of those who did testify on behalf of the gypsies as they left the courthouse. The Canningites also openly encouraged anti-gypsy hysteria, which Gascoygne felt had prejudiced the trial.

Elizabeth Canning claimed that she had been kidnapped by two men while returning to her mother's house from a visit to her aunt on 1 January 1753. (This day would have been a holiday for only the second time in Britain's history, as parliament had adopted the Gregorian calendar only from the start of 1752, thus making the first of January New Year's Day; previously the first day of the year was Lady Day, 23 March.)

Elizabeth claimed that the two men had attacked and beaten her and taken her to the house at Enfield Wash where she was further abused and robbed of her undergarments because she refused when the gypsy women asked her to 'go their way'—evidently a euphemism for becoming a prostitute.

Elizabeth also claimed that she had been imprisoned in the loft for a month and only been given a jug of water and a quarter loaf of bread in that time. She testified that she eventually took some boards off the window, jumped to the ground and walked back along the London Road to her mother's house without seeking any help along the way.

There were many things about Elizabeth's story that made no sense to Gascoygne and Gundry. Upon inspection, the room at Enfield Wash proved to be nothing like the one she had described, nor could she give any reason why she waited four weeks to make an escape attempt, or why she did not seek help instead of making the long walk back to her mother's house. Nor could she explain how she managed to survive for a month on a jug of water and a quarter loaf of bread and still have the strength to walk home.

Gascoygne felt the Canningites had not only obstructed the course of justice physically, but had prejudiced the case by publicly demonising the old and, unfortunately, rather ugly Mary Squires (who Gascoygne called 'the poor creature'). To the judge, this was a dangerous example of the 'common people' getting out of hand, exerting mob influence and developing aspirations to which they were not entitled.

He began a crusade to discover the truth and rather quickly found evidence from 'reputable people', including clergymen, to corroborate the alibis given by the gypsies—that they were actually travelling in other parts of the country during the time Elizabeth Canning claimed they were holding her prisoner.

He also interviewed Susannah Wells in Newgate Prison and, being impressed by the logic of her testimony, interviewed the chief witness for the prosecution, a woman named Virtue Hall, who told him that Henry Fielding had threatened her with imprisonment if she did not lie in the witness stand to corroborate Elizabeth Canning's story.

Gascoygne published *The Story of Elizabeth Canning Considered* in response to an attack on his persistent re-examination of the case in a pamphlet by Fielding, titled *A Clear Statement of the Case of Elizabeth Canning*. A war of words ensued between the Canningites and Gascoygne's supporters, who were given the title 'Egyptians'. Just about every literate person of note in London joined in and the furore caused by the case, and the attention given to the arguments involved, had far-reaching results.

By far the most significant of these was a move to reform the way in which the courts dealt with witness testimony, and the system of pre-trial hearings by magistrates. Until that time magistrates were able to interview witnesses ad hoc, separately or in groups in their private rooms, rather than individually before the court.

The debate also led to Elizabeth Canning being tried for perjury in April 1754. She was found guilty and transported as a convict to the American colonies. Her supporters, however, helped her financially and managed to get her assigned to a Methodist minister's household in Connecticut, where she lived as a free woman. She married in 1756, had four children, and died in 1773.

The case also led, quite controversially, to King George II pardoning a gypsy and thus being seen to give tacit support to a despised and feared ethnic minority, who were, at that time, denied the civil rights that were given to all other British commoners. Still, the prejudice against gypsies continued throughout the empire, and beyond.

JAMES SQUIRE

The name James Squire is a well-known one in Australia today, as a brand name for a range of beers made by the Lion Beer Company, whose advertising claim—that he was the first man to grow hops and brew beer in Australia—is doubtful. Squire was, however, the first man to successfully grow large quantities of hops and brew beer commercially on a large scale in the colony of New South Wales. His real-life story is a truly remarkable one that demonstrates what an egalitarian and wonderful place Australia could be.

Transported on the First Fleet to serve seven years for stealing, James Squire had a 'secret' that he probably chose to keep to himself once he was aboard a convict transport, 'bound for Botany Bay'. It was a characteristic he shared with only one other man in the entire group of 753 convicts who arrived at Sydney Cove. Oddly enough, that other man had a part to play in the story of Thomas Barrett, which is also told in this collection. His name was Henry Lovell.

What James Squire and Henry Lovell had in common was their ethnicity, and the fact that they were legally *persona non grata* under British law. They were gypsies ... aka Romanies, Roma, Travellers, Egyptians and, most derogatory of all, 'gypos'.

James was born on 18 December 1754. His parents, Timothy Squires and Mary Wells, were from the two gypsy families involved in the Canning Case, in which prejudice against gypsies led to a scandalous miscarriage of justice in 1753, almost two years before his birth.

On his father's side James's great-grandmother was Mary Squires, while Susannah Wells was a relative of James's mother, Mary Wells.

As a gypsy, James grew up in the aftermath of all this, to a life of crime as a despised fringe-dweller, smuggling and stealing. Gypsies were feared, persecuted and denied civil rights in 18th century Britain. They did, however, have good knowledge of hop cultivation as they provided the itinerant workforce for the hop planting and picking seasons.

The transformation of James Squire from a despised criminal of the lowest social rank imaginable in England, to a respectable and revered citizen of Sydney, is an amazing story. It shows how the convict system could achieve social reform by simply putting people in a place where their past was irrelevant to whatever they might achieve.

Squire's criminal behaviour had begun in 1774, when he was found guilty of either highway robbery or stealing from a house and running out onto the road (records are unclear about the exact crime). He was sentenced to transportation to the American colonies for seven years but apparently served the sentence, or part of it, in the army instead, which was not uncommon. He is sometimes referred to as a 'former soldier' in subsequent colonial newspaper articles.

In 1776, aged 22, James Squires (the 's' on the end of the name was dropped later) married Martha Quinton, also 22, at Kingston-upon-Thames, some 20 kilometres from the centre of London. They continued living in Kingston for the next nine years, during which time Martha gave birth to two sons and a daughter.

In 1785 they were living in a tavern in Heathen Street, Kingston. It is possible that James was the landlord, or manager, and the tavern he ran was, by all accounts, a den of thieves, smugglers, prostitutes and gypsies, so it is no surprise that, on 11 April 1785, James found himself again in court accused of stealing, 'four cocks, five hens . . . and other goods and chattels', which were the property of a Mr Stacey, who had recently moved into Heathen Street. The theft was almost certainly only one of many petty crimes James had committed since his return from the army. It was, however, the only one he was nabbed for.

So, found guilty of stealing nine chooks and a few sundries, James Squire was transported on the First Fleet to what was to become a totally different life in New South Wales. He was originally assigned to the convict transport *Friendship,* but records show him disembarking in Sydney from the *Charlotte.* Some convicts changed ships to balance the cargoes when the fleet took on extra supplies at the Cape of Good Hope, perhaps that was when James Squire joined the *Charlotte.*

Whatever ships he travelled on, he arrived safe and sound at Sydney Cove and disembarked with the other convicts from the *Charlotte* on 27 January. He was assigned as a servant to Surgeon John White.

It took a while for James Squires, gypsy and thief, to transform himself into Mr James Squire, Esquire, respectable and successful businessman, philanthropist and local constable.

Old habits die hard.

On Saturday, 14 November 1789, Squire was sentenced 'to receive 300 lashes, 150 now and the remainder when able to bear it' for the theft of medical supplies from Surgeon John White's store.

We don't know exactly what Squire stole from the store, but we do know why he stole the medicines. They were for his girlfriend, the convict Mary Spencer, who was pregnant and was sent to Norfolk Island on the *Supply* on 11 November 1789.

The items that Squire stole were found in a bag that he had given to John Frederick, a crew member of the *Supply*, to take on the ship to Norfolk Island and then give to Mary Spencer, the lover from whom James was now being permanently separated.

As a gypsy, James probably had some knowledge of herbs and natural medicines and it has been suggested that one of the drugs in the bag could have been the herb horehound, a plant often used to relieve period pain and discomfort during pregnancy. It has also been suggested that Squire stole the herb because it could be used as a substitute for hops in the brewing process.

This theory falls down somewhat when you consider, firstly, that there is no written evidence that horehound was among the items stolen. Secondly, it is very unlikely that there was enough of the herb in John White's medical store to use in brewing ale and, finally, that the stolen goods were found in a bag Squire had given to John Frederick to take on board the *Supply* and therefore, whatever they were, they weren't a large amount.

The version of the 'stealing from the medical stores' story used by the Lion Beer Company to promote a beer called '150 Lashes' is not even vaguely true. The company's 'simplified' version of the event claims that Squire stole hops, which he most certainly did not, though he was to grow hops successfully quite a few years later.

The rest of the Lion Beer Company's version of 'history' is pure fairy story. It suggests that the magistrate in the case made sure the punishment was never administered, because Squire had been making ale for him. The magistrates sitting on that day were Captain John Hunter and Judge Advocate Collins, both of whom were sticklers for the letter of the law.

This tale about the 'crooked magistrate' derives from the fact that Squire made ale for officers and soldiers who did act as magistrates, but that did not occur until after his trial for stealing. Hunter was a naval officer and, although Collins's military rank was officially captain, he was a captain in the marines, who kept law and order in the colony until December 1791, when they were replaced by the New South Wales Corps (Collins stayed on in the colony as judge advocate), and it was the officers and men of the New South Wales Corps for whom Squire later brewed beer, not the marines.

Records, including Squire's own statement to Commissioner Bigge in 1820, clearly show that he began brewing beer, in small quantities, for the officers and soldiers of the New South Wales Corps in 1793, more than three years after he was found guilty of stealing anything from the medical store.

James Squire told Commissioner Bigge in 1820:

> I have been in the Colony from its earliest establishment and for 30 years I have been a brewer. At first I lived in Sydney, and brewed beer in small quantities. I sold it then for 4d per quart and made it from some hops that I got from the Daedalus. I also brewed for General Grose & Col. Paterson for their own consumption from English Malt.

The *Daedalus*, a supply ship used by the British explorer George Vancouver, called into Sydney Cove on 19 April 1793 and sailed to rejoin the expedition in Alaska on 1 July that year. During her stay she was commissioned by Lieutenant-Governor Francis Grose to be sent back to the colony from America with supplies and she arrived back in Sydney Cove on 5 April 1794.

So, it seems James Squire was not brewing in the colony before 1793, probably 1794. He certainly never brewed ale for any magistrates before that time and, if he avoided the lash in 1789, it was because it was not uncommon for convicts of reasonably good character to be spared some, or even all, of their allotted punishment.

There is evidence to show that James Squire was regarded as one of the better class of convicts. He gave evidence before the magistrates on 5 March 1789, which led to two female convicts being found guilty of stealing cabbages, and he was assigned as a servant to Lieutenant Ralph Clark of the marines, who allowed him to carry firearms on their explorations of the Lane Cove River and seems to have had a good opinion of him.

Perhaps the fact that he had been a soldier, along with the obvious evidence that his crime was committed to benefit a pregnant female convict, rather than himself, may have helped him to avoid the lash but, whether he was flogged or not and, if he was, how many lashes he received, we shall never know—150 is a reasonable guess.

In his doctoral thesis, *Brewing in Early Australia*, David Hughes notes that, in reply to a letter from the Secretary of State for the Colonies, Henry Dundas, dated 10 January 1792, Arthur Phillip was not optimistic that the New South Wales Corps could be supplied with the normal ration of spirits and beer when they arrived in the colony but he hoped that, 'supplying the deficiency of spirits with beer may be done hereafter'.

Hughes goes on to say:

> Despite Phillip's pessimism, it is likely that small scale brewing was already going on. Certainly, in 1793, the year after Phillip returned to England, beer was being produced from imported hops and malt. The man who produced this beer was almost certainly James Squire, who went on to be the colony's foremost brewer before his death in 1822.

James's skill as a brewer was certainly recognised by Lieutenant-Governor Major Francis Grose, who was in control of the colony from Arthur Phillip's departure in December 1792 until his own departure in December 1794, and Captain William Paterson, who took over as lieutenant-governor when Grose departed and served until the arrival of John Hunter, nine months later. Both of these men provided Squire with imported malt, in order that he might provide them with a regular supply of ale.

So, it seems that James robbed the medical stores in 1789 simply in an attempt to make Mary Spencer's life on Norfolk Island a little more comfortable. Mary gave birth to a son, Francis, on 1 August 1790. When she returned to Sydney in 1796, James was in a relationship with his convict servant Elizabeth Mason and had fathered four more children. Mary was in a permanent relationship with a soldier named John Palmer, who had apparently arranged for Francis to be enlisted in the New South Wales Corps. Amazingly, little Francis went on the payroll on his seventh birthday as a drummer boy, served out a career in the army and died in Melbourne, aged 61, in 1851.

James Squire's attitude to caring for his offspring was determined by the harsh realities of his life. He left a wife and three children behind in England and fathered another eight children in Sydney, seven of them with Elizabeth Mason. In the seven years since he bade a sad farewell to Mary Spencer and their unborn child, many things had changed for James. He was now not only a free man, having completed his sentence in 1791, but a man of property, having been given a grant of land in 1795 at Kissing Point, in the area that is today the Sydney suburb of Ryde.

James's cunning was apparent in his land dealings. He added twelve other land grants to his own 30 acres (12 hectares) at Ryde and eventually had an estate of more than 800 acres (324 hectares) along the Parramatta River. He cleverly complained to the colonial secretary about neighbouring land grants not being taken up and consequently purchased several of them for a shilling each. He also purchased land cheaply from other settlers and ex-convicts, who had been given small land grants adjacent to his own but could not be bothered clearing and developing them.

James successfully cultivated hops and grain and became the first commercially successful brewer in Australia. He obtained a licence to sell liquor in partnership with another emancipist, Simeon Lord, in 1798, and set up the Malting Shovel Tavern near his home on the

Parramatta River at Kissing Point. It was at the halfway point on the river between the two settlements of Sydney and Parramatta and proved a great success.

Oddly enough, the brewing of beer was seen as a good thing for a colony that was corrupted by the trade in rum. Rum had become the currency of the colony and led to a rebellion and massive military corruption. It was considered a sobering influence to get the inhabitants of New South Wales to drink beer rather than rum, and Squire was much praised for his efforts in growing hops and grain and producing and selling a decent brew. Beer was actually considered to be a healthy and efficacious beverage!

This belief was partly due to the fact that 'small beer', very mildly alcoholic beer (less than 1 per cent), was universally consumed in parts of Europe, especially Northern Europe and the 'low countries', throughout medieval times and into the 17th and 18th centuries. Small beer was brewed in most households for consumption by workers, children and servants because water sources were polluted and the brewing process meant small beer was a much safer way to quench the thirst. It was common for men doing heavy manual labour in hot weather to consume 6 litres or more a day of small beer.

Governor King was keen to provide the colony with a regular supply of good ale and he set up a government brewery in 1803. When this proved financially unsuccessful, possibly due to the fact that the employees drank most of what they produced, the governor encouraged local settlers to take up the challenge.

It was in this spirit of free enterprise that James Squire, whose gypsy background provided him with a good knowledge of hop picking and cultivation, successfully answered the call. Having produced a bumper crop of good quality hops in the summer of 1805–06, he decided to present evidence of his success at Government House. Governor King was overjoyed at Squire's achievement, according to the *Sydney Gazette* of 6 March 1806:

> On Friday Mr. Jas. Squires, settler and brewer at Kissing Point waited on His Excellency at Government House, with 2 vines of hops taken from his own grounds. On a vine from a last year's cutting were numbers of very fine bunches; and upon a two years old cutting the

> clusters, mostly ripe, were innumerable, in weight supposed to yield at least a pound and a half, and of a most exquisite flavour.
>
> As a public recompence for the unremitted attention shewn by the Grower in bringing this valuable plant to such a high degree of perfection, His Excelency [*sic*] has directed a Cow to be given to Mr. Squires from the Government Herd.

This reward was not a spontaneous random act. James Squire was in need of a cow, according to the *Sydney Gazette* of 17 November 1805, three months earlier:

> A cow belonging to Squires at Kissing Point, that had calved the day before, by accident found her way to a tub of grains, and eat so immoderately that she died in three hours after. When the carcase was opened, a quantity of grains little less than three bushels was found; and on Friday a second cow, the only one remaining to him, was taken ill, perhaps from a like cause, and yesterday was not expected to survive.

In spite of having greedy cows, Squire was an industrious and successful farmer. The hop vine he cultivated in 1806 covered 5 acres (2 hectares) by 1812 and produced 700 kilograms of hops. As a brewer he was similarly successful; by 1820 his brewery was producing 40 hogsheads (about 10,000 litres) of beer a week.

One of the most amusing aspects of this gypsy's truly remarkable life is that he was one of only a few ex-convicts to be ever appointed a district constable. After half a lifetime of thieving and stealing, he applied to be made a constable for the district of Eastern Farms (the modern suburbs of Putney and Ryde) on the grounds that there was too much stealing and thieving going on in the area, especially from his properties! On several occasions he placed ads in the *Sydney Gazette* stating that people trespassing on, or taking timber from, his property without permission would be well advised to cease doing so.

He did not take up the position of constable, however, merely in order to protect his own property. There is ample evidence that he exercised his position in the pursuit of justice for others and had quite a talent for detective work. The *Sydney Gazette* of 15 December 1805 records:

> Abraham Smith was yesterday night secured by J Squires, constable for the district of Kissing Point, and several articles found upon him that had shortly before been taken out of a neighbourhood house. He was brought in a prisoner the same day, and lodged in safe custody as apprehended was effected in the house of J Newton, who has been repeatedly robbed by offenders that had betaken themselves to the woods from an aversion to labour.

One of the things that made James Squire, ex-convict, such a success was that he certainly did not have 'an aversion to labour'. As well as his successful farming and brewing enterprises, he also established a bakery, a butchery and a credit union, and he served as district constable and was appointed by the governor as a trustee of the common pastures in January 1805. He is a perfect example of the fact that, once free of the British class system and given half a chance, any man with initiative and work ethic could succeed in Australia. Our hero was also possibly the first law enforcement officer in history to make use of the special talents of an Aboriginal tracker.

According to the *Sydney Gazette* on 21 July 1810:

> Early on Saturday morning last several armed ruffians broke into the house of Richard Jenner, at Kissing Point, which they plundered, after exercising much violence towards the wife of Jenner and a man servant; both whom they left bound in the house.—Information being shortly after made to Mr. Squires, district constable, he used every exertion to discover the perpetrators, but no discovery was made till Monday, when assisted by the native, young Bundle, a footstep was traced by the marks of two prominent nails in the sole of a shoe, which was found shortly after in a neighbouring hut, the owner of which . . . said he had lent his shoes on the previous Friday night to a man of the name of Kean, a labourer at Lane Cove. Mr. Squires, attended by the man and woman, went thither, and from the description given by them challenged Kean as being one of the persons; and as soon as seen by Mrs. Jenner he was immediately recognized as such. Another labourer, named McHugh, was apprehended at the same time; and a third, whose name was Wright, has since been secured . . . The three are consequently in custody.

All three were sentenced to be flogged. McHugh served two years hard labour, and Kean and Wright served one year each.

By far the most amusing, and ironical, report on the exploits of Constable Squire in the *Gazette* can be found in the edition dated 29 January 1805, in which the reporter, obviously unaware of the truth about the constable's background, gives a light-hearted report of his apprehension of two homeless men, referred to by the reporter as 'a couple of modern Egyptians' (meaning gypsies) who:

> ... were pursued on Thursday by J. Squires, resident constable at Kissing Point, on vehement suspicion of sheep stealing one, we hear, had the luck to be apprehended but as in all countries wherein this Mercurial race are tolerated they usurp a right of now and then selecting a fat wether from a flock, the delinquent may incline to defend himself upon a plea of privilege founded in ancient custom. The offence was committed within the above district, and the animal made choice of devoured in the woods by night. It is not altogether improbable, that predators of the above description are more destructive to the shepherd's charge than the whole host combined of native dogs and reptiles.

There is no further record to tell us whether or not the one 'modern Egyptian' who was caught, having devoured the evidence 'in the woods by night' before being apprehended, was ever sent to trial. Had the intrepid reporter from the *Sydney Gazette* had even the vaguest clue that the arresting constable was himself one of 'this Mercurial race', it might have occurred to him to ponder whether the case presented against the miscreant was rather weak.

James Squire was a very canny businessman with a gypsy's nose for horse-trading, but what I like about him is his egalitarian spirit and support of the underdog, which I have no doubt came from his gypsy background. He set up a credit union for emancipated convicts and helped many less fortunate than himself. He assisted many with financial backing to work honestly and set up small businesses once they received their ticket of leave.

He was also a friend to Aboriginal people and especially to Bennelong, who was befriended by Governor Phillip and had been to Britain and back. When Bennelong fell on hard times later in life, he spent much of his time on Squire's farm and he was buried there, with a memorial erected by James Squire.

There is ample evidence to show that James Squire's property at Kissing Point was a haven for Aboriginal people, who saw it as a safe refuge as their tribal lands were taken from them and their way of life destroyed. In researching his account of the life of Nanberry, the Aboriginal boy who was taken in and raised by Surgeon John White, after his family were wiped out in the smallpox epidemic of 1789, historian Keith White found conclusive evidence that corroborees and ritual fights, which were used to settle tribal arguments, were held on Squire's property at Kissing Point. Bennelong and his last wife were buried there and Nanberry, having been mortally wounded in a ritual fight in 1821, requested to be buried there also.

In 1791 James had begun a relationship with 32-year-old convict Elizabeth Mason, who arrived in Sydney in July of that year on the convict transport *Mary Ann* to serve seven years for stealing a tablecloth, two sheets, two waistcoats, a silver spoon, and some pillowcases and handkerchiefs.

The cunning gypsy arranged to have her assigned as his live-in convict servant, and they had seven children together. What seems odd and strangely touching is that three of their children were given the same names as Squire's legal wife and two of the children he had left behind in London.

Elizabeth died in 1809, aged 50, four years after giving birth to the last of their children, a daughter named Ann. After Elizabeth's death, James lived with his housekeeper Lucy Harding and they moved to a house in Castlereagh Street in Sydney in 1816.

When James Squire died, aged 67, in 1822, his funeral was the largest ever seen in the colony up to that time. His friend, the noted artist (and forger) Joseph Lycett, said of him, 'Had he been less liberal, he might have died more wealthy; but his assistance always accompanied his advice to the poor and unfortunate, and his name will long be pronounced with veneration by the grateful objects of his liberality.'

After Squire's death the brewery was carried on by his son James until his death on 7 March 1826, aged 29. It was then closed for a time but reopened in 1828 by Squire's son-in-law, Thomas Charles Farnell, a free settler who had married Ann, the youngest of Squire's children. Their son, the grandson of a gypsy thief and convict, proudly bore the name James Squire Farnell—and he was the premier of New South Wales in 1877 and 1878.

12

THE 'IMPRESSED' MARINER

THE PRESS GANG

Until the Battle of Waterloo in 1815, Britain had been at war with France almost constantly since 1793—the two nations were actually at war somewhere on the globe for 46 of the 70 years from 1745 to 1815! Consequently, the huge Royal Navy needed massive manpower to maintain control of the seas. This was achieved by 'impressing'—basically kidnapping—free men and forcing them to serve in the navy.

General attitudes to human rights and justice were very different then to those of today. Slavery was still legal, and flogging sailors was deemed an essential part of running a sailing ship; the 'cat-o-nine-tails' was not prohibited by law until the 1860s. (And it's hard to believe that caning or birching sailors was still legal in the Royal Navy in World War II.) These punishments were decided 'ad hoc' by officers—there were no trials or procedures necessary. Times were tough.

Half of the 120,000 men serving in the Royal Navy at the Battle of Trafalgar in 1805 had been impressed. The practice was so rife that, in 1812, the United States declared war on Britain partly due to the fact that American sailors were being impressed into the Royal Navy.

Official recruiting parties from the navy's 'impress service', or 'press gangs' as they were known, did not only prey on drunken sailors leaving dockside clubs, as we have seen portrayed in movies and novels of colourful adventures at sea; they were known to meet merchant ships as they docked at their home ports, and to take crew members before they could get ashore.

The majority of the merchant seaman impressed into the Royal Navy were, however, taken from merchant ships at sea, just off the coast, as they returned to port. This was a common practice and was done by individual warships, sometimes stationed along the coast for the purpose, rather than by the impress service ashore. It was actually a legal practice, so long as the navy replaced the man they took. Royal Naval captains used this system to improve the quality of their crew, by taking the best sailors from merchant ships and replacing them with troublesome, alcoholic or inexperienced crew members from their own ships. Another common practice was for trusted volunteers from Royal Naval ships to act as 'temporary substitutes' then desert as soon as the merchant ship docked, and return to their navy ship.

There was much resistance to the system of impressment. In 1740, a British merchant ship fired on a Royal Navy ship that was attempting to impress its crew. The British East India Company, a very powerful organisation which had a monopoly on British overseas trade in Asia, made official protests, as many of its sailors returning home from long voyages, often of several years duration, were taken by the Royal Navy and not seen by their families for at least another two years. This led to a system of 'protection', where men who were exempt from impressment were issued with a medallion to be carried at all times. The medallion could be shown to a press gang in order to avoid being taken. When the Royal Navy was desperately short of men or engaged in a war, however, a 'hot press' could be ordered, which meant the medallion offered no protection.

Impressment was harshly enforced during the 18th century by Acts of parliament passed in 1703, 1705, 1740 and 1779. From 1793 to 1815 an official impress service operated in British coastal towns. The impress officer would arrive in town and set up his headquarters in a dockside pub. He would use his 'gang', often made up of Royal Navy sailors on leave, or those who had retired from the navy, to 'recruit' the local seamen by force. As these gangs were often from other parts of the country, regional rivalry added an extra spice to the opposition of the practice.

Impressment, and press gangs, were very unpopular with the British public, especially in coastal ports where families depended on the merchant shipping trade to survive. The coal trade especially suffered from lack of able crewmen, which led to a rise in wages. Local officials often acted against the system, and were even known to imprison officers from the impress service.

It was also not unknown for local groups to organise and oppose the impress service by force of arms. This often gave the Crown the excuse of 'civil disobedience' and led to the army being sent in to assist the impress service.

This had actually happened in North Shields in 1793. A 'new wave' of impressment began that year, which led to a group of men from the ship-building and port towns of Newcastle, Sunderland and North Shields deciding to take action against the practice. They overpowered the press gang in North Shields and, in a show of contempt, removed gang members' jackets, turned them inside out, and forced the men out of town wearing their jackets reversed—to show they were 'turncoats', despised as traitors by all decent, seafaring men.

Several months later the inevitable reprisal was put into action. An army regiment was sent from Tynemouth and formed a military cordon around the town of North Shields. Then the press gangs moved in—and took away more than 250 able-bodied men.

The need for such harsh measures to ensure sufficient men to keep the Royal Navy afloat during the lead-up to the Napoleonic Wars is, perhaps, best illustrated by a report from Lord Nelson to the admiralty in 1803, which indicated that at least 42,000 men had deserted from the navy in the previous decade.

William Walker was just one of the countless sailors impressed into the Royal Navy, but that was only the beginning of his lifetime of adventures at sea. His exploits were ultimately so numerous and amazing that he needed seven identities to manage them all!

WILLIAM WALKER

Come all you sons of Freedom, a chorus join with me,
I'll sing a song of heroes and glorious liberty.
Of lads condemned from England upon Van Diemen's Shore,
Their Country, friends and parents, to never see them more.

'The Cyprus Brig', Frank McNamara ('Frank the Poet')

William Walker's own accounts of such things as his birthplace, age, name and past history were many and varied and frequently altered for convenience, or to hide evidence of his criminal activities. He was born in 1792, at either Sunderland or 12 kilometres away at North Shields. What is certain is that, from his early teens he worked on the colliers, boats that sailed out of the northern ports, providing London with coal and braving the treacherous North Sea to work at the Baltic trade in timber and other basic materials. It is likely that he was apprenticed as a seaman from the age of thirteen or fourteen, and learned the skills required to operate a sea-going sailing vessel and to navigate using a compass, sextant and the night sky. These skills, learned early in his life, would become second nature to him, making him a very valuable commodity on any sailing ship—and lead him into adventures and ordeals beyond the wildest imaginings of ordinary people.

Sometime around 1812, when Walker was about twenty, he was impressed into the Royal Navy. To understand William Walker's life, and his 'criminal behaviour', we need to acknowledge how impressment could change the lives of men like him. Walker served with the Royal Navy until the Napoleonic Wars ended in 1815.

Immediately after the war he secured a position as master of the trading brig *Liberty*, which shows what a respected sailor Walker was—certainly good enough to be offered a responsible position, probably by a shipping company that knew him before the war. A year later he married Susan Addison, set up home in Sunderland and left the *Liberty* to take a position as mate on a larger vessel, the *Florida*.

In early 1820 the *Florida* was wrecked in the Mediterranean and William, now a father of three, found himself unemployed. The Depression that followed the war showed no sign of ending. In fact, it was getting worse. Many thousands were out of work and the harsh Corn Laws, favouring the rich landowners who controlled the British parliament, had raised the cost of living, restricted British economic growth and reduced the disposable income of workers. With the Industrial Revolution underway, machinery was taking over traditional jobs—wages fell, taxation rose and an economic crisis developed.

William managed to find part-time work as a rigger in the shipyards but the amount he made was insufficient to feed a family of five. Working on the docks did, however, provide opportunities for theft and, on 22 October 1820, he was caught in possession of household goods—a tea canister, a quilt, two blankets and a curtain. He was arrested and imprisoned in Durham Gaol awaiting trial. As Durham Quarter Sessions were not due until January 1821, Walker, who had not been tried, spent three months in a prison where inmates were forced to pay for food and straw to sleep on, work on the treadmill and could be flogged for misdemeanours.

At his trial Walker at first pleaded not guilty but, after the jury valued the stolen goods at 10 pence, he changed his plea to guilty. This was because the British court system at the time enabled a jury to decide the value of stolen goods, and if the goods were valued at more than one shilling then the theft was one of the 222 crimes punishable by hanging.

Walker was sentenced to seven years transportation 'to parts beyond the sea', but it would be a while before he was finally transported. As the prisons were full to overflowing, old or unseaworthy warships and merchant ships served as extra prisons along the coasts and rivers of Britain and as reception centres for those awaiting transportation. He was to be held in the hulks on the Thames until a convict ship was leaving for what was then known as 'Botany Bay'.

William and at least one other prisoner were sent to London on the regular passenger and mail service, aboard the *Merchant Packet,* from Sunderland. As this vessel was not equipped to carry felons, the prisoners were confined in the forecastle storage. It seems that the seaman quickly discovered two things to his advantage. One was that there were a number of cork floats stored in their temporary prison, some of which he stuffed into his clothing. The other thing he quickly realised was that a fellow prisoner, a man named Dormer, was quite deranged and suicidal. As the ship made its way along the Suffolk coast to London, he evidently convinced Mr Dormer to jump overboard. The poor fellow did so and drowned within sight of the ship, while Walker cunningly used the diversion to slip over the other side and stay afloat using the cork he had found.

He managed to survive in the cold water for five hours and was miraculously picked up by another ship bound for London where he was subsequently put ashore. He explained his predicament, obviously rather convincingly, by claiming he was a sailor who had fallen from the rigging.

After earning some money around the London docks by finding work as a rigger, Walker grew a beard, called himself 'William Brown' and returned to Sunderland as a crewman on a collier, apparently determined not to desert his family. In spite of the beard, however, he was recognised as he approached Sunderland and arrested, tried in the very same court (this time at the April Quarterly Assizes) and convicted of 'being found at large before the expiration of his sentence'. Rather conveniently, there was a batch of convicts about to be sent to London from Durham via Newcastle and the judge thought it easiest to order Walker to complete his original sentence so he could join the group. He was again sent to the hulks moored at Woolwich on the Thames, to await transportation to Van Diemen's Land.

This time William was delivered safely and spent four months living in degradation and squalor aboard the hulk *Justitia* at Woolwich, along with about 480 other convicts. Prisoners were rowed ashore in chain gangs each day to work daylight hours in the naval shipyards. Three years previously, the reforming politician Henry Grey Bennet had inspected the *Justitia* and declared it 'unfit for any purpose of rational punishment'. Even those serving relatively short prison terms, and not sentenced to transportation, often volunteered to be sent 'beyond the sea' to avoid living on the hulks, where death rates from disease or violence were around 30 to 40 per cent.

In the second week of June 1821, the square-rigged three-masted merchant ship *Malabar,* which had been chartered for the task of transportation, began loading 172 convicts from the *Justitia* for a passage to Hobart Town. This was a procedure that was to occur similarly in British ports more than 800 times between 1788 and 1860, for voyages to various colonial destinations in Australia. The *Malabar* alone made ten such voyages in her working lifetime. On this occasion she sailed on 21 June and reached Hobart after a relatively uneventful 121 days at sea. Eight other convict transports arrived in Hobart Town that same year.

Upon their arrival the convicts were addressed by Lieutenant-Governor William Sorell (*Lieutenant*-Governor because Van Diemen's Land was still part of New South Wales until 1825) and inspected and questioned by Superintendent of Police and Chief Magistrate Adolarius William Henry Humphrey.

Humphrey was so renowned for his cruelty to convicts that Governor Macquarie at first refused to make him a magistrate, and in 1812 escaped convict William Howe and his bushranger gang had risked a special raid on his property to burn his farm buildings and ransack his house. By 1821 Humphrey was the second most powerful man in the colony.

He described William Walker as '29 years of age 5' 8¾" with blue eyes, brown hair and scars on his nose and chin—occupation mariner'.

We know nothing about Walker's life for the next eight months, there were no convict barracks and convicts were allowed to find board and lodging in the town, for which they were provided 5 shillings a week. They could also take outside work cutting firewood and fetching water and save the 5 shillings by building shelters and providing for their own food. This seems a lenient system, but punishment for attempts to escape were brutal: floggings or banishment to the most feared settlement of Macquarie Harbour, on the wild uninhabited west coast, isolated and surrounded by impenetrable forests, mountains and the raging Southern Ocean. Sorell had established a convict settlement on Sarah Island, in Macquarie Harbour, as 'a place of rigid penal constraint and coercion', because he needed some threat worse than flogging to make convicts hesitate before re-offending. William Walker would be sentenced to serve time on Sarah Island three times—he would arrive there only once.

Because of his stated profession, it is likely that William worked with boats and had relatively easy access to the river, because in early 1822, he and six other convicts stole a schooner—belonging to either influential grazier and merchant Anthony Kemp, or merchant, pastoralist and magistrate Edward Lord (reports vary)—from the Derwent River and escaped.

On 8 March 1822 the *Sydney Gazette* reported the dire news that a whaling vessel, the *Perseverance,* had been wrecked in 'Bass's Streights' but survivors in a whaleboat had landed at the Five Islands near modern-day Port Kembla, and made their way to Appin, some 50 kilometres northwest:

> Mr. Smith, of Appin, nephew of Charles Throsby, Esq. arrived in Sydney on Wednesday with unpleasant tidings. The following are the outlines of what comes within our knowledge :—The whaler Perseverance, Captain Dixon, of and from the port of London, has been very recently wrecked on some of the islands in Bass's Streights. Five boats, containing the captain, officers, and crew, left the wreck for this port ; one of which has providentially succeeded in gaining the Five Islands ; from whence three men peregrinated to Appin, where they were benevolently and hospitably received, having left behind with the boat two of their companions, who were too fatigued to travel. Two boats

> are strongly suspected to have perished, from the circumstance of their separation in a storm. The other two may be expected in Sydney Cove every hour. Two or three of the crew, we learn, were lost at the wreck. We shall exert ourselves to obtain a faithful account of the lamentable event.

The two survivors who arrived at Appin, calling themselves John Shields and William Anderson, were actually William Walker and his old friend from the *Malabar*, John Wilkinson. A week later the truth was being unravelled by some intrepid reporter in the *Sydney Gazette:*

> Last week we promised to exert ourselves in the procurance of further information relative to the reported loss of the Perseverance whaler. Such intelligence has been obtained by the Superintendent of Police these last few days as to set the matter of the wreck of the Perseverance quite at rest; the whole of which turns out to be a fabricated story.
>
> The two men, who reported themselves as being part of the crew of the boat, are now in custody. They say that their names are, John Shields and Wm Anderson. The following is the statement now given:—Shields and Anderson, with five others, now at large in the Colony, seized the pilot's boat in the Derwent River, and then succeeded in boarding and cutting out a small schooner belonging to Edward Lord, Esq. at Hobart Town, laden with sundries. They speedily put to sea, bearing away for the coast of New Holland.
>
> Off the Five Islands they were seen, for a considerable time, throwing articles overboard, by the men variously employed in that district; and the vessel was also observed to steer direct for the rocks, on which she soon was dashed to pieces. Shields and Anderson then proceeded to Appin, and gave the account reported in our last. The others have hitherto successfully eluded the adroitness of our Police; but the measures adopted for their speedy apprehension cannot very long be rendered abortive. What gave rise to suspicion in the first instance upon this transaction was, that the pirates in custody grossly prevaricated in their statements, and upon examining them apart, each had his own tale, so that at length confusion so possessed their minds, that the fact itself became reluctantly and necessarily disclosed.

The two men were taken into custody by John Redman, the chief constable and town gaoler of Sydney (who had arrived as a convict serving a fourteen-year sentence in 1790), and he reported to the Colonial Secretary Frederick Goulburn that the men were suspected of being part of the gang that stole the schooner from the Derwent River.

Goulburn sent descriptions of the two men to Lieutenant-Governor Sorell in June and received confirmation in August that they were, indeed, Walker and Wilkinson.

The brig *Deveron* was to leave Sydney on 22 September, carrying a detachment of the 48th Regiment to Hobart, so the two escapees were placed on board to return to face the consequences of their piracy.

The *Deveron* was almost wrecked in a huge storm on the way back to Hobart and attempted to take refuge in Adventure Bay, on the east coast of Bruny Island, where mountainous seas pounded the vessel for three days and three anchors were lost as the captain attempted to hold the vessel fast.

When the main topmast broke away and fouled the rigging, the boatswain attempted to free the broken spars and was swept away and drowned. In attempting to save him, the captain, William Wilson, was also swept overboard but was able to regain the ship.

It was William Walker who saved the day, by climbing along the broken mast as it hung over the side of the ship in the raging storm to cut away the fouled section with an axe. Captain Wilson then cut the remaining anchor cable, worked the vessel clear of the bay and made a run for Hobart in the teeth of the storm. They arrived two days later.

On 5 October the two men were tried by magistrate Reverend Robert Knopwood, who was not noted for his Christian kindness when it came to dealing with convicts. Knopwood had also presided when another three of the gang that stole the schooner were tried in April. They were sentenced to 150 lashes and banishment to Sarah Island for the rest of their sentences.

By the time Walker and Wilkinson were being tried, two of the men, Matthew Travers and Robert Greenhill, had already escaped and headed into the wilderness with five others, one of whom was the infamous Alexander Pearce, who had subsequently killed and eaten his six companions, including Travers and Greenhill. When Pearce was recaptured and confessed his cannibalism to Knopwood, the magistrate refused to believe his story, assuming he was lying to protect his fellow escapees, who were still at large. Pearce was returned to Sarah Island, escaped again a year later with another man and was apprehended alone, carrying lumps of human flesh in his pockets. Pearce was hanged at the Hobart Town Gaol on 19 July 1824, but immortalised as the character Matthew Gabbett in Marcus Clarke's melodramatic popular novel, *For the Term of His Natural Life,* in which the convict transport *Malabar* also features.

Knopwood repeated the sentence he had given to the other three 'pirates'—Walker and Wilkinson were to receive 150 lashes each and sentenced to be sent to Sarah Island.

However, William Walker did not go to Sarah Island. Perhaps this was due to his heroism on the *Deveron*. It is possible he was also spared the 150 lashes, we don't know, but we do know his transfer to Macquarie Harbour was cancelled. Apparently, Walker was a model prisoner for the next eight months in Hobart, at least there is no mention of him in any convict documentation.

To understand what happened next, we need to have some insight into the difficulties of keeping convicts in Hobart. Here is a part of a despatch from Lieutenant-Governor Sorell to Governor Macquarie in 1818, regarding the not uncommon practice among visiting ship's captains of adding suitable convicts to their crews. Experienced mariners were a valuable commodity on any sailing ship:

> Such is the facility which the extensive shores of this port offer, if a master be determined to carry off men, that it is next to impossible to prevent him.

In spite of measures such as a £200 bond for all ships entering Hobart, a £500 fine and two years imprisonment for carrying off convicts, and the precaution of sealing the holds of departing vessels and smoking them with brimstone (burning sulphur) to drive out stowaways, the practice continued to be a problem in Hobart until transportation ended in 1853.

Thus it was that when the *Deveron* departed Hobart, on 6 June 1823, she carried not only a cargo of '100,000 lbs weight of wool, several thousand sealskins and some Huon pine', as reported by the

Hobart Town Gazette and Van Diemen's Land Advertiser, but also eight escaped convicts, including that rather useful mariner, William Walker. Perhaps the *Deveron*'s Captain Wilson was repaying Walker's bravery and usefulness during that awful experience in Adventure Bay nine months previously, which had helped to save his ship.

The *Deveron* returned to England via Rio de Janeiro, and so did William Walker.

William was reunited with his wife and two surviving children. They moved to London and set up home in Bermondsey, on the south bank of the Thames near the dockyards, where William could obtain work as a mariner. He made at least one voyage on a ship working the Baltic trade and worked as a rigger, and later at the less skilled occupation of loading ships. At first, he used his old alias, 'Brown', but when he moved his family to the seedy district of Soho, he started to call himself 'William Swallow'.

Loading and unloading ships gave ample opportunity for pilfering. Men engaged in this occupation, usually on a casual basis, wore special coats with inside pockets and even special trousers with pockets inside the leg where small items stolen could be secreted.

Other opportunities for thieving from the docks came at night. This was known as 'tier ranging', as the various trading ships were moored in 'tiers' with wharves arranged like the branches of a tree (what we would today call a marina). Tier rangers would sometimes work in collusion with corrupt nightwatchmen, stealing canvas, rope, tools and other shipping equipment and selling it to dishonest ships' chandlers to be resold.

It seems that 'William Swallow' became an habitual criminal and petty thief in the six years he spent in London. *The Times* newspaper described him as 'being frequently apprehended by the Thames police and repeatedly fined and imprisoned for robbing vessels' and 'well known at all the London police-offices'.

It appears that, along with the change of address and name, there was also a change in William's criminal activities for, on 28 July 1828, he pleaded not guilty to a charge of house-breaking. He defended himself in court with an eloquent speech, in which he said that he had been walking with his wife to her place of work one morning, when he found the goods lying on the street. Of course, nobody believed a word of it and he was sentenced to death.

On appeal the sentence was reduced to transportation and William was sentenced to be held on the hulk *Dolphin* awaiting transportation to Van Diemen's Land, which must have filled him with a dreadful sense of foreboding. The thought of what was to come, when his true identity was realised, was enough to provoke him to attempt to escape from prison before being transferred to the *Dolphin.* When the attempt failed, his prison report noted, 'in prison before, character and connexions bad'.

On 1 December 1828 the convict transport *Georgiana,* carrying 170 convicted felons, left the Thames and anchored on 'The Downs', off the Kentish coast, waiting for a favourable wind to take her south. When a southerly gale set in, the vessel was almost wrecked and survived two days of horrific weather so bad that the captain was obliged to put into Plymouth where it took twelve days to repair the ship.

Two days of howling winds and massive waves crashing over the deck and spilling into the hold where the convicts were chained may not have bothered an experienced mariner like William Walker too much. It would, however, have no doubt terrified many of the other 169 prisoners, especially the 60 young boys with an average age of twelve, mostly the junior members of house-breaking gangs who were being transported as convicts on the *Georgiana.*

After the false start the *Georgiana* made excellent time of just 117 days to Hobart, completing the journey on 18 April 1829, with a brief stopover at Cape Town. Three convicts died on the voyage, all from diseases they had contracted in the hulks.

In Hobart there was now a governor, Colonel George Arthur, as Van Diemen's Land had become a separate colony in 1825. There was also a new system of dealing with arrivals. The 'muster master' boarded the ship as it neared the port and was given the history of each man. He would have learned William Swallow's criminal record but was also told he had mended sails on the voyage and was recorded as being 'a good man' while at sea by the surgeon-superintendent on the *Georgiana,* Dr Conway.

Much to his relief, our hero was not recognised as William Walker when the convicts disembarked three day later, but he knew it was only a matter of time. The penalty for 'being at large before the expiration of a sentence' was death. He had escaped that penalty once before. He had to escape again before he was recognised.

On the recommendation of Dr Conway and Captain Thompson of the *Georgiana*, William was made coxswain of the guard boat. After a month of that work he was sent back aboard the *Georgiana* to work as a sail-maker. Having completed her assignment to carry convicts to Hobart, the ship had been chartered to carry a load of potatoes, wheat and onions to Sydney.

After the final inspection for stowaways, the ship's mate helped William to hide in among the cargo, but the departure was delayed and a second inspection revealed his hiding place. He was charged with 'absconding from the public works with the intention of escaping' and sentenced to 50 lashes and transportation to Sarah Island.

Evidently, he managed to avoid the lashes by claiming he had fallen asleep while loading the cargo. He possibly might have avoided Sarah Island, too, except that around this time someone recognised him as William Walker. The official final 'distribution list' from the *Georgiana* (detailing what happened to those transported aboard her—dated 30 May 1829) notes that two convicts were gaoled for 'being runaways returned for a second sentence'. Almost certainly the two were William Walker and a convict who was to play a part in later events in Walker's life, George James 'Jim' Jones. Jones was 29 years old and an ex-mariner, like Walker. His arms were heavily tattooed, which may have led to him being recognised when he escaped and returned to Britain after being transported to Sydney in 1822. Both Jones and Walker were spared the death penalty and sentenced instead to Sarah Island, Walker for a second time.

Knowing that there was little chance of escaping and surviving once there, the two men turned their minds to escaping in transit. The greatest adventure of Walker's truly amazing life was about to begin.

The vessel used to convey supplies, convicts and military personnel from Hobart to Macquarie Harbour was the 110-ton, two-masted government brig, *Cyprus*. In a strange twist of fate, she hailed from the same place as William Walker, having been built in Sunderland in 1816. Ten years later she had been purchased by the colonial government of Van Diemen's Land, to replace an ageing similar vessel, the *Duke of York*.

The *Cyprus* was 22 metres long and 7 metres wide. She was in good condition and had been sheathed with copper below the waterline to prevent marine growth, which slowed the speed of sea-going vessels and led to costly maintenance. Purchased at a cost of £1700 by the colonial government in 1826, she was a good investment. If the *Cyprus* were to be lost, it would cause great inconvenience to the growing colony. That particular fact, however, meant little to Walker, Jones and certain other convicts being transported to Macquarie Harbour.

There are quite a few different versions of the story of the seizure and theft of the *Cyprus*. Let us begin with the most likely scenario.

The crew of the *Cyprus* consisted of thirteen men: the captain, first mate, second mate and ten sailors, four of whom were convicts 'of good character'. Her cargo consisted of three months supplies for the Macquarie Harbour prison (flour, beef, pork, tea, soap, rum, wine, live sheep and fowls) and 33 convicts who had been sentenced to continue their punishment in that most inhospitable of all penal settlements.

In addition, on this voyage, the ship carried a sergeant and nine privates of the 63rd Regiment, under the command of Lieutenant Carew. Their job was to guard the convicts and then take up duty as prison guards at Macquarie Harbour. Assistant surgeon Walter Williams was also on board, in charge of convict welfare, as were a clerk in charge of cargo, Lieutenant Carew's wife and two children, two soldiers' wives and another child.

The voyage from Hobart to Macquarie Harbour would normally take four to five days but bad weather was common and once, in 1826, it had taken 53 days to complete the journey. On this occasion, the vessel departed on 21 July and immediately ran into bad winter weather. As was usual in such circumstances, the *Cyprus* took refuge in Recherche Bay, near the very bottom of the island of Van Diemen's Land. Even in this relatively sheltered bay, the ship lost two anchors and cables, and even the windlass, which forced it to return to Hobart.

Another reason to return was the fact that the captain became so ill that he could no longer take command of the vessel. The only replacement was a 63-year-old superannuated ship's captain named Robert Harrison who is described as having 'increasing infirmities and a fondness for drink'. The repairs to the *Cyprus* took sixteen days, during which time the 33 convicts remained chained below decks. By the time the ship departed once more, on 5 August, under the command of Captain Harrison, there had been ample time for Walker and Jones to prepare a desperate escape plan.

A brief description of some of the likely accomplices, secretly recruited into the plot by Walker and Jones, may give us a clearer picture of the type of men who were chained below the decks of the *Cyprus* brig.

Leslie Ferguson, aged 28, a labourer from Carrickfergus in Ireland was serving life for horse stealing. Since his original sentence, he had received a total of 375 lashes—for absconding, stealing, being an accomplice to fraud and receiving stolen goods.

James Camm, a labourer from Nottingham, aged 53, had received 200 lashes for assaulting another convict and for beating his wife and another man while on a ticket of leave. He had attempted to escape on seven occasions, five of them while working on a road gang.

Matthew Pennell, another labourer, aged 23, from Middlesex, originally sentenced to seven years for stealing, was now serving life for 'being at large before the expiration of his sentence' and for being a member of a gang accused of stealing £1200 from the colony's treasury.

William Brown, a 37-year-old mariner from County Wicklow, was serving life for burglary. He had attempted to escape three times, had received a total of 700 lashes, and had already served two terms at Macquarie Harbour.

Robert McGuire, a farm labourer from Ireland, aged 37, was originally serving seven years for theft but was one of a gang of seven men originally sentenced to death for another theft in May 1829. He was on his way to Macquarie Harbour for life with fellow gang members Michael Herring and William Templeman. The other four had been hanged.

George James Davis was a well-educated engraver from London, sentenced to seven years for petty larceny. For attempting to escape and stealing, he was sentenced to serve a further fourteen years at Macquarie Harbour. Davis was the only one of the group not facing a life sentence on Sarah Island.

On the second attempt to convey its cargo to Macquarie Harbour, the *Cyprus* encountered favourable weather until it neared the southern tip of the island. At that point a fierce westerly gale set in, against which it was impossible to make headway. Once again, the *Cyprus* sought refuge from the storm in Recherche Bay and remained anchored up in the relatively calm conditions, waiting for the wind to change. Captain Harrison made good use of the time and was able to retrieve the two anchors the ship had lost on its previous visit to the bay.

Within several days of the ship's second visit to the bay that winter, William Walker either genuinely suffered or feigned an attack of abdominal pain, which Dr Williams diagnosed as a urinary tract infection. If it was merely a ruse, part of the plan to take over the ship, Walker paid a high price for the pretence, as Dr Williams performed an abdominal operation with a scalpel and the patient was placed in the forecastle to recover. His chains had already been removed so that he could help the crew to manage the ship during the storm.

The normal procedure was for the convicts to be allowed on deck to exercise five at a time, but there is evidence that this rule was relaxed while the ship rode anchor in the bay. Discipline among soldiers was also noted to be rather lax and their muskets remained unloaded. It seems also that Captain Harrison took to drinking in his cabin.

Late in the afternoon on 14 August, Lieutenant Carew, Dr Williams and John Burn, the first mate, took the longboat to go fishing. They took one of the soldiers and a convict, named John Pobjoy, ostensibly to row the boat. Both William Walker and John Pobjoy had been working as part of the crew while the *Cyprus* was anchored up in Recherche Bay. Pobjoy would play an important part in the events that were to follow but there are several contradictions regarding his actual role in the affair, which involve his loyalty, intentions and even the primary reason he was in the longboat to begin with.

There are different versions of what happened next.

One version says security was lax and, when Lieutenant Carew and Dr Williams went fishing in the longboat with Pobjoy, their negligence allowed the mutiny to unfold. Another version has it that the fishing trip was a ploy to enable Pobjoy to inform Carew and Williams that a plot was afoot against the ship by Walker and some others. A third version suggests that Pobjoy was part of the plot and suggested the fishing trip in order to remove Carew, Williams and Burn from the vessel, thus facilitating the piracy.

What is obvious is that there were now three less authority figures aboard the *Cyprus*. This provided the gang of would-be pirates with the perfect opportunity to put their plans into action.

Privates Scully, Devine and Wallace were on sentry duty guarding the hatchway, deck and quarterdeck during the absence of the fishing party. In spite of Carew's rule that only five unchained convicts could exercise on deck at any one time, there were at least eight unchained felons on deck and six of them were Leslie Ferguson, James Camm, Matthew Pennell, Robert McGuire, Michael Herring and George Davis.

When the convicts' behaviour became disorderly, described as 'riotous' in a later court hearing, Private Scully ordered them to go below but they refused, stating that they were not feeling well and Carew had given them permission to come up for fresh air. While Scully was arguing the point, McGuire crept upon him from behind and knocked him out with a piece of wood. Several of the convicts also rushed at Wallace, who fled below leaving his musket behind. On the quarterdeck Private James Devine saw the attack begin but, before he could prime his musket, Ferguson, Herring and another convict Watts rushed at him and beat him unconscious with an axe handle.

As soon as this was done, Camm and several others closed the hatchway over the soldiers' quarters and piled the hen coops and one of the recovered anchors on top of the hatch, effectively imprisoning the rest of the soldiers below deck.

During this process, Captain Harrison appeared on deck and was knocked out, or at least knocked down, with a large scrubbing brush. Private Scully came to and rushed at the nearest of the convicts, only to be knocked out again with a belaying pin.

Then the remaining prisoners were freed and their chains removed with hammers and chisels from the ship's store.

Realising they were trapped, the soldiers fired up through the decks, but the convicts threatened to pour boiling water and pitch down on them unless they ceased firing and told the soldiers they would not be harmed if they surrendered their weapons. After making a futile attempt to break through into the main cabin, the soldiers realised resistance was useless, and surrendered.

On hearing the shots, the fishing party returned to the *Cyprus.* When Lieutenant Carew made an attempt to board the vessel, he was met with the sight of ten armed convicts leaning over the side. Matthew Pennell aimed a musket at Carew and attempted to fire twice, but the weapon did not discharge. Fearing for his family's safety, Carew complied with the convicts' directions.

All passengers and crew, and any convicts unwilling to take part in the plan, were taken ashore in the longboat with rations. This took five trips and each group was landed on a different part of the shoreline to prevent them joining up and formulating any plan that might foil the success of the escape plot.

Interestingly, the last to leave the ship was Pobjoy, who claimed he dived overboard as the *Cyprus* set sail and swam ashore. At another time he claimed to have slipped ashore with one of the groups landed from the longboat.

Apart from two privates who were knocked on the head at the beginning of the takeover, no one was badly hurt and the *Cyprus* sailed off with eighteen men aboard, leaving 44 people marooned on the beach at Recherche Bay, from whence there were no roads back to Hobart, just 120 kilometres of unexplored wilderness or 150 kilometres of rocky coastline.

What happened to those left onshore is another story altogether. As we are concerned with the story of William Walker and his pirate crew of seventeen convicts, a brief summary will have to suffice.

Some bark shelters were built and two convicts set out to walk back to Hobart along the coast. After swimming the Huon River, they encountered hostile Aborigines and fled without their clothes, swimming back across the river and returning to the others. Another five convicts then set off for Hobart, going inland through the bush. Meanwhile, a Welsh convict named Morgan constructed a coracle from canvas and wattle, made waterproof with wax and soap brought ashore with personal effects. Morgan and Pobjoy used the flimsy craft to cross the D'Entrecasteaux Channel to Partridge Island, where they finally found the ship *Orelia,* which they had attempted to signal a few days earlier as they saw it pass by as they trudged along the coast. The *Orelia* sent a boat to pick up those on the beach. Another boat from Hobart found the other five convicts a few days later.

Lieutenant Carew was court-martialled, found guilty of negligence and cashiered, but then pardoned and allowed to keep his commission. He later served with the regiment in India, fathered three more children and died in Ireland in 1847.

As John Pobjoy has a further part to play in the adventures of William Walker, let's take a brief look at his life story.

Like Walker, John Pobjoy was a mariner by trade sentenced to fourteen years transportation for stealing a horse worth £5. He arrived in Sydney in 1817 and his convict record notes that he was 'a notorious bad character' and he served terms of hard labour in the Newcastle coalmines twice and also in Hobart and Port Macquarie, before making an escape attempt in 1824, which led to him being sent to Sarah Island, in Macquarie Harbour. A change in behaviour, and experience as a sailor, saw him made coxswain of the pilot boat which was used to guide ships through the treacherous opening which led into the harbour.

By 1828 he was back in Hobart, assigned to the public works. Old habits, however, die hard and Pobjoy soon found himself back in court, charged with violently assaulting a sailor and attempting to steal his watch. As it was three months before the case came to trial, and the sailor had subsequently left the colony, Pobjoy was discharged. It was decided, however, that it was much better for him, and the town of Hobart, if he returned to his old position as coxswain of the pilot boat at Macquarie Harbour; when the mutiny occurred, he was returning on the *Cyprus* to complete his sentence there.

Pobjoy stood just 160 centimetres tall and his arms were covered with dozens of tattoos, which today would, no doubt, be the envy of many football players. Although I doubt if any football player's tattoos include the prayer 'From roaring guns and women's tongues, O Lord deliver me', which was one of several prayers adorning Pobjoy's arms, in among the mermaids, anchors, royal coat of arms, sun, moon and stars, Masonic symbols and the figure of Britannia.

For the part he played in the rescue of those abandoned at Recherche Bay, John Pobjoy received a full pardon and subsequently returned to London, where he was soon in trouble again—arrested and brought before the Thames Street magistrates for house-breaking. In court he used his self-proclaimed 'patriotic exploits' in Van Diemen's Land as character references to secure his acquittal. Before long, however, he again came to the notice of the police when he bashed the father of a woman he was 'courting'. And his role in the '*Cyprus* drama' was not yet played out.

Meanwhile, back on the *Cyprus,* the pirates knew full well that, if they were caught, they would be hanged. William Walker convinced his seventeen shipmates that there was not enough fresh water on board to sail directly to America. Also, although there was a compass, quadrant and sextant on board, the *Cyprus* carried no charts of the Pacific Ocean and was not equipped with a chronometer, which meant that calculating longitude would have to be done by the inaccurate method of 'dead reckoning'.

Considering all these facts, Walker had decided, prudently, to set sail for New Zealand.

A week later the *Cyprus* was anchored up in a secluded bay on the west coast of New Zealand's South Island (we are not sure which bay it was) and there she was transformed into an American trading ship, the *Friends of Boston.* Her hull was painted completely black and her distinctive figurehead, of a Scottish Highlander, was sawn off. Walker also forged a set of ships papers for the *Friends,* and a ship's log which showed her current voyage to have originated in Manila.

With a new identity the vessel headed north, entered Cook Strait and, on 22 August, sailed into Cloudy Bay, on the northern coast on New Zealand's South Island, and followed the coast 10 kilometres westward to a safe anchorage at Kakapo Bay, where they found Jack Guard's whaling station.

Jack was an ex-convict who had served his sentence of seven years for house-breaking in Sydney and then gone sealing in the southern islands of Cape Horn, become captain of a trading vessel and established two whaling stations in New Zealand, one at the bottom of the North Island and the other at Kakapo Bay, on the northern tip of the South Island.

Jack boarded the *Friends* and must have thought it odd that the crew of an American ship spoke with a variety of British accents and the ship's figurehead was missing, but he said nothing and the pirate crew spent the day fetching fresh water to the ship.

Later that day another ship, the sealing schooner *Elizabeth and Mary*, entered the bay. This vessel was returning from Campbell Island, some 680 kilometres south of the New Zealand mainland, where she had rescued survivors from the wreck of another sealing vessel, which had been lost close to the island in October 1828.

(Truth being stranger than fiction, the name of the wrecked vessel was the *Perseverance,* the same name that Walker and his old friend John Wilkinson had given to the imaginary wrecked whaling ship from which they claimed to be survivors, after their escape from captivity in 1822. Perhaps they knew this ship was whaling and sealing in the Southern Ocean in 1822 and hoped it would remain at sea long enough for their lie to go undiscovered until they could get away to sea themselves—we will never know but the coincidence of the ships' names seems remarkable if this is not the case.)

When Captain Worth, of the *Elizabeth and Mary*, sent his first mate across to the *Friends* to ask if they had any fish hooks to spare, a quantity of hooks was given, wrapped in newspaper, which on inspection was seen to have come from a three-week-old copy of the *Hobart Town Courier.*

It was not unknown for honest sea captains or others to apprehend and recapture runaway convicts. Three years previously 31 convicts had seized the government brig *Wellington* on a voyage from Sydney to Norfolk Island and had forced the crew to sail to New Zealand where the vessel was apprehended and attacked by two whaling ships which had fired upon her, freed the crew and returned the convicts to Sydney, where five of them were hanged.

Neither Jack Guard nor Captain Worth, however, made any attempt to apprehend the crew of the *Friends*, although they obviously had suspicions about the vessel's legitimacy. Jack Guard was more concerned with protecting his whaling station and avoiding trouble. The *Elizabeth and Mary*, at 70 tons, was a smaller unarmed vessel and had a precious cargo to protect.

One month later, on 24 September, the *Sydney Gazette* reported the return of the *Elizabeth and Mary*: 'From New Zealand and Macquarie Island, same day, the schooner Elizabeth and Mary (70 tons), Captain Worth. Lading, 18 tons of elephant oil, and 330 seal skins.' 'Elephant oil' was, of course, obtained from elephant seals.

Captain Worth had much to report: 'The brig Perseverance and schooner Hunter, both of this port, are totally lost, the former in October last, at Campbell's Island, and the latter on the 8th of June last, at Entry Island, Cooke's Straits. Both crews saved.'

The information he passed on regarding the *Friends* was also reported in the *Sydney Gazette* and, on 17 October, in the *Hobart Town Gazette*, which recorded the following:

> By the arrival of a vessel at Sydney from New Zealand we learn, that a brig had put in there for water called the Friends of Boston, bound ostensibly from Manilla to South America, but answering in all other respects to the description of the Cyprus. She was commanded, the account says, by a man named Walker, and the whole crew was in perfect order and discipline. The vessel had been fresh painted black, and had a complete set of ships papers filled up agreeably to their account of themselves. The mate of the Sydney vessel had requested the favour of some fish hooks from the strange brig, which were wrapped up in a piece of a Hobart town newspaper. There is no doubt but this was the Cyprus.

The *Hobart Town Gazette*, which had previously predicted that the escaped convicts would soon murder each other or be lost at sea in the Pacific without charts, was also hopeful that the *Cyprus* would 'in all likelihood have the luck to meet his Majesty's ship Success, which has gone cruising in that quarter'. The Royal Navy sloop, HMS *Success*, however, returned to Sydney in October without having sighted the stolen vessel, which by then was making its way east in bad weather towards the Chatham Islands.

The *Friends* had left Kakapo Bay with one more crew member, a man called John Wright who had been living at the whaling station for two years and was perhaps himself a runaway or ex-convict. A few days later, however, the crew was reduced to its original number when William Brown was lost overboard in bad weather and drowned.

William Walker's ship's log gives the lost man's name as John Brown, possibly because most of the convicts had by now chosen new names.

The Chatham Islands lie 800 kilometres to the east of New Zealand, on approximately the same latitude as the bottom of Tasmania. In 1829 the islands were inhabited by the Moriori people, a peace-loving subgroup of Maori/Polynesians who had arrived around 1500. They were few in number and had been joined on the islands by semi-permanent settlements of sealers and whalers since their discovery by Europeans in 1791.

It was here that the group of escaped convicts, having now become the competent crew of a stolen sea-going vessel, decided to play at being real pirates. Having landed in a sheltered bay on the main island, they proceeded to raid the Moriori village and then a sealers' camp, from which they took virtually anything of value. Encouraged by their success they then attempted to row up the river which flowed into the bay in order to raid another settlement. When their boats were swamped in the surf, however, they decided to end their piratical adventure and, considering themselves lucky to have escaped unscathed, returned to the comfort of their ship and set sail northeast for Tahiti.

Whether Tahiti was now the final destination, or merely another stepping stone on the way to America, is uncertain. Having no charts, they had to trust Walker's confidence in his own navigational skills to get them from one landfall to the next. So far he had successfully guided them to New Zealand and the Chatham Islands and it appears that he was confident that he could find Tahiti, more than 3800 kilometres to the northeast, although the tradewinds blowing east to west across the tropics would not make this an easy task.

After a month at sea they sighted Tahiti, far off to the southeast, only to be told by Walker that it was not now possible to make landfall with the prevailing winds blowing strongly westward. When the others asked Walker to suggest another safe haven that could be reached, he later recorded: 'I replied that there were the Friendly Islands which were in the same parallel latitude 18° south and nearly the same longitude as New Zealand.'

To some in the group, this suggestion that they head to the Friendly Islands (Tonga) appeared to be a bad move. They were going back towards British colonies. On the other hand, they had the wind at their backs and could easily make a run from there to an Asian port where they could find a passage on ships departing to anywhere in the world.

By now discipline was beginning to break down, partly because of the change of plan and also, no doubt, due to the fact that they had been a long time at sea. Walker records that some of the crew became 'distrustful' and 'committed acts of disorder'.

Luckily it took just a week for them to make landfall on Keppel's Island, known locally as Niua, one of the northernmost of the Tongan islands, which Walker recorded in his log as 'Nowey'. Here they were welcomed by the local chief and were surprised to find an African-American shipwreck survivor named Roberts, described by George Davis as 'an American Black', who was able to act as translator and thus enable good communication and understanding between the convicts and the locals.

During the six weeks that the *Friends* was anchored at Keppel's Island, the eighteen runaways split into two groups. One group of eight, including Ferguson, Templeman, Camm, McGuire and the man who had joined the ship in New Zealand, John Wright, wished to stay on the island, join the locals and spend the rest of their lives as beachcombers.

An opposing group of eight wished to leave the island immediately and head for either Japan or China before their whereabouts were discovered and a British warship appeared on the horizon. In spite of Walker assuring them that neither China nor Japan welcomed foreigners or accepted unknown foreign vessels into the ports, this group stuck doggedly to their proposed plan.

William Walker and the convict named Watts, now calling himself Charles Williams, belonged to neither party. Walker's plan was to stay on 'Nowey' island for some time until things settled down, and either join a visiting whaler and make his way home, or make a run for some Asian port where the crew could separate and each man could trust his luck to find his own way to wherever he wished to go. His one wish, throughout the whole business, was to eventually find his way home to his wife and family.

After six weeks on the island, the whole matter came to a head when the group who wished to leave sent a message to the island chief, via

Mr Roberts, stating that, unless the chief forced Walker and Watts to join their group, go back aboard the ship and make sail for Japan, they would cause the chief and his people as much trouble as they possibly could, by burning their huts and destroying their canoes.

The chief then apparently ordered his warriors to prepare his war canoe and convey Walker and Watts, either against their will or with their reluctant consent, back to the ship. With her crew reduced to just ten members, the *Friends of Boston*, made sail for Japan.

According to an account given later by a crew member, John Denner, they made one stop for water at one of the Marshall Islands, before the final 2000-kilometre leg of the journey to Japan. While they were anchored there in an unknown bay in the Marshall Islands, an American whaling ship sailed in and several of the convicts went on board. At that point, Denner said, he suggested that he and those with him should abandon their fellow convicts and join the crew of the whaling vessel. Upon hearing his suggestion, he reported that his fellow crewmates, 'pointed their muskets at me and forced me to return on board . . . I was ironed on board by order of Herring and the Captain, sometimes called Walker, his real name was Swallow. They were afraid of my having them hanged.'

Evidently the fear of being caught, the obvious problems resulting from having a crew of only ten men, and the paranoia caused by sailing west instead of east, were beginning to take a toll. Only three of those remaining, Walker, his fellow ex-mariner George Jones and a man named Stevenson, had ever hauled a rope or climbed the rigging before that day in Recherche Bay when they took over the ship, although the other seven had no doubt become better than amateur sailors by now. Denner also reported that, after leaving the Marshall Islands, fights broke out on board but luckily 'no one was killed'.

On 16 January 1830 the *Friends* sailed into Mugi Cove, a small bay near the town of Mugi, in the Tokushima district on the southeast coast of Shikoku, the second smallest of Japan's five main islands. Although William Walker knew, by hearsay, that Japan did not allow or welcome foreign vessels, he would not have known that any 'barbarian' vessel had to be reported and, if it refused to leave, driven away by force.

Japan had followed a policy of total isolation from European influence since 1639, in the time of the Tokugawa shogunate. Apart from a small colony of Dutch traders, forced to live in isolation on an artificial island in Nagasaki Harbour and pay regular homage to the shogun, there was no trade or contact with foreigners. Indeed, a law enacted as recently as 1825 had demanded that any foreign ship was to be driven away by force by the local authorities.

Makita Hamaguchi, the local samurai whose job was to write reports of local events, recorded 'An Illustrated Account of the Arrival of a Foreign Ship' which was rather remarkably not properly translated into modern Japanese (and then subsequently into English) until 2017, when Nick Russell, a British-born teacher of English and amateur historian living in Mugi, came across a wonderful illustrated manuscript in the Tokushima District Archives. Russell, who has lived in Japan for 30 years, asked one of his students, 82-year-old Mr Shinoda, to help him and they made translating it into modern Japanese into a learning/teaching project.

The account includes the actual comments of a local samurai commander called Mima, who observed and monitored the ship from the moment it arrived:

> 'I've been suspicious of that ship since it arrived yesterday afternoon,' he reported, 'through the spyglass, I can see a floor halfway up the mast and one of the crew climbs up there to look out. The men on the ship do not look hungry at all.'

An agent, evidently disguised as a local fisherman, was sent to inspect the ship and check for weapons. He also carefully painted the details of the foreigners' equipment and clothing, right down to an accurate detailed painting of the *Friends*, flying a British red ensign (obviously the only flag available on board, although they were ostensibly still pretending to be American), and a portrait of William Walker, with a dog that had apparently joined the crew somewhere between Hobart and Japan!

Even the painter's comments are recorded in Makita Hamaguchi's report, including some observations that show certain cultural differences:

> As we approached the barbarian ship the dog wagged its tail and whined at us. Its face looks like my illustration. It did not look like food. It looked like a pet . . . Some of them were painting the outside of the ship with tar, one was climbing the mast and another was mending the sail. Each of them was involved in some task. All of them stopped work and looked at us . . . At first, we kept our distance at about 50 metres, but they waved to us to come closer and did not seem to be hostile so we rowed over to get a better look.

The agent was given a letter by Walker, which evidently explained, no doubt by way of a series of lies, where they were from and who they were. In the letter Walker asked for permission to repair the boat and take on wood and water. A local samurai commander, named Yamauchi, however, had clear orders regarding foreign ships, from the shogunate in Tokugawa: 'All foreign vessels should be fired upon. Any foreigner who landed should be arrested or killed.'

He ordered the letter be returned unopened and a samurai was ordered to go on board and, using sign language, ordered the ship to leave, or be fired on:

> Go aboard the barbarian ship and with sign language tell them to leave immediately . . . If they do not comply, show them the large ball and tell them that we are ready to fire it at them from Teba Island and reduce them to matchwood.

Also in the archive is a second report, 'A Foreign Ship Drifts in Off Mugi Cove', transcribed from an account given by a local farmer called Harada:

> The crew then tossed gifts: something shaped like this [there is a rough drawing of what looks like a boomerang] a metal bell and what looked like a religious icon of a woman framed in black and covered with glass into our boat . . . we returned each of them.

According to the archive documents, the ship showed no signs of departing, so a cannon on Teba Island fired a warning shot which flew low over the ship and landed beside it. When the *Friends* still did not weigh anchor or set sails, the samurai cannon fired twice more and hit the vessel near the waterline: 'They ordered fire to be directed at the waterline in the red copper sheathed area. Two cannon balls hit and shook the ship badly.'

William Walker's account of the incident, as transcribed in the British court records at a later date, states that lack of any wind made their getaway very difficult:

> In Japan he anchored in a convenient bay, and a Mandarin came off, to whom he stated that they were in great distress, and in want of wood and water. The Japanese threatened to fire at the ship, unless they made off by sunset, which he could not do in consequence of a calm. The Japanese then opened fire upon them from the batteries. One shot struck the vessel between wind and water under the counter, but, a breeze springing up, they departed, and the Japanese ceased firing.

For 287 years many sceptical historians dismissed Walker's claim that the *Friends* visited Japan and was fired upon by the samurai, believing the story to be a concoction of lies to cover up the fact that he had simply scuttled the vessel off the coast of China. The discovery and translation of the illustrated documents in Tokushima District Archives in 2017 prove conclusively that he had told the truth.

With the ship in a bad state of repair, and now further damaged by the samurai cannonballs, they made their way south and came to an area that Walker called the 'Ten Thousand islands', a chain of islands which extends through the East China Sea from the southern Japanese island of Kyushu towards Taiwan—known as the Ryukyu Arc, or the Nansei Islands.

On one of these islands they took on water and reprovisioned the ship. John Denner and a convict named Samuel Thacker were left ashore with provisions at this point. Thacker, who had been fighting with Michael Herring, left the ship willingly while Denner, who was no longer trusted, was less happy about being abandoned.

The remaining eight convicts then set sail for Canton, where there was an international trading station which included an agency of the

British East India Company. With the *Friends* now in a bad state of repair and in danger of sinking, they formulated a plan and prepared the longboat with provisions. The idea was to claim to be survivors of an imaginary English brig called the *Edward* which had foundered off the Chinese coast. The name *Edward of London* was painted on the longboat.

When they met up with a Chinese junk, an argument developed between the crew as to whether they should scuttle the *Friends* or keep going until she started sinking. Four of the original plotters, Davis, Jones, Herring and Pennell, paid the captain of the junk eight dollars each to be taken to the port of Whampao at the mouth of the Pearl River—after Pennell had slipped below and cut through some of the timbers in the hold, below the waterline.

At this point the ship was still some 25 kilometres from land and the four remaining on board—Walker, Watts, Stevenson and Beveridge—steered the sinking ship towards the coast, while Walker attempted to repair the leak with sailcloth.

Around midnight they took to the lifeboat, taking only some food and the ship's compass, telescope, quadrant and charts. They rowed past Macau and the island that is now called Hong Kong and eventually paid the captain of a junk $24 to tow them to the port of Whampao, where they were delighted to see several British East India ships but no British naval vessels. They went aboard one of the British trading vessels, the *Charles Grant*, where Walker, now calling himself Captain Waldron, told the concocted story of the wreck of the *Edward*.

The story seemed plausible enough to Captain Roger Everest and he offered the four men the opportunity to join his crew for the voyage home, but he also insisted that they make a report on the loss of the *Edward* to the man in charge of the British trading station, the senior supercargo (supervisor of cargoes and trade) William Baynes. Walker, in an exhausted and highly nervous state, met the official later that day and, according to Baynes, 'told his narrative in so incoherent a manner, that it produced an impression that the man was either in liquor or suffering under some derangement of mind'.

Evidently, Baynes did not believe a word of it and suspected the four had deserted from one of the British East India Company's opium ships visiting the harbour at Lintin Island, in the Pearl River estuary. So, when Captain Everest presented his papers for departure two weeks later, and Baynes saw the men's names (all aliases, of course) with 'William Waldron' listed as quartermaster and the other three as crew, he again questioned Walker, alias 'Captain Waldron', and was given a clearer, more coherent account of the wreck of the *Edward*, which was taken down by a clerk, signed by Walker and Beveridge (using their aliases) and witnessed by Baynes.

This, plus the fact that *Edward of London* was painted on the longboat, satisfied Baynes and he agreed that the four men could sail for London on the *Charles Grant*, which they did.

Several days after the *Charles Grant* departed, Baynes received word that four more men claiming to be survivors of the *Edward* had arrived at Macau. One of them (George Davis using the name Huntley) had made his way to Whampao and joined the crew of another East India ship, the *Kellie Castle*. The other three (Pennell, Herring and Jones) had joined the crew of a Danish ship which had sailed for Mexico—they were never heard of again.

Baynes ordered that 'Huntley' be brought to Canton to appear before the select committee of supercargoes, of which he was the chairman. Davis/Huntley gave his long and detailed account of the voyage of the *Edward*, which differed in almost every detail from that given by Walker and Beveridge—to begin with, he said the captain's name was Wilson not Waldron. The select committee's report concluded, quite correctly, 'that there is every reason to entertain suspicions that some nefarious proceedings are concealed in the mysterious affair'.

Davis was sent back to the *Kellie Castle* to be conveyed as a prisoner to London, along with the longboat from the *Friends/Edward*, a copy of the select committee's report and descriptions of the four men who had left on the *Charles Grant*, a week before the *Kellie Castle* sailed.

Next to turn up were Denner and Thacker, who had managed to get into a fracas with some of the locals on the island where they had been left. A local magistrate had sent them to the mainland and they had been forwarded on to Canton where the governor, realising they were English sailors, had sent them on to Baynes, who was now forced to sit through another concocted story of imaginary voyages and shipwrecks.

In the meantime, news had finally reached Canton of the seizure of the *Cyprus* six months previously, which caused Baynes to develop certain suspicions. These proved to be justified when Denner broke down under further questioning and blabbed the whole story, including the whereabouts of those left on Keppel's Island, in an attempt to paint himself as an unwilling participant who was press-ganged into the affair and often kept in chains below deck by the rest of the dastardly, piratical crew.

Baynes realised he was duty-bound to get Denner and Thacker back to New South Wales or send them to London to stand trial. In Canton harbour there was a small trading vessel, the *Austen*, which was preparing to sail for Sydney. Baynes asked the captain if he would take the two runaways on his ship. The captain replied that, as his vessel only carried a small crew of lascars, he feared that carrying two desperate and possibly dangerous escaped criminals on a long sea voyage would possibly invalidate his insurance. He did, however, take a letter from Baynes to Governor Darling in Sydney, which explained all that had happened in Canton and included a copy of Denner's confession and information as to the possible whereabouts of other members of the gang in the Friendly Isles and Mexico.

Denner and Thacker were confined in chains aboard a British East India Company vessel, the *Samarang*, which was being loaded and prepared to leave for London.

It is London which now becomes the setting for the next act of this far-ranging melodrama, as many members of the cast assemble in that bustling city in order to play out what we may call the 'court scene'. They are indeed a motley crew—and there will be many surprises and quite a few twists and turns to the narrative. You will need to concentrate—do try to keep up!

The first twist in the tale is that the *Kellie Castle*, having left China a week after the *Charles Grant*, made a better time to London and arrived a week ahead of the other vessel. This meant that George Davis alias Huntley was the first of the felons to be delivered into the hands of the London police who, at this stage, had no idea what crime he could possibly be charged with. All they had to go on was a definite knowledge that he was one of a group of men who were lying about who they were and where they had come from. When examined by magistrate William Ballantine, the suspect was reluctant to answer any questions and was remanded in custody.

Exactly one week later the *Charles Grant* put in at Margate, on the Kent coast at the mouth of the Thames Estuary. At that point William Walker, who had efficiently carried out his duties on the voyage as William Waldron, quartermaster, asked permission of Captain Everest to leave the ship in order to find his wife and children. This was granted. The *Charles Grant* then made its way up the Thames to the East India dock with Beveridge, Watts and Stevenson still aboard (calling themselves John Anderson, Charles Williams and Alexander Telford).

With Davis/Huntley now in police custody and the Thames police in possession of information sent by Baynes on the *Kellie Castle*, it will come as no surprise that the police were waiting at the dock to arrest 'John Anderson', 'Charles Williams' and 'Alexander Telford' on 'suspicion of having committed a crime'. They were questioned individually by Magistrate Ballantine and, when Davis was brought in after they had been questioned, they claimed to have never seen him before in their lives. The four men were ordered to be detained in separate cells.

And about this point in the saga there is a truly dramatic moment when the arresting officer, James Evans, remarked to the magistrate that it had just dawned upon him that these men bore a remarkable resemblance to those described months earlier in the police bulletin *Hue and Cry* as having been involved in the seizure of the *Cyprus* brig, in faraway Van Diemen's Land.

Fake news is not a modern phenomenon. This sensational revelation caused a media frenzy with the British press concocting possible scenarios of the *Cyprus* pirates violently capturing the *Edward* in mid ocean and sailing her to China, leaving a trail of murder and mayhem in their wake. Pirates were big news in London. Sir Walter Scott's novel, *The Pirate*, and Lord Byron's poem, 'The Corsair', had both been massive bestsellers throughout the 1820s.

Although it seems highly questionable to me to call the eighteen convicts who stole the *Cyprus* in order to escape from custody, 'pirates', in the true sense of the word, this was what the British media now wanted them to be, and the British public lapped it up.

The whole affair began to develop momentum. George Huntley was identified as George James Davis, sentenced to seven years transportation at the Old Bailey in July 1820 for stealing some silver spoons. Records of criminal proceedings and court sessions from different parts of Britain soon revealed the true identities of the other three and witnesses were called into court to identify them.

On 22 September 1830 there was another sensation when a surprise witness, one of the leading players in the melodrama, theatrically re-entered the action. The four accused men must surely have turned pale when John Pobjoy was called to the witness stand.

Having received a free pardon for his part in rescuing those left ashore in Recherche Bay, Pobjoy had worked his passage back to London on a ship called the *Ionia*, after having being dismissed from the crew of another ship, the *Hugh Crawford*, before it even set sail from Hobart 'on account of bad character'. Back in London it wasn't long before he was again in trouble with the law for attempting to break into a house. In his defence he spun a wonderful tale of his bravery in Van Diemen's Land, where he had, according to his accounts, been solely responsible for saving the lives of 40 people. He then called as a character witness a beadle who had last known him when he was thirteen, who swore everything Pobjoy said was true. At this point the magistrate dropped the charges and added that he hoped Pobjoy would be further rewarded for his bravery.

To Pobjoy, the opportunity to be involved in a court case against the *Cyprus* brig 'pirates' must have seemed like manna from heaven and he used it to further embroider his own version of the affair and exaggerate his role in saving the survivors, in order to seek further rewards from the Crown. He identified the men, testified that Davis, Watts and Beveridge had been armed during the 'mutiny', and said Davis had handcuffed him and took him below decks with the other crewmen of the *Cyprus*. He also implicated Walker in the plot, stating that it was Walker who had taken the ship's papers from Captain Harrison's cabin.

Various crew members from the *Charles Grant* testified that they had either bought or been offered various items which had originally been stolen from the *Cyprus*, including a small desk which had belonged to Dr Williams, in which Walker had kept the ship's papers. There was an outburst of laughter when Thomas Wardell, the boatswain's assistant on the *Charles Grant*, testified that he had bought silk stockings and women's clothing from Watts (obviously the property of Mrs Carew or the soldiers' wives). At this point the magistrate's curiosity got the better of him and he asked Wardell why he had purchased the items, to which the sailor replied, 'Because I intended to be married when I came to England.'

Another sensation was caused by the appearance in court of the Chief Constable of Hobart Town, Thomas Capon. How he came to be in London is quite a bizarre tale in itself. The notorious Jewish criminal Ikey Solomon (the inspiration for Dickens' character Fagin in *David Copperfrield*) had escaped from the police van taking him to Newgate Prison and fled to Rio de Janeiro in 1827. Hilariously, it was later revealed that Solomon's father-in-law had been driving the van. Recaptured in Rio he was transported to Hobart and then escorted by Capon back to London to stand trial, which resulted, again quite hilariously, in him being transported for fourteen years . . . back to Hobart!

Although he had obviously not been present when the *Cyprus* was seized, Capon corroborated Pobjoy's evidence about later events and could identify the prisoners from having known them in Hobart.

Meanwhile, William Walker, now calling himself William Todd, had tracked down his wife Susan only to find that, supposing he would never return, she had married a grocer's assistant named Tom Fluke. The whole sad story of what happened subsequently is summarised in the court records this way:

> After he left the country his wife, (by whom he had three children) concluding that he would never return, married another man named Flook [*sic*]; and the woman, hearing lately that her husband had again arrived in this country, and was in the neighbourhood of his old quarters (Lambeth), lived with him for a few days, when Flook demanded her and she returned to him. She afterwards gave information to a man named Taylor where her husband was to be found, in order that he might be got rid of; and Taylor communicated the information to the Queens Square officers, by whom the prisoner was apprehended.

It is reasonable to suggest that it was Fluke, rather than Susan, who passed on the information via Taylor to the police, although she certainly risked being charged as an accomplice, as well as with bigamy, if information about Walker's whereabouts was not given to police. Also, with a reward being offered and notices in all London police stations describing Walker, it was really only a matter of time before he was apprehended. Walker had also returned to his old profession of tier-ranging. He was arrested at a boarding house in Lambeth on 15 October, where he was living as a 'Mr Watson'. In his room the police found pawn tickets for a quadrant, telescope and coat—all recently stolen from a ship berthed on the Thames.

In court at the preliminary hearings, Walker maintained that he had been forcibly taken as part of the convict crew as he was the only one of those being transported who was capable of navigating the ship. He made a voluntary confession in which he stuck fairly closely to the truth, apart from attempting to protect those left on the Friendly Islands by claiming that they had sailed to Hawaii where a mutiny had occurred and the men had left the ship. He claimed that he was on his sickbed below decks when the ship was seized in Recherche Bay: 'I was below very ill when the ship was taken, and was forced above to take the command by the convicts.'

Every other witness, including the others accused and John Pobjoy, claimed that Walker was the ringleader of the entire operation, and captain of the vessel throughout the entire voyage. With all the evidence presented, the case was sent to trial and Walker was allowed to access the quartermaster's wages owed to him by the East India Company. He used the money to hire a barrister, William Bodkin. Davis also had a barrister, paid for by his family.

During the trial, which began on 4 November 1830 at the Admiralty Sessions, Bodkin made reasonably successful efforts to discredit Pobjoy, who had done his own reputation no good when he had been brought before the magistrate on 18 October for having beaten up his girlfriend's father, a certain Mr Stapes. According to Pobjoy's statement (quoted verbatim), Mr Stapes 'don't think it proper to let us alone'.

The magistrate had responded by telling Pobjoy: 'You must not make love to the daughter by beating her father . . . that can't be allowed. Promise him you will not molest him again, and I will discharge you.'

The trial preceded in a similar way to the preliminary hearings, with four of the accused men sticking to highly improbable stories, while the evidence given by Pobjoy, Capon, Evans and the crew of the *Charles Grant* continued to build a fairly obvious, and ominous, case against them. William Walker, who was known as 'Swallow' throughout the proceedings, continued to give a fairly accurate account of his adventures, while maintaining all along that he had been coerced into joining the runaways.

As the trial (and, indeed, the entire saga) moved towards its conclusion, the greatest sensation of all was yet to be played out. In the grand theatrical style of Victorian melodrama, or perhaps French farce, one of the *dramatis personae* from the beginning of the story made a dramatic reappearance, when Mr Bodkin, Walker's barrister, called Dr Walter Williams to the witness box!

The doctor had arrived in London only a few days before, so now there was a second eyewitness account to be put up against Pobjoy's. Bodkin had worked hard, in his cross-examination of Pobjoy, to cast doubt upon the credibility and character of the habitual criminal. It was not a difficult thing to do.

Much of the doctor's evidence corroborated that given by Pobjoy, including the fact that Watts was armed with a sword and was a major player in the takeover.

The good doctor, however, identified Ferguson as the ringleader and further testified that Walker/Swallow did not come on deck until the longboat, carrying the doctor himself, along with Lieutenant Carew and his family, was about to depart for the shore. At that point, according to the doctor, Walker had leaned over the rail and said to them, 'I am a pressed man. I am unarmed and surrounded by armed men.' The witness then added that, when Mrs Carew asked for some blankets for the children, Walker was about to go below and get them, when he was stopped by Ferguson.

At this point the prosecutor, a Mr Wightman, asked the doctor if the prisoner had been under his care, to which the doctor replied, 'Yes for some days previous . . . His complaint was a very serious one.' Thus the prosecutor, very wisely, told the judge he had no more questions and sat down.

When Mr Bodkin asked the doctor if he had feared for Walker's life at the time when he went fishing with Carew, the doctor stated:

> Yes, I did. He was exceedingly weak, but not so much but he had it in his power to exert himself if he chose. His disease was of about a week's duration. The operation I had performed the evening before saved him. He was below as a sick person when we went out in the boat.

Whether the doctor's evidence, which contradicted that of all the other witnesses, was given honestly or through some connivance with Bodkin, we will never know. It did, however, save William Walker's life. At the conclusion of the trial the jury, sensationally, found him not guilty.

The other four, Davis, Watts, Stevenson and Beveridge, were all found guilty and the judge sentenced them to be 'hanged by the neck until dead', although the jury recommended mercy for Stevenson and Beveridge, as they appeared to have been 'not so active' in the seizure of the ship as Davis and Watts.

On 8 December the King's Council met to consider petitions for leniency from those condemned to hang—there had been 130 hangings already in London that year. Stevenson and Beveridge had their sentences commuted to life imprisonment, but Watts and Davis were not reprieved. Their executions were ordered on 9 December, death warrants were signed the next day and they were hanged on 16 December, as pirates. This meant that they were hanged at Execution Dock, on the foul-smelling mudflats near Wapping at low tide, and not cut down until the incoming tide had washed over their feet. They were the last men ever hanged for piracy in Britain.

Stevenson and Beveridge sent a petition to King William to have their sentences lessened, stating that they had been forced to join the convict crew by Ferguson and Walker, on account of their respective skills as a sailor and a carpenter. This was denied and they were transported to Van Diemen's Land in February on the *Argyll*. Both men took part in a failed mutiny in the mid-Atlantic, and finally ended their long adventure in Macquarie Harbour.

Denner and Thacker arrived back in London from Canton under guard in March 1831 and appeared in front of the Thames Police Office magistrate charged with piracy. They claimed that Walker was the ringleader and had forced them at gunpoint to join the runaways.

When Dr Williams was called to identify the men, he said he could not do so and commented that, as the two men had spent so much time in a tropical climate, their appearances could have changed. The magistrate decided to send the two back to Hobart and, while Denner arrived there via Sydney sometime in December, Thacker apparently managed to escape along the way and was never heard from again.

Meanwhile, in August, James Camm had been apprehended in Tahiti, having somehow managed to get himself there from Keppel's Island. Camm and Denner stood trial together in Hobart with Chief Justice John Pedder presiding. After the jury delivered a verdict of guilty, Pedder asked the foreman of the jury if he considered a vessel anchored in a bay to be 'on the high seas' and the foreman replied, 'yes'. The judge then reminded the foreman that the *Cyprus* had been at anchor in the bay 'in between two heads' and asked again, 'Do you find that to be on the high seas?' When the foreman answered, 'We do', it made the crime 'piracy' and the judge had no option other than to sentence the men to death. Governor Arthur issued a reprieve for Denner, whose sentence was commuted to life imprisonment. James Camm was hanged in Hobart on 30 April 1832.

While James Camm was mounting the gallows steps in Hobart, his majesty's sloop HMS *Zebra* was heading towards Rotuma. This island, situated between Fiji and Tuvalu, was a favourite stopover for whaling ships in need of water and provisions but had become a haven for runaway sailors, deserters and escaped convicts.

Acting perhaps on rumours and information provided by the trial of the *Cyprus* 'pirates', Captain MacMurdo took HMS *Zebra* to Boscawen's Island (Tafahi), situated a mere 5 kilometres from Keppel's Island. The longboat took a landing party ashore and soon returned with Robert McGuire as their prisoner. The *Zebra* picked up another escaped convict on Rotuma before heading home.

Six months later McGuire was tried for piracy in Hobart, Chief Justice Pedder again presided and Private Scully testified that it was McGuire who split his head open. The verdict was guilty and the sentence was death, later commuted to life on the notoriously savage 'last resort' penal colony on Norfolk Island.

After the trial of Walker, Davis, Watts, Stevenson and Beveridge concluded, John Pobjoy, outraged that Dr Williams had stolen the limelight and that Walker, the man he had been at pains to show as the ringleader, had escaped the noose, attempted to secure a pension as a reward for his part in the affair and wrote dozens of petitions claiming Walker was guilty. However, after the Home Secretary's Department responded by giving him a paltry £5 reward, he petitioned Queen Adelaide, the Duke of Wellington, and the lords of the admiralty, who all either refused or ignored the requests. Finally, Pobjoy wrote directly to the Home Secretary, Lord Melbourne, and, in a reply written by the Home Secretary's secretary, was reminded that he had already been paid three shillings a day for his services as a witness and an extra five quid and he was not entitled to anything more. Pobjoy went back to working as a mariner and died when swept overboard from a ship returning with a load of timber from Canada, in August 1833. He had married in June 1832, and a daughter was baptised two months after his death.

On 2 March 1831, William Walker—alias Brown, Shields, Swallow, Waldron, Todd and Watson—having petitioned unsuccessfully to be pardoned or have his original life sentence commuted, began his third voyage as a transported convict, this time along with 289 others, aboard the transport *Exmouth,* bound for Sydney, where the convicts were duly disembarked five months later on 28 July. After being transferred at some point to Hobart he found himself in chains, in company with his old shipmate John Denner, on board the government brig *Tamar*, on 10 May 1832, bound for Macquarie Harbour—this time Walker would finally arrive at his destination.

The captain of the *Tamar* was well acquainted with both the convicts—it was John Burn, previously second mate of the *Cyprus*, who had been one of the fishing party in the longboat, along with Lieutenant Carew, Dr Williams and John Pobjoy, on that fateful day three years and nine months earlier.

William Walker was finally delivered to Macquarie Harbour penal colony on 4 June 1832, but he was not there 'for life'. Some fifteen months later he and his fellow 'pirates', Beveridge, Stevenson and Denner, were all transferred to the new convict prison at Port Arthur, much closer to Hobart, on the other side of Van Diemen's Land. Macquarie Harbour was closed as a prison, maintaining the penal colony so far from Hobart had proved too difficult. Although he was only 42 years old when he left Macquarie Harbour, William Walker was already terminally ill and he died of tuberculosis at Port Arthur on 12 May 1834. He was buried in an unmarked grave on The Isle of the Dead.

Amazingly, his official convict record noted that he was 'a very good man'.

THE CYPRUS BRIG

By Frank McNamara ('Frank the Poet')

Come all you sons of Freedom, a chorus join with me,
I'll sing a song of heroes and glorious liberty.
Of lads condemned from England upon Van Diemen's Shore,
Their Country, friends and parents, to never see them more.

A second sentence being incurred we were ordered for to be
Sent to Macquarie Harbour, that place of tyranny.
The hardships we'd to undergo are matters of record,
But who believes the convict, or who regards his word?

Starved and flogged and punished, deprived of all redress,
The Bush our only refuge, with death to end distress.
Hundreds of us all shot down, for daring to be free,
Numbers caught and banished to life-long slavery.

But Swallow, Watt and Davis, were in our noble band,
Determined at the first chance to quit Van Diemen's Land.
In heavy chains and guarded, on the Cyprus Brig conveyed
The topsails being hoisted, the anchor being weighed.

The wind it blew Sou'Westerly and on we went straightway,
And found ourselves all wind-bound, in gloomy Recherche Bay.
'Twas August eighteen twenty-nine, with convicts all on board,
Lieutenant Carew left the Brig, and soon we passed the word.

The Doctor too was absent, the soldiers off their guard,
A better opportunity could never have occurred.
Confined within a dismal hole, we soon contrived a plan,
To capture now the Cyprus, or perish every man.

We first addressed the soldiers 'for liberty we crave,
Give up your arms this instant, or the sea will be your grave,
By tyranny we've been oppressed, by your Colonial laws,
But we'll bid adieu to slavery, or die in freedom's cause.'

While some lads turned faint-hearted and begged to go ashore,
Eighteen boys rushed daring, and took the Brig and store.
We brought the sailors from below, and rowed them to the land
Likewise, the wife and children of Carew in command.

Supplies of food and water, we gave the vanquished crew,
Returning good for evil, as we'd been taught to do.
The Morn broke bright the wind was fair; we headed out to sea
With one more cheer for those on shore and glorious liberty.

For our elected captain, Bill Swallow was the man,
Who laid a course out neatly to take us to Japan.
Then sound your golden trumpets; play on your tuneful notes,
The Cyprus Brig is sailing, how proudly now she floats.

May fortune help the Noble lads, and keep them ever free
From Gags, and Cats, and Chains, and Traps, and Cruel Tyranny.

SELECTED BIBLIOGRAPHY

We have used the resources of the National Library of Australia, particularly *Trove* for newspaper articles, notably the *Sydney Gazette*, Project Gutenberg online transcripts of First Fleet journals of Surgeon John White, Lieutenant-Captain Watkin Tench, Governor Arthur Phillip and Judge Advocate Collins, *A Voyage to Terra Australis* by Matthew Flinders and *Western Australia: A history from its discover to the inauguration of the Commonwealth* by J.S. Battye.

Online, we accessed census, court registers and *British Almanac* records, convict registers, shipping lists, ancestry.com and other various websites. Also the Mitchell Library at the State Library of New South Wales, the Grainger Museum at the University of Melbourne, the Hinkler Hall of Aviation in Bundaberg, and the following books and articles:

Bird-Walton, Nancy, *My God, It's A Woman*, Collins, Sydney, 1990

Cobley, John (ed.), *Sydney Cove 1788, Vol. 1*, Angus and Robertson, Sydney, 1963

Cobley, John (ed.), *Sydney Cove 1789–1790, Vol. 2,* Angus and Robertson, Sydney, 1963

Cobley, John (ed.), *Sydney Cove 1791–1792, Vol. 3*, Angus and Robertson, Sydney, 1963

Cobley, John (ed.), *Sydney Cove 1793–1795, Vol. 4,* Angus and Robertson, Sydney, 1963

Cobley, John (ed.), *Sydney Cove 1795–1800, Vol. 5*, Angus and Robertson, Sydney, 1963

Cowan, Peter, *A Unique Position: A biography of Edith Dircksey Cowan*, University of Western Australia Press, Perth, 1978

Cowan, Peter, *Maitland Brown: A view of nineteenth century Western Australia,* Fremantle Arts Centre Press, Fremantle, 1988

Crowe, David *A History of the Gypsies of Eastern Europe and Russia*, Palgrave Macmillan, New York, 2004

Cuthbertson, Bern, *Around Tasmania in a Whaleboat 1986: In the wake of Captain James Kelly 1815–1816*, Cuthbertson, Hobart, 1989

de Moore, Greg, *Tom Wills: First wild man of Australian sport,* Allen & Unwin, Sydney, 2011

Gibson, Emily and Firth, Barbara, *The Original Million Dollar Mermaid*, Allen & Unwin, Sydney, 2005

Hirst, Warwick, *The Man Who Stole the Cyprus*, Rosenberg Publishing, Sydney, 2008

Hughes, David, *Brewing in Early Australia*, (thesis submitted for the degree of Doctor of Philosophy of the Australian National University, Canberra), March 1998

Humphries, Glen, *James Squire: The biography,* Last Day of School Publishing, Wollongong, 2017

Kellerman, Annette, *How to Swim*, William Heinemann, London, 1918

Kellerman, Annette, *My Story*, Kellerman Papers, ML MSS 6270, State Library of NSW, Sydney

Lo Hui-min (ed.), *The Correspondence of G.E. Morrison*, Cambridge University Press, Cambridge, 1978

Mealey, Rachel, 'The brig Cyprus: How an English surfer solved the mystery of an Australian pirate ship in Japan', *ABC News*, 2017

Morrison, George, *An Australian in China, Being the narrative of a quiet journey across China to Burma,* Angus and Robertson, Sydney 1972 (first published 1895)

Nemec, Belinda, '"I am hungry for fame-after-death", Percy Grainger's quest for immortality through his museum', *reCollections*, Vol. 2, No. 2, National Museum of Australia, Canberra, 2016

Paterson, A.B. 'Happy Despatches', *Complete Works,* Ure Smith Press Sydney, 1991

Sayer, Mandy *Australian Gypsies: Their secret history*, NewSouth Publishing, Sydney, 2017

Smith, Keith Vincent, 'Nanbarry', *Dictionary of Sydney*, 2010

Thompson, Larry Clinton, *William Scott Ament and The Boxer Rebellion,* McFarland & Co, Jefferson, North Carolina, 2009
Woollacott, Angela, *Race and the Modern Exotic: Three 'Australian' women on global display*, Monash University Press, Melbourne, 2011

ACKNOWLEDGEMENTS

I wish to credit and thank the following:

- Jillian Dellit for collaboration, contributions, research, suggestions and proofreading.
- Rebecca Kaiser for her good-humoured support and encouragement.
- Tom Bailey-Smith for professionally managing the whole process.
- Susin Chow for her perceptive editing, attention to detail, support and ideas.
- Julia Cain for her meticulous proofreading.
- Phil Campbell for the cover design.
- All at Allen & Unwin.
- My wife Robyn.

I have written about several of these life stories, in shorter forms, in previous collections published by Allen & Unwin.